GROWING D·E·S·E·R·T PLANTS from Windowsill to Garden

◆GROWING

Above
The combination of strawberry cactus, Torrey yucca, and creosote bush creates a beautiful natural garden in Big Bend National Park in Texas.

Right Page
A late afternoon thunderstorm is silhouetted against the setting sun. Bringing much needed moisture to the Chihuahuan Desert, the summer monsoons are a welcome relief to desert plants and dwellers alike.

•DESERT•PLANTS•

from Windowsill to Garden

THEODORE B. HODOBA

SANTA FE

To my wonderful wife, Candy, without whose support this book would not exist; and to my son Nate and my daughter Hannah, who, like blossoms in springtime, bring great joy to our lives.

Cover and book design by Jos. Trautwein
Text drawings by Mimi Kamp
Cover photograph by Charles Mann
Interior photographs by Charles Mann and Theodore B. Hodoba
Map of Chihuahuan Desert Region by Carol Cooperrider
U.S.D.A. Plant Hardiness Zone Map compliments of U.S.D.A.

First Edition

Manufactured in Hong Kong

Library of Congress Cataloging-in-Publication Data

Hodoba, Theodore B., 1950–
Growing desert plants : from windowsill to garden / Theodore B. Hodoba ; illustrated by Mimi Kamp ; photography by Charles Mann and Theodore B. Hodoba. — 1st ed.
p. cm.
Includes bibliographical references and index.
ISBN 1-878610-54-6 : $24.95
1. Desert gardening. 2. Desert plants. 3. Native plant gardening. 4. Native plants for cultivation. 5. Desert plants—Chihuahuan Desert. 6. Native plants for cultivation—Chihuahuan Desert. I. Title.
SB427.5.H63 1995 94–49008
635.9′5179—dc20 CIP

Red Crane Books
2008 Rosina St. Suite B
Santa Fe, New Mexico 87505

CONTENTS

ACKNOWLEDGMENTS

Growing Desert Plants: From Windowsill to Garden is based on my experiences growing every plant listed in the book. But without encouragement, advice, information, and support from others, I would not have been able to grow the plants or make this book a reality. Among those I would especially like to thank are Helen and Lawrence Cummings, Jean Dodd, Evelyn and the late John I. Kroft, Horst Kuenzler, Lisa Mandelkern, Pat Nott, Erma Pilz, Lucille Wilson, Tom Wooten, and all of my friends in the Native Plant Society of New Mexico.

I would also like to thank a number of people who helped with the production of this book. I am grateful to David Eppele for reviewing the manuscript and making suggestions for its improvement. I would like to thank Dennie Miller of the Chihuahuan Desert Research Institute for sending information regarding the mapping of the Chihuahuan Desert. This book would not be nearly so beautiful without Charles Mann's lovely photographs, Mimi Kamp's elegant drawings, and Jos. Trautwein's excellent book design. I'd also like to thank Mimi for suggesting Red Crane Books as a publisher. The folks at Red Crane Books have been absolutely wonderful to work with. A big thanks to them all, especially Carol Caruthers, whose hard work pulled this book together, and Ann Mason, whose editing and suggestions for organization made this a much better book. I am grateful also to Marianne and Michael O'Shaughnessy for their foresight and decision to accept my manuscript for publication.

Finally, I would like to express my appreciation to my family for their understanding and support during the times when I was consumed with preparing this manuscript for publication. I'd like to thank Nate and Hannah for their patience when I had to work on this book instead of going outside to play. Most of all I am grateful to my wife, Candy, for all her hard work on this book. She spent many hours typing and retyping the manuscript as well as proofreading it at various stages. To all of these people and to those who garden in the desert, I owe many thanks.

PHOTOGRAPHIC CREDITS

Charles Mann: Cover, Pages iii, viii, ix, x, 2(l), 4, 8, 10, 11, 12, 17(r), 21(r), 23(l), 24(l), 26, 27(r), 30, 31(l), 32(r), 35(r), 43, 48(l), 54, 68(l), 69(t), 72(r), 73, 76(l, tr).

Theodore B. Hodoba: Pages i, ii, v, 2(r), 3, 7, 9, 17(l), 21(l), 23(r), 24(r), 25, 27(l), 28, 31(r), 32(l), 35(l), 38, 41, 42, 44, 48(r), 49, 65, 68(r), 69(b), 70, 71, 72(l), 74, 75, 76(br).

INTRODUCTION

When we think of the Southwest, one of the first images that comes to mind is the exotic, fantastical desert: its brilliant light, its strange creatures, its intriguing plant life. Among plants of the desert there is a vast variety of shapes, sizes, and textures. From the succulent, armored leaves of the amazing-looking agaves to the delicate, airy foliage of the fragrant-flowered acacias, they have evolved into some of the most unusual and beautiful plants in the world.

In this book the term "desert gardening" is used to define the style of gardening with natives presented here in the same manner as woodland gardening is used to describe the native gardens of the eastern states. Desert gardening is a more specific and appropriate name for gardening in the region of the Chihuahuan Desert than commonly used, generic terms such as naturalistic-style gardening or wildflower gardening. By using native plants and working with arid soils and limited rainfall, this style of gardening is well adapted to the unique conditions of the desert. Unlike traditional landscaping, it uses fewer poisons such as nonorganic fertilizers and pesticides. Desert gardening (and gardeners!) welcomes the return of lizards, butterflies, and other indigenous creatures to their desert homes. Most of all it seeks ways to save water while creating a beautiful landscape. In essence desert gardening is based on living in harmony with the desert.

There is a popular form of landscaping in the Southwest consisting of large, bleak expanses of rock and gravel interspersed with an occasional yucca, cactus, pinyon, or other plant. Unfortunately, this type of landscape is what many people think of when they hear of desert gardening; however, the style of desert gardening described and advocated in this book is very different. The former is neither aesthetically pleasing nor environmentally appropriate. Desert gardening is just the opposite: it is beautiful to look at and in tune with the desert and the arid grassland surrounding it.

Landscaping with native plants is not a new idea. Some people have been gardening with them for many years; however, only recently have native plants grown in popularity. For much of our history, we have tried to emulate the formal landscapes of the European aristocracy. Part of this inherited style is foundation plantings and large expanses of mowed lawn. By controlling the ornamental landscape, by "civilizing" their environment, people felt a sense of security and order in the world. As long as water was plentiful and fertilizer was cheap, little attention was given to using native plants in desert landscapes. However, with our increasing awareness of the pollution caused by some fertilizers and pesticides, and the more frequent water shortages in some communities, attitudes are changing. Although many gardeners and people in the landscape industry are still planting non-native, nonadapted plants with high water and fertilizer needs, they may not have this choice in the near future. In the Southwest 35 to 70 percent of urban water consumption is used for watering our landscapes. Not only is this becoming more expensive for the home gardener, but many cities in the region are beginning to regulate water use more strictly, including the passage of ordinances requiring the use of native and drought-tolerant plants.

In the fall, the bright red berries of Texas madrone are a striking feature of this evergreen tree.

In addition to using large amounts of water, the average non-native landscape requires an excessive amount of fertilizers and dangerous pesticides, many of which are made from petrochemicals. As we continue to deplete our oil reserves, we will no longer be able to afford this luxury. Pesticides and fertilizers also pollute our groundwater, streams, and rivers through infiltration and runoff. Many people are ready to change their gardening habits and switch to a more rational approach to landscaping. Xeriscaping, which seeks to conserve water in landscaping, is becoming quite popular in arid regions. Its principles are easily applied to desert gardening. (There is more information about Xeriscaping in Chapter 2.)

The urban areas of the Southwest were developed with a hostile attitude towards the desert environment. Having come from other areas with higher rainfall, people wanted landscapes that reminded them of home. Such an oasis concept of gardening is nothing new; the Egyptians and Persians practiced a similar form of gardening. With careful plant selection, natives that prefer extra watering can be used with other plants to create lush areas close to outdoor living spaces. Beyond this, however, we should be using native plants to celebrate the beauty of the desert, to live in harmony with our environment. The Southwest is a unique area of the United States, and we should enhance this uniqueness instead of imitating the landscaping of other areas to the point where we will no longer be able to distinguish Albuquerque from Atlanta, or El Paso from Denver. As with much of modern architecture, the homogenizing effects of modern landscaping practices are leaving us with little sense of place. By using natives we can regain a regional identity.

It may seem that it should be obvious what a native plant is. However, the term "native" is defined differently by various authors, gardeners, and others. To encompass as many varieties of plants as possible, "native" is usually defined as those plants found within a larger biological region rather than a smaller one. For example, instead of only including plants from the immediate vicinity of a town or city, native plants also could include plants indigenous to the grasslands surrounding a city. An even wider list of possibilities becomes available if we include in this definition plants from the larger Chihuahuan Desert region. Some people go beyond this to include adapted plants from other arid lands. What definition is used is largely a matter of personal preference. All of the plants listed in this book (except those under the category "related species" in the "Desert Plant Encyclopedia") are native to New Mexico; most are also native to Texas, and many are found in Arizona. There is one impostor: the yellow bird-of-paradise, originally from Argentina, has escaped cultivation and now grows wild in the three states just mentioned.

Many people haven't noticed the native plants growing around them. They have a misconception that native plants and landscapes are weedy, sparse, and unkempt. However, once they have become familiar with these plants, they are surprised to find that there are a lot of lush, green, and beautifully flowered plants native to the Chihuahuan Desert.

Chihuahuan Desert plants are very much at home in the garden, as well as in the desert itself in the arid regions of northern Mexico. The Mexican states of Chihuahua, Coahuila, Durango, Zacatecas, San Luis Potosí, Nuevo León, and Tamaulipas all contain portions of the Chihuahuan Desert within their borders. Centered in

Because of their wide range of textures, colors, and forms, desert plants can be combined to produce lush and attractive landscapes while using only a limited amount of water.

With a wider selection of native plants becoming available at nurseries, the gardener can create a colorful landscape of arid-adapted plants in harmony with the desert environment.

northern Mexico, the Chihuahuan Desert enters the United States in parts of New Mexico, Texas, and Arizona. It includes Trans-Pecos Texas, including El Paso; southeastern Arizona almost to the Sonoran Desert of Tucson; and a large part of New Mexico containing the majority of the state's population—from Albuquerque to Las Cruces, Roswell to Carlsbad, and Alamogordo to Deming. It is an arid region that includes desert scrub, grasslands, and smaller areas of riparian and montane habitats; within its borders there are about 3,500 species of plants. With such a large number of species to choose from, there is a native choice for almost any landscape situation. This area is the heart of the Southwest, and we can retain the splendid character of this region by our own desert gardening style of landscaping. Over thousands of years native plants have adapted to the Southwest's alkaline soils and unpredictable climate. As a result, they require less maintenance and resources than plants from other areas. In fact, their adaptations make them a better buy at the nursery since their chances of survival are much greater than that of a non-native plant.

Native plants are becoming ever more available in nurseries, but it can still take some hunting to find the less commonly available species. Until recently, nurseries hadn't given much attention to the native plants of their regions. With the realization of the benefits of desert gardening has come a demand for more native plants in the nursery trade.

Growing plants of all kinds in containers has revolutionized the industry. Originating in California, this trend has spread nationwide. Until containers became popular it was difficult to grow many of our southwestern natives since they didn't do well bareroot, nor could they be easily transplanted due to their extensive root systems and/or long taproots. Once the roots could be confined to a container, the problem was solved. We are now seeing a much wider choice of native plants at nurseries, with more new plants being introduced to the market each year. Now that this is happening, there will be a continuing need and desire for more information about Chihuahuan Desert plants. Even gardeners in other parts of the United States and in other countries around the world have begun growing these plants in outdoor beds and indoor collections. This is due not only to the plants' interesting forms and beautiful flowers but also to the fact that people are finding out that many plants of the Chihuahuan Desert are quite cold hardy.

Following a discussion of the characteristics of the Chihuahuan Desert and plant adaptations to the desert's conditions, *Growing Desert Plants: From Windowsill to Garden* presents information on designing a desert garden; on propagating desert plants from seeds, offsets, and so forth; and on maintaining a desert garden, with an emphasis on water conservation. For those who don't live in the

Southwest, there is a discussion on how to grow desert plants in non-desert climates. This book also contains an extensive "Desert Plant Encyclopedia" with specific information on a large number of native plants. The "Desert Plant Encyclopedia" is divided into five separate sections: wildflowers, cacti, succulents, shrubs, and trees. Each entry has a description of the plant, including its natural range and hardiness zone (as specified by the United States Department of Agriculture Plant Hardiness Zone Map, which is based on the average annual minimum temperatures across the United States). Information about planting and care is given for each species along with remarks concerning the plant's uses in landscaping. The book also contains appendixes listing places where desert plants can be seen in the wild and in cultivation, and mail-order sources of seeds and plants.

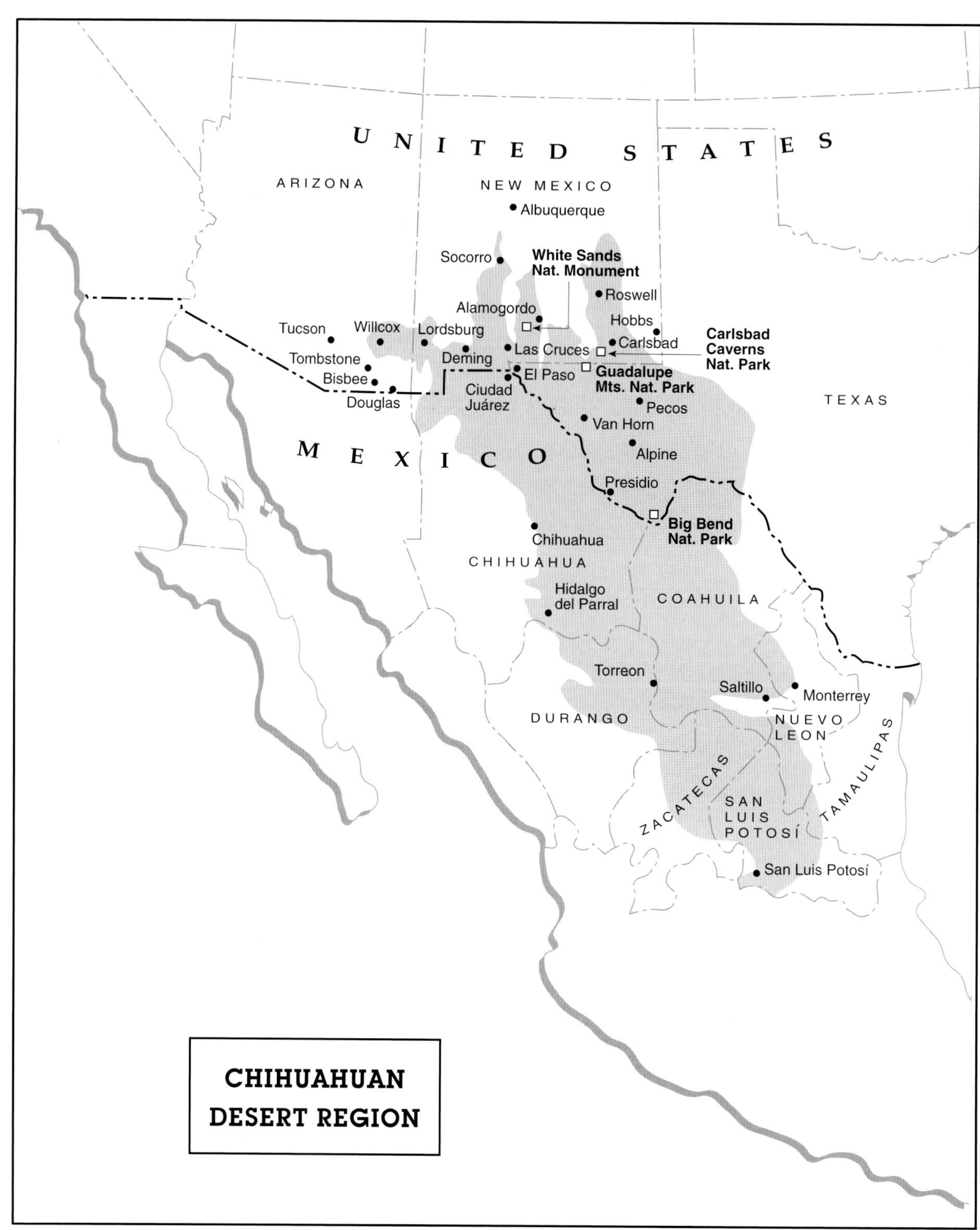
UNITED STATES
ARIZONA
NEW MEXICO
Albuquerque
Socorro
White Sands Nat. Monument
Roswell
Alamogordo
Hobbs
Tucson
Willcox
Lordsburg
Carlsbad
Carlsbad Caverns Nat. Park
Tombstone
Deming
Las Cruces
Bisbee
El Paso
Guadalupe Mts. Nat. Park
Douglas
Ciudad Juárez
Pecos
TEXAS
Van Horn
MEXICO
Alpine
Presidio
Big Bend Nat. Park
Chihuahua
CHIHUAHUA
Hidalgo del Parral
COAHUILA
Torreon
Saltillo
Monterrey
DURANGO
NUEVO LEON
ZACATECAS
SAN LUIS POTOSÍ
TAMAULIPAS
San Luis Potosí
CHIHUAHUAN DESERT REGION

CHAPTER 1 Climate and Plant Adaptation in the Chihuahuan Desert

It's dawn in the desert. The sun has just risen over the sharp edge of a small mountain range. The cool night air is beginning to give way to the warmth of the new day. This is one of the most active times for many of the creatures of the Chihuahuan Desert. Quail scurry to a watering hole, constantly nervous and aware, for they know that coyotes and hawks are hunting for them. A variety of lizards sit on desert rocks absorbing the first warm rays of the sun. Horned toads (actually lizards in thorny armor) are about to begin searching for the ants that constitute their diet. Roadrunners are also taking advantage of the solar heat. Once they are warmed up, the lizards had better beware, for the roadrunners have hungry young ones in nests in the chollas, and they must hunt for snakes, lizards, insects, and other small animals to feed their voracious appetites. Jackrabbits are busily gnawing on the tender stems of desert willows. They are just one of the many creatures that feed on plants of the desert, and they, in turn, are prey for other animals. The rattlesnakes are retreating after a successful night's hunt to their refuge in the rocks, to digest their kangaroo rat dinners in peace and comfort.

While its wildlife is familiar to most of us, much of the Chihuahuan Desert remains a vast, unfamiliar land to many. Unlike the better- known Sonoran and Mojave deserts to the west, it doesn't have a well- known image like the Sonoran saguaro and the Mojave Joshua tree of western movie fame. The Chihuahuan Desert does, however, have its own unique, beautiful plants.

It seems ironic that so little has been written about the Chihuahuan Desert, as it is the largest of the North American deserts. Depending on the authority, and his or her perspective, it ranges in size from 150,000 to just over 200,000 square miles (240,000 to just over 320,000 square kilometers). Much of the debate about its size centers around the argument of what to include in defining geographic boundaries. Does the Chihuahuan Desert include the non-arid mountain ranges surrounded by desert, such as the Organ Mountains of southern New Mexico and the Chisos Mountains of the Big Bend region of Texas?

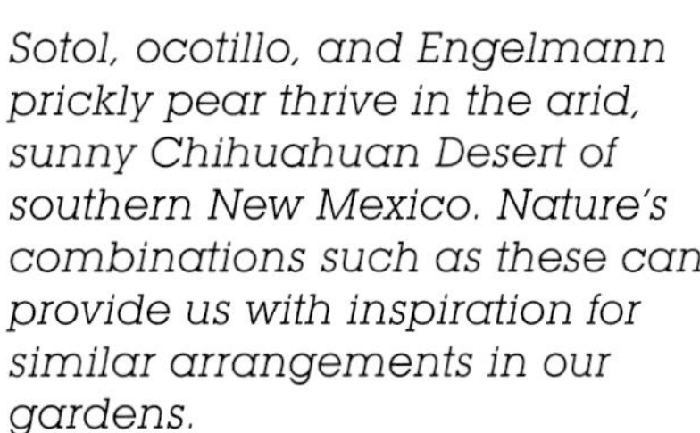

Sotol, ocotillo, and Engelmann prickly pear thrive in the arid, sunny Chihuahuan Desert of southern New Mexico. Nature's combinations such as these can provide us with inspiration for similar arrangements in our gardens.

Does it include the former grasslands, now being invaded by desert shrubs and other plants? How far north, south, east, and west does it go? While no one has been able to agree on its boundaries, for our purposes the Chihuahuan Desert will be defined as being centered in northern Mexico, including the states of Chihuahua and Coahuila, and extending across Trans-Pecos Texas from Del Rio north and west into the Pecos Valley as far as Roswell, New Mexico, then north into the Tularosa Basin and the Rio Grande Valley of New Mexico to just south of Albuquerque. There are pockets of creosote bush at Isleta Pueblo that are considered the northern limit of the desert by some. The Chihuahuan Desert is further defined geographically by three surrounding mountain ranges: the Sierra Madre Occidental, the Sierra Madre Oriental, and the Rocky Mountains. There are those who also include the areas around Douglas, Tombstone, and other locations in Arizona as part of the Chihuahuan Desert. Others contend that this is more of a transition area between the Chihuahuan and Sonoran deserts. In any case, many of the plant species described in this book are found here, and the desert gardening style is very appropriate for this region.

Soaptree yucca has impressive flower stalks which can grow 6 feet (180 centimeters) or taller. It is one of the most abundant plants in the Chihuahuan Desert and surrounding desert grassland.

Dryness and heat are two of the more common characteristics we associate with a desert. The Chihuahuan Desert is characterized by both of these during parts of the year, but it is also wet and cool at other times. Afternoon temperatures in early and midsummer are usually in the 90°F to 100°F (32°C to 38°C) range. In late summer monsoons in the form of intense afternoon thunderstorms bring relief from the high temperatures and also provide most of the Chihuahuan Desert's yearly precipitation. Total yearly rainfall varies from 7 to 12 inches (18 to 30 centimeters), with the usual amounts ranging from 7 to 8 inches (18 to 20 centimeters). During the non-monsoon months, rainfall averages less than ½ inch (1 centimeter) per month. In winter nighttime temperatures frequently fall

Left
Occurring in dense stands, lechuguilla is considered the indicator of the Chihuahuan Desert. In the garden it needs room to spread.

Right
A native of the desert grassland, horse crippler has injured horses which have stepped on its stout, sharp spines; however, its unique appearance, lovely flowers, and brightly colored fruit make it a desirable addition to the garden.

below freezing and may even drop below the 0°F (-18°C) mark. It is not uncommon for snow to fall in the desert; however, it does not stay on the ground for long. During the day the temperatures rise; the overall climate is mild, and winter is more of an extended autumn when compared to non-desert areas.

The Chihuahuan Desert contains large areas of desert scrub, consisting mainly of shrubby species, desert grassland, and smaller areas of riparian and montane environments. Most of the trees that are found in the desert grow along washes and the few perennial streams and rivers. In the American portion of the Chihuahuan Desert, there are a few large chollas (*Opuntia* species); however, most of the numerous species of cacti are small. Dense stands of agaves, yuccas, and sotols are major components of this desert and in large part give it its character. One of the agaves, in fact, is considered an indicator plant of the Chihuahuan Desert. This plant, lechuguilla (*Agave lechuguilla*) is one of the most abundant of the agaves and is found in southern New Mexico, Trans-Pecos Texas, and northern Mexico. The soaptree yucca (*Yucca elata*) is another of the commonly occurring plants of the northern Chihuahuan Desert, and it is found in "forests" throughout the area, including the surrounding desert grasslands. These and other desert plants are often described as struggling to survive in a hostile environment. While the desert may seem hostile to some, it is the perfect environment for these plants that have adapted to life here. Not only don't they struggle, they actually thrive in the heat and intense sunlight. In order to see cactus flowers at their fullest, you must be willing to go out in the midday sun when they are wide open.

The Desert Grassland

Surrounding the desert proper is an area referred to as desert grassland. At one time it was much more extensive than it is now. With the arrival of European man to the region, a period of overgrazing began that continues to the present day. Large areas that once were grassland are now dominated by desert scrub vegetation such as creosote bush, honey mesquite, snakeweed, and burroweed.

The remaining grassland is an area of high plains and rolling hills in southern New Mexico, Trans-Pecos Texas, and southeastern Arizona. It usually occurs at elevations between 3,000 and 5,000 feet (900 to 1,500 meters) but sometimes as high as 8,000 feet (2,400 meters). The desert grassland consists largely of grama grasses, threeawns, sacatons, and tobosa grass. At the lower elevations there are often other species associated with the Chihuahuan and Sonoran deserts such as mesquite and creosote bush. At the higher elevations there is often a mixture of grasses and shrubs, including acacias, mimosas, sotols, beargrass, and yuccas. The desert grassland includes a number of cacti species from areas above and below the grassland, as well as many species that are found primarily in this habitat, such as horse crippler *(Echinocactus texensis)* and early bloomer *(Echinocactus intertextus)*.

As in the desert below, most of the moisture received in the grassland falls during monsoon thunderstorms in July, August, and September. Annual precipitation is higher here than in the lower desert, between 10 and 20 inches (25 and 51 centimeters), and is responsible for this grassland habitat. It is not enough, however, to support trees. As in the desert, they are restricted to washes and other riparian areas and are generally small in size.

Geologically, the Chihuahuan Desert, including the desert grassland, is part of the Basin and Range Province, consisting of large, flat basins separated by relatively small mountain ranges. For the gardener, the area is challenging, with a climate unlike

Consisting of various grasses, including the sacaton shown here, the desert grassland forms a transition zone between the desert and the Southwest woodlands.

those with which most people are familiar. By studying and learning more about the desert itself and the plants which grow here, the ease of desert gardening as a style appropriate to the region becomes more apparent.

Climate

The desert is a land of contrasts: hot and cold, dry and wet. For the gardener, the extremes of this climate are the factors that most affect plant choice. Because of this it is important to go into more detail regarding southwestern weather. In terms of climate this region includes parts of Arizona, New Mexico, and Trans-Pecos Texas. Portions of California, Colorado, Nevada, and Utah are similar.

Roughly half of the yearly moisture comes in July and August during summer monsoons. It falls as afternoon thundershowers from systems that generally originate in the Gulf of Mexico. With 8 to 10 inches (20 to 25 centimeters) of precipitation, the Tularosa Basin, Jornada del Muerto, and the Rio Grande Valley of New Mexico are among the region's driest areas. A plant has little choice but to adapt in some manner to use this precious resource as efficiently as possible.

There is a definite winter season in the Chihuahuan Desert, with temperatures dipping below freezing more than one hundred nights a year. From December through February average minimum temperatures range from 24°F to 31°F (-4°C to -6°C). One of the lowest temperatures recorded for the area was -17°F (-27°C) at Albuquerque, New Mexico. This was a freakish cold front, however, and was a very abnormal occurrence. During the winter months most of the moisture comes from the Pacific via the Northwest, usually falling as snow. The Rio Grande Valley of New Mexico, for example, receives 2 to 5 inches (5 to 13 centimeters) of snow annually.

The lack of rainfall in the desert not only means the additional watering of plants, but it also requires dealing with soils that are usually alkaline, even saline. There is not enough rain to leach out mineral salts. Dry, high winds complicate the process by blowing away leaf litter and other plant debris before it can decompose into humus and by increasing the amount of moisture lost due to evaporation. The combination of low organic content, alkaline soil, and salinity inhibits the absorption of many nutrients and water. Fortunately, we have a wide choice of plants that survive these conditions and are actually easy to grow.

While much of the above has dealt with average rainfall and temperatures, there are wet years with 13 or more inches (33+ centimeters) of rain followed by dry years with as little as 4 inches (10 centimeters). Gardening in the desert means adapting to lots of changes, sometimes very rapid ones. Temperatures not only vary from winter to summer, but from day to night they can differ by as much as 40°F (4°C) or more.

One of the most common events that affects the desert garden is mild spring weather followed by a late freeze. Most native plants have adapted to this phenomenon by breaking winter dormancy later in the season than non-native plants. After such a freeze, it's easy to see the advantage of using native plants when compared to the frozen, dead non-natives. Two of our most common natives, mesquite and catclaw acacia, are considered an indication by desert dwellers of when to plant tender vegetable crops such as beans, corn, and tomatoes. Once these natives have leafed out, frost is most likely gone for the season.

Drought Adaptations

Perhaps a desert plant's greatest challenge is surviving in a land of perpetual arid or semiarid conditions (drought is the term used when rainfall falls below normal). Native plants have found many ways to meet this challenge, starting with their roots. Some plants, including yuccas, have thick, fleshy roots which can store moisture. Others, such as the agaves, have developed extensive fibrous root systems that go far beyond the plant body. These roots grow close to the soil surface, and they can absorb moisture from very light rains. Many native plants, including desert willow, mesquite, and soaptree yucca, have developed long taproots capable of growing down very far in order to reach underground water. Yuccas, mesquite, and other plants have developed both fibrous roots and taproots in order to increase their chance of survival.

Leaves are another plant part that has been modified to withstand an arid lifestyle. The thick, succulent leaves of the agaves are very good at conserving moisture. Many desert plants, such as creosote bush, have reduced the size of their leaves. Smaller leaves have less surface area and, as a result, less moisture is lost. Some plants have covered their leaves with tiny hairs or waxlike resins to prevent further moisture loss. Other shrubs and trees are drought deciduous, shedding their leaves to minimize water loss during hot, dry spells. Some of these, such as honey mesquite and ocotillo, can still carry on some photosynthetic activity in their stems.

Perhaps the most uniquely adapted and well known of the drought-tolerant desert plants are cacti and other succulents. By storing water in their tissues, they avoid the need to search for water deep in the ground. During periods of dry weather they shed their small root hairs to avoid water loss. They can regrow these root hairs within twenty-four hours after a heavy rain.

In contrast to most other plants, cacti also prevent loss of moisture to evaporation by opening their stomata (minute surface pores that allow the plant to exchange gases) at night when the relative humidity is higher and closing them during the day when there is lower, 10 to 20 percent, humidity.

When water is available, cacti and succulents can absorb moisture rapidly by means of finely branched roots and the previously mentioned root hairs. Water is taken up by the plants and stored in ribbed stems or stems with tubercles, in the cacti, for example. Agaves store water in large, fleshy leaves. There is a limit, however, to the amount of water that can be stored; beyond this limit, these plants will rot.

Desert cacti have also taken the route of giving up leaves altogether as another way to minimize water loss (opuntias have tiny leaves when the pads are young, but these are quickly shed as the pads mature). All the functions of leaves are conducted by the stems of a cactus. Other adaptations cacti have made for conserving water are spines for shading as well as for protection, waxy coating of the epidermis, and wool or hairs covering the sensitive growing area on the tops of some types, such as blue barrel (*Echinocactus horizonthalonius*). The ribbed stems of some cacti and the rosettes of succulents such as agaves and yuccas have evolved to direct water down to their fibrous root systems.

Winter-Hardy Cacti's Adaptations to Cold

While other plants shed their leaves in the fall, cacti, which have no leaves to shed, prepare for the winter by giving off moisture. The plants shrivel regardless of the fall weather. By the time the plants are very desiccated, their cells are dry enough that severe freezing does not kill them. Amazingly, the cells can shrink to as much as one-sixteenth of the size they are during the growing season. In spring the tissues will swell, the cacti will break dormancy, growth will resume, and flowering will begin. Without this dormant period many cacti will fail to flower.

LEFT
The leaves of a New Mexico agave form a rosette which channels water down to its root system. Its unique shape also makes it an attractive accent plant.

RIGHT
Hidden by the showy flowers is an area of woolly fibers which protects the new growth of a blue barrel cactus from the intense desert sun.

Wildflowers brighten the desert floor as the sun sets behind the Organ Mountains in New Mexico. With such landscapes as inspiration desert gardens can be created which will reflect the region's natural beauty.

Keeping these plants dry in winter requires taking a couple of precautions. Obviously no more water should be given to the plants than is necessary to keep them alive. A mulch of gravel as much as 2 to 4 inches (5 to 10 centimeters) thick should be placed around the plants. This will help keep the surface dry as well as the bases of the cacti, which are especially prone to rot. In the Southwest this may or may not be necessary, depending on soil type, elevation, and the amount of rainfall an area receives. Those areas with desert pavement, a natural layer of weather-varnished pebbles, already have the right conditions for these plants.

A desert is uniquely defined by the very nature of its climate. Nothing looks sadder than seeing an ill-adapted, non-native tree suffering the effects of wind burn, sun scorch, iron chlorosis, and so forth. Working with already adapted native plants, we can have gardens of beauty without fighting the elements.

CHAPTER 2 Designing a Desert Garden

Desert plants are known for their interesting shapes, colorful flowers, wonderful textures, and unique adaptations. In designing your own desert garden, combining all of these attributes will result in a beautiful landscape in balance with the natural desert environment. Although there are many excellent works on the technical aspects of landscape design, some of which are listed in the Bibliography, this book focuses more specifically on designing with native plants of the Chihuahuan Desert.

Our goal is a garden that is self-sustaining as much as possible as well as being beautiful to look at. In many areas of the country water conservation has become of paramount importance, and a number of communities, including several southwestern cities, are passing ordinances banning the use of lawns and/or high-water use plants in front yards. An ideal garden is one that can survive on natural rainfall within three years of planting, as some California cities are advocating. Such a garden is attainable by using desert plants, both native and introduced. However, there are also ways we can conserve water and still use otherwise desirable plants that would not be able to survive without extra watering. The desert gardening landscape style and the plants discussed in this book are a means of achieving the above, and it can be done on anyone's budget. Cacti, succulents, and native shrubs and trees are easily propagated and grown. Other materials, such as rocks and mulches can be gathered locally, often free for the asking. If you're not the do-it-yourself type or just need some additional help, a landscape architect or designer can be hired to design your plan, and/or a landscape contractor can be hired to do the site work and planting.

New Mexico agave, Engelmann prickly pear, and bird-of-paradise are combined into a distinctive arrangement in front of a stuccoed wall, evoking the popular image of the Southwest desert.

Desert gardening is a naturalistic approach to landscaping. At first glance, this may seem simple, but making desert landscaping look natural takes experience and a knowledge of native plants. However, by reading and studying, anyone can learn to take care of these plants' needs. Fortunately, many of them are forgiving and do well with very little care.

Left
Lush yet drought tolerant, this garden of Apache plume, desert olive, and little bluestem grass looks as if it had occurred spontaneously in nature.

Right
Surrounded by a bed of wildflowers, such as the vibrant verbena here, sotols make dramatic accent plants. Although they have small prickles, sotols lack the needlelike tips of their relatives, the agaves and yuccas, making them easier to use in the garden.

If you are lucky enough to move into a home where there has been little disturbance to native vegetation, landscaping can be a process of adding plants here and there for various purposes. Most native plants (those that have been collected, that is) are difficult to transplant due to their root systems. For this reason, preserving any existing plants should be an important consideration. Regrettably, developers frequently level and scrape the land bare of all native vegetation, building houses without regard to terrain, solar aspect, and so forth—a practice that should be stopped. In the meantime we can restore these home lots by planting both species that were removed and others native to the region.

A desert garden, like any other, has a link with its surroundings; that is, the overall climate dictates what plants can be grown. Using native trees, shrubs, and other plants, a regional identity is maintained. Often in the Southwest there are broad vistas which the gardener can deliberately take advantage of, incorporating the larger view into the landscape design. The opposite approach, the creation of a courtyard, is another common means of dealing with an arid environment. The walled courtyard was brought to this area by the Spanish settlers by way of Mexico. This hidden oasis protects the garden and its occupants from the desert winds and provides some shade and privacy from others. Native plants, especially the fragrant and finely textured ones such as the acacias and the sculptural ones such as the cacti, can be effectively used here.

With this relaxed style of gardening, be careful not to overdesign. Allow for some serendipity in the naturalistic desert garden. Although your plan should define the areas to be planted with wildflowers, trees, shrubs, succulents, and so forth, don't be surprised when some of them, especially the wildflowers, show up where you least expect them. Often the combinations resulting from these in-garden migrations are better and more beautiful than those we plan.

Non-desert plants can look very much out of place in the desert garden. The most frequently made mistake is the use of evergreens, whose character suggests high mountain forests, as specimen trees. They create too much of a contrast with desert plants unless they are carefully used. However, as with all rules, there are exceptions. Pinyon pines and native junipers are small evergreens that can be successfully incorporated into a desert design. As windbreaks they not only serve as a barrier, they also become a background for the rest of the landscape. The easiest way to avoid planting a tree or shrub that is aesthetically out of place is to use the plants listed in the "Desert Plant Encyclopedia" (see p. 88) and other native or adapted plants.

The aim in designing a desert garden is to achieve a landscape which looks as if it had been created by nature. In order to convey such a feeling, careful planning is required concerning where to place individual plants or groups of plants. Be aware of the mature size of the plants in order to avoid planting too closely, a common mistake when planting young, small plants. The fact that different species have different rates of growth must also be taken into account. Color, both of flowers and foliage, is another factor to keep in mind, as well as how foliage textures vary and can complement or contrast with each other. With all these factors to consider, it is very important to have a knowledge of native plants before beginning your design.

When reading about garden designs and various styles, you'll

Arid-adapted wildflowers, including paperflower and pine-leaf penstemon, grow alongside a dry stream bed of rocks, creating an illusion of a wetter area.

Having a knowledge of plant varieties allows the gardener to select native plants such as chollas, grasses, and shrubs with a wide range of colors and textures.

often come across references to "garden rooms," that is, areas separated from one another to form individual gardens within a landscape. This is usually done in a formal garden style with low or tall hedges. In the desert garden the same effect and purpose can be accomplished by using a line of shrubs such as creosote bush, bird-of-paradise, or cholla, a mixed shrub or wildflower border, or a low planting or edging with plants such as crimson sage, fringed sage, or agaves.

As in a painting, you'll need to establish foreground, middleground, and background. In the foreground you might want to use low-growing plants such as small cacti, chocolate flower, desert zinnia, and blackfoot daisy as ground covers or perhaps a native grass lawn. For the middleground you may want to grow smaller shrubs, larger perennials, and larger succulents such as fairy duster, bush penstemon, and New Mexico agave, which have visual interest in the form of flowers, sculptural shapes, or colorful foliage. The background could consist of larger trees and shrubs such as mesquite, screwbean, or desert willow. By observing plants in the wild and paying attention to the way they grow, you can imitate nature's patterns in the garden. As an example, in nature it's rare to see a single specimen of a plant alone in the desert; usually there are colonies of plant species. You can imitate this by planting small odd-numbered groups of three, five, and so on of the same species.

When selecting plants for a specific site, choose plants with similar water requirements and eliminate any whose needs cannot be easily accommodated with a minimum amount of soil amendments. In short, avoid trying to grow a lot of different species with a variety of cultural needs. Instead, plant in groups as mentioned above and limit those to larger groups of a few species, thereby effectively producing a harmonious naturalistic design.

Once you've gathered ideas, it's time to begin designing on paper. Start by drawing a plot plan (also known as a site analysis) of your land. The easiest way to do this is to use 1/8- or 1/4-inch (3- or 6-millimeter) graph paper, with each square equal to 1 foot (30

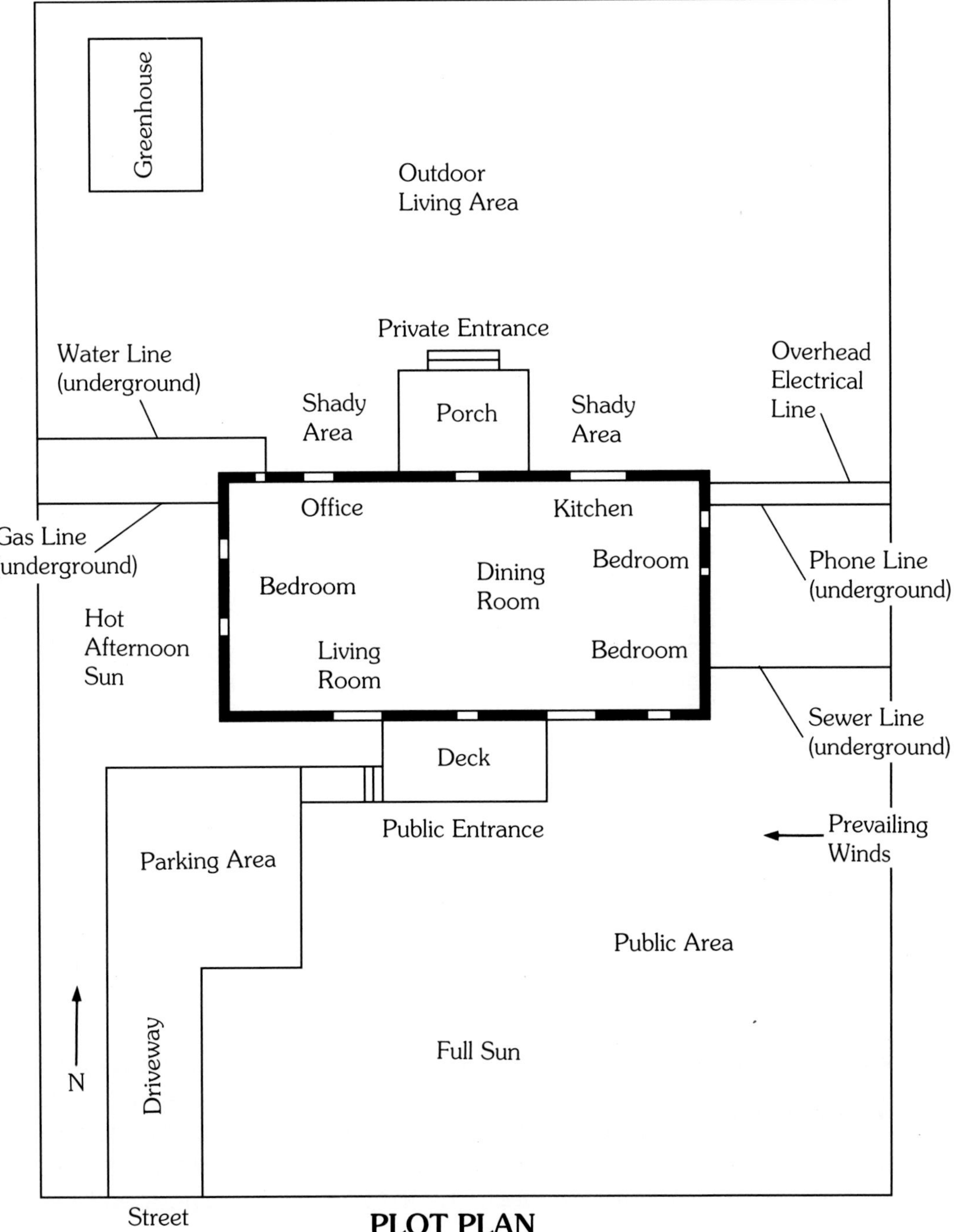

PLOT PLAN

centimeters). Include all the structures and existing landscape features, such as the house (indicating windows, doors, and overhangs), fences and walls, property lines, utility lines, pavement, and existing trees and other vegetation. Also, indicate such things as wind directions, an arrow pointing north, good and bad views, slopes and drainage, and shade and sun.

Next, decide what purposes plants are to serve in your garden, where they will go, what size plants are needed, and which ones are compatible companions. Some of the uses for native plants are as windbreaks, erosion control, shade, privacy, and noise control, as well as decoration. Look through the "Desert Plant Encyclopedia" (p. 88) and choose a selection of plants you like and which will serve your needs.

Perhaps the easiest way to determine the uses of various areas in your design is to draw a bubble diagram (also known as a use analysis). This is a process of dividing up the plot plan into smaller areas, each with its own purpose and planting plan. Keeping in mind that each area should be unified with the rest of the landscape by your overall design, these garden rooms can be enjoyed as separately viewed and used areas. Such garden rooms might include an herb garden, a vegetable garden, or a small orchard, as well as natural desert landscaping. After taking an inventory of your particular needs and desires, begin by drawing large outlines, "bubbles," of various areas and labeling them as to their individual purposes.

Once you have created your bubble diagram, (see p. 15 for an example) it's time to take the final step in designing—the placement of plants and structures (walls, paths, and so forth) on paper. This is the difficult, but fun, part of imagining what your desert garden will eventually look like. Using your bubbles, add to each one any structures you wish such as paths and fences; then draw in the plants you've chosen for that particular area, always keeping in mind their mature size and drawing them that way. Try to tie the garden together by repeating species and groups of plants in the various areas you've defined.

Don't be afraid of designing your own garden. It's fun, and it will give you a sense of direction and your landscape a unity difficult to achieve without a plan. Allow for changes that may become necessary when you actually begin to plant. As the plants grow and mature, they will soften and blend your design into a unique desert garden of your own creation.

Zoning for Water Use

There has been a lot of discussion about dividing the landscape surrounding a residence into zones (not to be confused with U.S.D.A. hardiness zones) from high-water to low-water use plants as a means of conserving water. This is an excellent idea, one that has been practiced by a

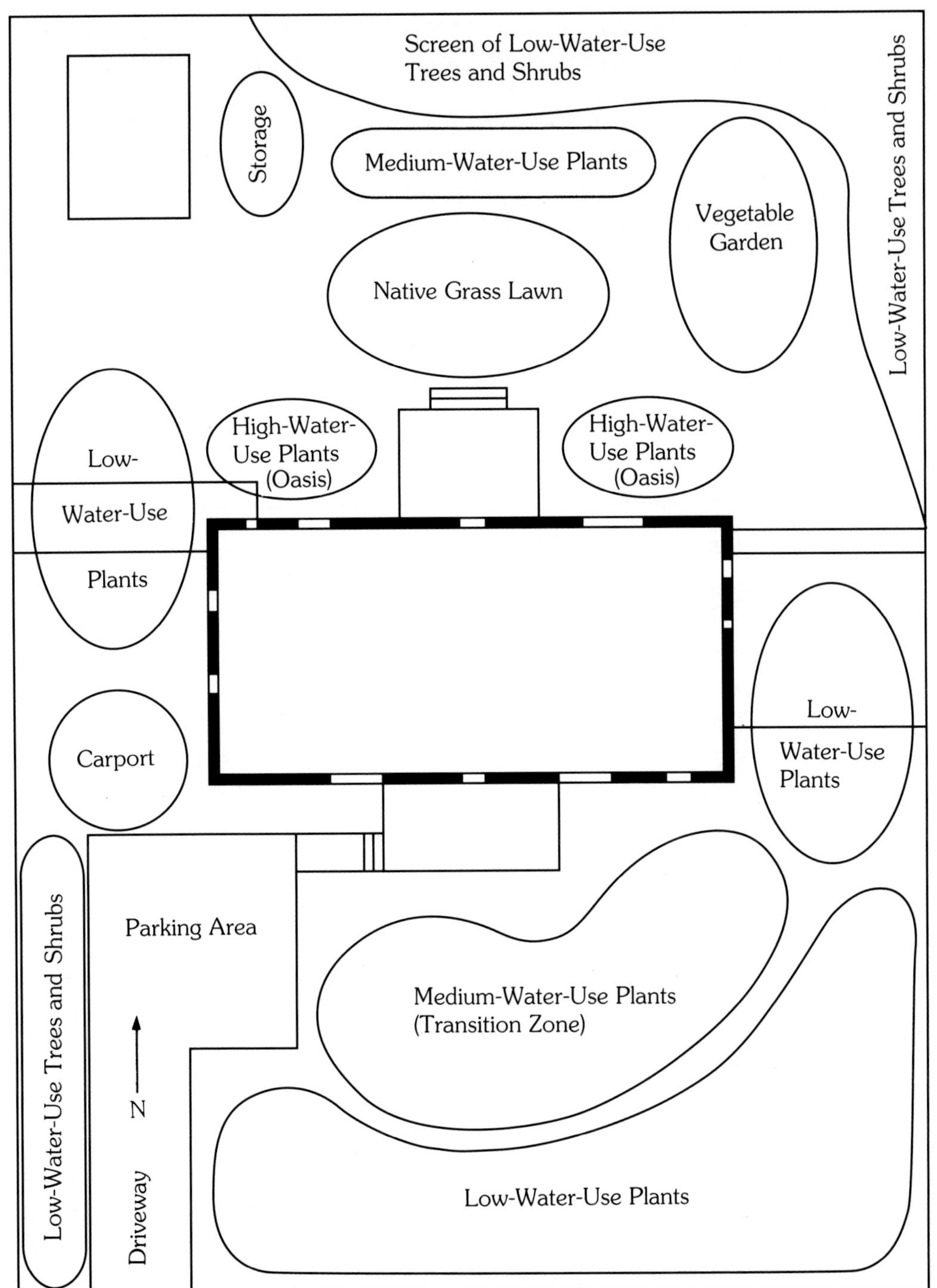

BUBBLE DIAGRAM

few wise people in the past and one that is gaining new converts through a design concept known as Xeriscape. The term Xeriscape is derived from the Greek word *xeri*, meaning dry; that is, a dry landscape. Xeriscape, originated by the Denver Water Department in 1980, is now being used nationwide as a term to describe water-conserving landscaping, no matter what the style. In the book

Landscaping for Water Conservation: Xeriscape, edited by Kimberley M. Knox, the principles of Xeriscape are summarized:

> Xeriscape, water conservation through creative landscaping, uses seven simple landscape principles. Depending on the landscape and the use of these principles, water savings from 30 to 80% have been obtained with the use of Xeriscape. The seven steps are:
>
> 1. *Planning and design*
> 2. *Limited turf areas**
> 3. *Efficient irrigation*
> 4. *Soil improvement*
> 5. *Use mulches*
> 6. *Use low-water demanding plants**
> 7. *Appropriate maintenance*

*"Limited turf area" is now referred to as practical turf area, and use of "low-water demanding plants" is referred to as appropriate plant selection.

These seven principles are easily applied in the desert garden. A good design is essential if the end result is to be both aesthetically pleasing and water-conserving. Using the information in this chapter and elsewhere in the book, you can create a good garden design. This is the first principle.

Turf grass is the largest consumer of water in the landscape. It is, however, often among the most useful areas. Children like to play on the grass, while adults might use it for entertaining company. By using native grasses and limiting the size of the yard, we can follow the second principle: practical turf area.

Watering our gardens is the focus of the third principle. A lot of water can be wasted because of inefficient and/or broken sprinklers. Using drip irrigation, soaker hoses, and the right sprinkler for the right area can save water. Catch run-off water in basins around shrubs and trees until it can soak into the ground. And water during the early morning hours so that less water will be evaporated by the hot, midday desert sun.

Soil improvement is usually not necessary since the plants in this book are well adapted to our desert soils. There are special situations, however, which require the addition of amendments, primarily organic matter, to the soil. Vegetable gardens, for example, will benefit from the added soil fertility as well as the extra water-holding capacity of improved soil.

The use of mulches, the fifth principle, is important in growing desert plants in both the Southwest and elsewhere. Mulches help even out soil moisture. In clay soils gravel mulches help keep the soil from drying out too fast at the surface, which can cause large cracks. In sandy soils mulches can help keep water from evaporating too quickly at the surface, allowing the plants more access to moisture before it drains through. Mulches can also help control weeds by keeping weed seeds from coming in contact with the soil.

Appropriate plant selection is simply a matter of choosing the right plants for the right location. Use the Water Zone Plant List on page 19 to determine which plants need more or less moisture and plant accordingly. By using low-water demanding plants such as desert willows, cacti, and penstemons, we can save water yet have beautiful gardens.

Finally, appropriate maintenance is important in order to keep the plants healthy and the landscape looking good.

Using these principles, water conservation doesn't mean doing without lawns and other vegetation that require extra water. Instead, place them in the high-water zone of your landscape, such as near a patio or entryway where they will be seen the most, or close to your source of water, an outside faucet, for example. You can have a shady oasis surrounded by drought-tolerant desert plants, resulting in less maintenance overall.

Another means of water conservation that can be used in conjunction with the above is simply substituting water-hungry plants with arid-land plants. For example, creosote bush and four-wing saltbush make good hedge substitutes for plants such as euonymus and photinias. Even in high-water use areas, natives that are more tolerant of sun and wind but require extra water, such as desert olive, can find a home. Again, an understanding of a plant's needs is necessary for a successful landscape.

LEFT
Plants in this garden are divided into several zones of water use: high-water-use bluegrass turf in the background, middle-water-use plants such as roses in the middle ground, and low-water-use plants such as desert penstemons in the foreground.

RIGHT
Four-wing saltbush is an excellent shrub for use as a hedge or windbreak. Its seeds are a favorite of wildlife, including quail and other birds.

LANDSCAPE PLAN–PLANT KEY

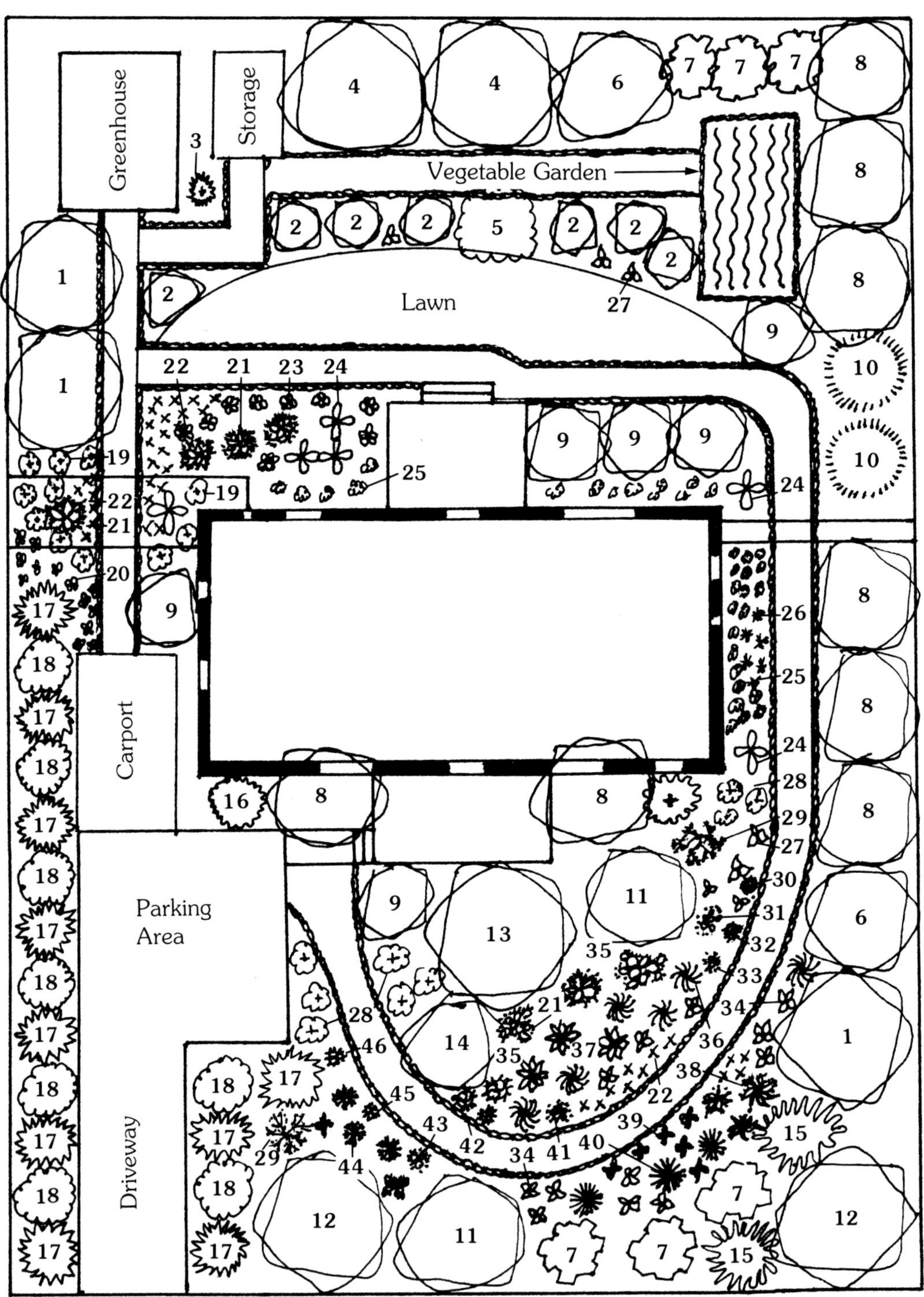

1. *Leucanea retusa* (goldenball leadtree)
2. *Caesalpinia gilliesii* (bird-of-paradise)
3. *Calliandra eriophylla* (fairy duster)
4. *Celtis reticulata* (netleaf hackberry)
5. *Amorpha fruticosa* (indigo bush)
6. *Prosopis pubescens* (screwbean)
7. *Acacia neovernicosa* (Chihuahuan whitethorn)
8. *Chilopsis linearis* (desert willow)
9. *Forestiera neomexicana* (desert olive)
10. *Pinus edulis* (pinyon pine)
11. *Acacia greggii* (catclaw acacia)
12. *Prosopis glandulosa* (honey mesquite)
13. *Sapindus saponaria* (western soapberry)
14. *Ungnadia speciosa* (New Mexico buckeye)
15. *Rhus microphylla* (little-leaf sumac)
16. *Sophora secundiflora* (Texas mountain laurel)
17. *Larrea tridentata* (creosote bush)
18. *Fallugia paradoxa* (Apache plume)
19. *Penstemon ambiguus* (bush penstemon)
20. *Psilostrophe tagetina* (paperflower)
21. *Agave neomexicana* (New Mexico agave)
22. *Zinnia grandiflora* (desert zinnia)
23. *Berlandiera lyrata* (chocolate flower)
24. *Fendlera rupicola* (cliff fendlerbush)
25. *Aquilegia chrysantha* (golden columbine)
26. *Silene laciniata* (Mexican campion)
27. *Penstemon superbus* (superb penstemon)
28. *Salvia greggii* (autumn sage)
29. *Opuntia imbricata* (tree cholla)
30. *Echinocereus fendleri* (Fendler's hedgehog cactus)
31. *Opuntia macrocentra* (purple prickly pear)
32. *Echinocereus chloranthus* var. *chloranthus* (New Mexico rainbow cactus)
33. *Echinocereus cocineus* var. *gurneyi* (red-flowered hedgehog cactus)
34. *Penstemon pseudospectabilis* (desert penstemon)
35. *Opuntia engelmanii* (Engelmann prickly pear)
36. *Nolina texana* (beargrass)
37. *Yucca torreyi* (Torrey yucca)
38. *Agave lechuguilla* (lechuguilla)
39. *Glandularia wrightii* (purple verbena)
40. *Yucca elata* (soaptree yucca)
41. *Escobaria orcuttii* var. *koenigii* (Koenig's pincushion cactus)
42. *Echinocactus texensis* (hc crippler)
43. *Escobaria vivipara* var. *neomexicana* (New Mexic pincushion cactus)
44. *Dasylirion wheeleri* (sotol
45. *Mammillaria wrightii* var. *wrightii* (Wright's pincushi cactus)
46. *Coryphantha macromeris* (Doña Ana cactus)

WATER ZONE PLANT LIST

High to Moderate Water Zone:

Non-native plants
Plants from montane habitats
Crimson sage (*Salvia henryi*)
Desert olive (*Forestiera neomexicana*)
Fragrant ash (*Fraxinus cuspidata*)
Golden columbine (*Aquilegia chrysantha*)
Indigo bush (*Amorpha fruticosa*)
Mealy-cup sage (*Salvia farinacea*)
Mexican campion (*Silene laciniata*)
Mexican elder (*Sambucus mexicana*)
Screwbean (*Prosopis pubescens*)
Western soapberry (*Sapindus saponaria* var. *drummondii*)

Moderate Water Zone:

Acacias
Beargrass (*Nolina texana*)
Bird-of-paradise (*Caesalpinia gilliesii*)
Blackfoot daisy (*Melampodium leucanthum*)
Blue stars (*Amsonia hirtella*)
Cassias
Chocolate flower (*Berlandiera lyrata*)
Cliff fendlerbush (*Fendlera rupicola*)
Crimson sage (*Salvia henryi*)
Desert olive (*Forestiera neomexicana*)
Desert willow (*Chilopsis linearis*)
Desert zinnia (*Zinnia grandiflora*)
Fragrant ash (*Fraxinus cuspidata*)
Goldenball leadtree (*Leucanea retusa*)
Indigo bush (*Amorpha fruticosa*)
Mealy-cup sage (*Salvia farinacea*)
Netleaf hackberry (*Celtis reticulata*)
New Mexico buckeye (*Ungnadia speciosa*)
Penstemons
Purple prairie clover (*Petalostemum purpureum*)
Screwbean (*Prosopis pubescens*)
Sumacs
Texas madrone (*Arbutus texana*)
Texas mountain laurel (*Sophora secundiflora*)
Tufted evening primrose (*Oenothera caespitosa*)
Verbenas
Western soapberry (*Sapindus saponaria* var. *drummondii*)
Yuccas

Low Water Zone:

Acacias
Agaves
Apache plume (*Fallugia paradoxa*)
Beargrass (*Nolina texana*)
Bird-of-paradise (*Caesalpinia gilliesii*)
Blackfoot daisy (*Melampodium leucanthum*)
Broom dalea (*Psorothamnus scoparia*)
Bush penstemon (*Penstemon ambiguus*)
Cacti
Cassias
Chocolate flower (*Berlandiera lyrata*)
Creosote bush (*Larrea tridentata*)
Desert marigold (*Baileya multiradiata*)
Desert willow (*Chilopsis linearis*)
Desert zinnia (*Zinnia grandiflora*)
Fairy duster (*Calliandra eriophylla*)
Four-wing saltbush (*Atriplex canescens*)
Goldenball leadtree (*Leucanea retusa*)
Mesquite (*Prosopis glandulosa*)
New Mexico buckeye (*Ungnadia speciosa*)
Ocotillo (*Fouquieria splendens*)
Paperflower (*Psilostrophe tagetina*)
Screwbean (*Prosopis pubescens*)
Sotols
Sumacs (some)
Threadleaf groundsel (*Senecio douglassii*)
Verbenas (some)
Yuccas

Microclimates In the Southwest, as elsewhere, there are pockets where the overall climate is modified by one or more factors creating what is termed a microclimate. The location of your garden, its elevation, slope, and so forth can determine if it is a warmer or cooler zone than that of the overall climate. In fact, it can be a hardiness zone (United States Department of Agriculture—see p. 80) above or below your zone. Using these microclimates, it is obvious that plants from other areas can thus be accommodated, adding to the variety of species available to gardeners.

South-facing slopes are sunnier and therefore warmer than north-facing slopes. Cool air will follow a slope downhill, resulting in a warm spot at the top of the hill and a cool area at the bottom. Just as a south-facing slope is warmer, so is the south wall of a building; a north-facing slope is cooler, so is the north wall of a building. Plants from lower, hotter elevations will often survive much farther north than their normal range if planted along a south wall. The north wall can be used for plants that require cooler and moister conditions, such as those native to the local mountains.

On some land there may be areas where the drainage is such that there are low spots where runoff can be utilized to water plants. Take notice of the direction of the prevailing winds; some plants may need protection from its drying effects. Wind is especially deadly to plants when combined with low temperatures. This combination prevents transpiration, causing dehydration and death. It is best not to begin planning and planting your land until you've been able to observe the weather patterns and microclimates of your property. Doing this will allow you to place your plants where they will be most likely to flourish.

Windbreaks As with people, some of our desert plants, such as Mexican elder and fragrant ash, need protection from cold winter and blowing spring winds. The combination of sun and wind increases evaporation from plants and the surrounding soil. Essentially what we must do is create protective microclimates in the form of windbreaks. A windbreak can be a fence, a wall (adobe is perfect), or, as more commonly thought of, a planting of trees and shrubs. Avoid planting rows of monocultures, that is, one or two species only. Instead, plant four to five rows of four or five different species of trees and shrubs, ascending in height, in order to lift and divert the wind. Listed in order of ascending size, the following species are among those that make a good windbreak: Apache plume, four-wing saltbush, little-leaf sumac, Texas mountain laurel, desert olive, desert willow, netleaf hackberry, and western soapberry. Starting with

Century plant and autumn sage thrive in the warm microclimate created by surrounding adobe walls in this garden located in the pinyon-juniper woodland found above the desert grassland.

small shrubs and trees on the windward side, build up to medium and taller plants. In a small garden where there is not enough room for four or five rows, a double row is the most effective alternative. Mixed rows of shrubs and trees will be more successful because diseases and insects will be less likely to wipe out more than one or two species at a time. Acting as hedgerows, mixed plantings will bring the extra bonus of attracting wildlife.

Left unmowed, blue grama grass has wonderfully decorative seed heads. This native grass is easy to grow and requires very little fertilizing or watering.

Native Grass Lawns

As an alternative to conventional grasses and other ground covers, a native grass lawn in the desert garden is an excellent choice, as it won't look out of place and will use less water and fertilizer. Lawns should be limited in size and to areas where they will be used, such as play areas for children and game areas for adults.

Most of the native grasses suitable for turf in desert areas are warm-season grasses; that is, they grow and are green during the hot times of the year, and go dormant and turn brown during the cooler seasons. Two of the best for meadows or lawns are blue grama grass and buffalograss.

Blue Grama Grass

Blue grama grass *(Bouteloua gracilis)* is both a bunch and a sod-forming grass that is easy to get established. Its tolerance of dry conditions and poor soils and its cold hardiness make this adaptable plant a favorite of environmentally aware gardeners. Blue grama grass grows 1 to 1½ feet (30 to 45 centimeters) tall.

Buffalograss

Buffalograss *(Buchloe dactyloides)* is one of our best native grasses, known for its ability to withstand foot traffic. As with blue grama, it is tolerant of dry conditions, poor soils, and cold weather. Buffalograss only grows 6 to 9 inches (15 to 23 centimeters) tall and doesn't need mowing. Unmowed it has a wonderfully soft, almost furry-looking appearance. Buffalograss establishes itself by spreading with aboveground runners.

The soil for a native grass lawn must be prepared in the same manner as for a conventional lawn. Till in some natural soil amendments such as peat moss or compost, and any starter fertilizer made for lawns. Mixing the seed with sand or peat moss will make it easier to hand broadcast the seed. Sow in a pattern by swinging your arm from side to side, distributing the seed mix first in one direction, east to west, and then in the other, north to south, for example.

Rake the soil lightly to cover the seed up to 1/2 inch (about 1 centimeter) deep. Then cover with a light mulch of peat moss, manure, sand, or straw. Water immediately and keep watering several times a day for the first three weeks. After germination keep well watered until the grass is established, when only an occasional watering will be needed. Pay attention to natural cycles and let nature help with watering during the summer rainy season.

Blue grama grass and buffalograss are best sown during the warm times of the year, up to a month and a half before the first killing frost. The seed will germinate better if it is cold stratified by placing it in the refrigerator for three weeks prior to sowing.

These grasses, especially when planted in a fifty-fifty mixture of each, will make an excellent turf that can be mowed in those areas where a more manicured appearance is desired. Some places have ordinances requiring this type of maintenance.

Color in the Garden

Desert plants have some of the brightest flowers in the world. The foliage of these plants also has a wonderfully broad spectrum of colors ranging from yellow-green to gray-green. When siting plants, use color as a tool to create special effects. For example, the warm colors of blanketflower complement the same warm colors (red and yellow) of bird-of-paradise. Cool colors, such as blues, purples, and pale pinks, can create moods of peace and serenity.

Gardens can also be based on a single color. White-flowered gardens have become popular because they create a peaceful, restful mood without the bright, attention-getting colors of other flowers. White-flowered gardens are often called moon gardens since many white flowers bloom at night and are fun to view on a warm summer evening. Some white-flowering and cream-colored desert plants include Apache plume, beargrass, blackfoot daisy, bush penstemon, cliff fendlerbush, desert willow (white-flowered forms), desert zinnia (*Zinnia acerosa*), early bloomer, little-leaf sumac, night-blooming cereus, soaptree yucca, sotol, Torrey yucca, tufted evening primrose, and white sand stars.

Other colors can also be used in single-color schemes. Since yellow is the dominant flower color in desert regions, a garden based on yellow would be the easiest to create, with a wide variety of plants to choose from. Yellow draws the eye into the garden, as it is the color which is first picked up by the eye when looking into a garden. Some good choices for a yellow-flowered garden are Chihuahuan whitethorn, chocolate flower, club cholla, desert marigold, desert senna, desert zinnia (*Zinnia grandiflora*), Engelmann prickly pear, goldenball leadtree, New Mexico agave, paperflower, purple prickly pear, Scheer's pincushion cactus, screwbean, and Texas rainbow cactus.

A garden can also be created focusing on colors such as red or pink. Even green can be a dominant color if foliage is the main attraction. There are also a couple of green-flowered cacti, green-flowered torch cactus and desert Christmas cactus.

Clashes of color can occur in the garden just as they do in clothes or elsewhere. Nature, however, has a way of blending even the harshest color combination with harmonious results. Experiment with color in your garden much as a painter experiments on a canvas; plant a living creation of your own design and mood.

A garden path winds through a variety of wildflowers and other plants, following the natural contour of a small arroyo that bisects this property.

The Garden Path

The desert gardening style is essentially informal, and consequently paths should follow the natural contours of the land whenever possible. The idea is to plan the path so that you are drawn into the garden to

Native gardens can be full of color, a pleasant surprise to many people who are unaware of the wide variety of desert flowers.

wander, to see if a prized cactus is blooming, or if the leaves are out yet on the mesquite, and so on. Your path should go somewhere. Turns, rocks, slopes, and plants should be placed so as to entice you to wander through your desert walk. Bend your path around a corner and place a sculpture or sculptural plant such as an agave there to create a visual surprise. Provide places along the way to sit, look, and contemplate the garden and its inhabitants, to check their health and study their form. If there are any features on your property that are special enough to serve as focal points, route the path to go there.

Materials for a desert path range from bare, compacted earth to pavements of various types, such as brick or concrete. Bark mulches can even be used without seeming out of place as one might think. The most natural-looking covers for a path, however, are small gravels or crusher fines. A thin layer 2 to 4 inches (5 to 10 centimeters) thick will provide a comfortable walking surface and is easily kept weed free.

Paths in the desert garden can vary in width from less than 1 foot (30 centimeters) for maintenance routes to 3 to 6 feet (90 to 180 centimeters) for main walkways. Let your path take you and your garden's visitors on an inviting stroll through a desert landscape of unique natural beauty.

Rocks

Anyone who has been to the Southwest has noticed rock outcrops and ledges, a striking feature of the landscape. In the desert garden rocks should be used as specimens or in odd-numbered groups of three, five, seven, and so on. For a natural look, bury rocks part way instead of just setting them on top of the ground. Rocks are much like icebergs; in nature you generally only see part of them above the ground. Rocks can also act like mulch, conserving moisture underneath their surfaces that nearby plants can take

Left
An excellent plant for the dry-country rock garden, desert zinnia has bright yellow flowers that are guaranteed to cheer up any gardener. Rocks and desert plants are a natural combination.

Right
New Mexico agave, fishhook barrel cactus, hedgehog cacti, ocotillo, and other desert plants form a colorful border between the house and sidewalk in this front yard.

This garden consists of various hedgehog cacti and barrel cacti, which look like living sculptures.

advantage of. A mixture of various rock sizes and gravel will contribute to the desert garden's appearance. Larger rocks or boulders can be used as focal points or as accents; but be careful of overdoing it. For borders and edgings, rocks are among the most successful and easily used materials. Rocks can be purchased or gathered. A good place to find free ones is along recently graded dirt roads or road cuts into hillsides.

Desert Icons: Cacti and Succulents in the Landscape

Many authors who have previously written about southwestern native plants have been reluctant to include agaves, cacti, and yuccas, some of our most representative regional plants. There are several reasons for this. First and foremost is their association with the rock and gravel landscaping style discussed in the introduction. Second, they are perceived as difficult to keep tidy, especially the cacti. This is most often the result of incorrect placement in the landscape and a general lack of knowledge as to the many different species that exist. The only cacti many people are familiar with are the opuntias: prickly pears and chollas. Their impressions of cacti are due to painful experiences while weeding or when brushing up against these sharply spined and barbed plants. Large opuntias do require careful placement and generally may not be among the best plants for a small landscape; however, many of our other cacti and succulents are very good plants for desert gardens.

Cacti and succulents of the Chihuahuan Desert range in size from tiny plants such as button cactus (*Epithelantha micromeris*), a couple of inches across, to very large plants such as soaptree yucca (*Yucca elata*), several feet wide and tall. Smaller varieties are easier to use in the garden. Larger varieties, on the other hand,

Soaptree yucca, ocotillo, and prickly pears are dramatic plants that require careful placement in the landscape so their forms can be appreciated.

need to be chosen carefully and should be planted where they won't become a problem when they reach mature size.

This group of plants can be used in all areas of your garden or to create separate gardens. In addition to the general guidelines for landscaping previously discussed, there are some additional ways to use cacti and succulents in the garden. Use your imagination when designing with these fascinating plants. An individual giant Torrey yucca (*Yucca torreyi*) or New Mexico agave (*Agave neomexicana*) can make a strong sculptural statement in the landscape. Place them in an open spot where their dramatic forms can be appreciated or against an adobe wall, which will show them off beautifully. Large rocks and a gravel mulch will keep the planting looking neat, keep the weeds down, and add a natural appearance to the overall composition.

The smaller cacti and succulents, such as pincushions, hedgehogs, or agaves, can be used very effectively as part of your foreground and middleground areas. Additionally, in a garden with several vertical layers they can be a part of the understory layer. In these situations groups of the same species will create a strong, geometric statement. These plants, especially the pincushion cacti such as some of the mammillarias, coryphanthas, and escobarias appreciate being grown under the light shade of the branches of airy shrubs such as acacias, bird-of-paradise, and mesquite. Not only is this healthier for the plants, but they can also be "discovered" on garden walks, especially when they are in bloom.

Finding the right spot in the garden for a clump of purple prickly pear is rewarding. This plant bursts with yellow flowers followed by the appearance of decorative red fruit.

In recent years island beds have become popular for perennials, and they also can be used effectively with this group of plants. Island beds consist of raised mounds of earth arranged in oval, kidney, and other fluid geometric shapes. Larger plants should be grouped on top of the mound and smaller ones around them to the bottom of the mound. One advantage of island beds is that they can be viewed from all sides, thus showing off the plants; another advantage is that they are raised and drain better, especially with soils amended with gravel, sand, or scoria (crushed volcanic rock).

Succulents can make good ground covers. Lechuguilla (*Agave lechuguilla*), for example, will spread extensively by offsets. Some opuntias such as club cholla (*Opuntia clavata*) are also spreaders. Obviously, succulent ground covers cannot be placed anywhere there is going to be foot traffic, as neither the plants nor the people can take it.

Yuccas and sotols are usually included in works on succulents even though they are correctly identified as semisucculents. They are certainly good companions for other desert plants. There is a yucca variety for every Southwest garden, and every garden should have a yucca since their character is so symbolic of the region.

The very large and showy flowers of strawberry cactus contrast dramatically with the sharply spined stems of the plant.

When planting cacti and succulents, care should be taken to ensure their survival. Many nursery plants begin life in a greenhouse and are protected for much of their early life in lath houses or by other means. They will need to be acclimated to the change in growing conditions gradually. Cacti and succulents should be planted after all danger of frost is past and preferably during the hottest times of the year. Plant them early enough in the summer so they can establish themselves before winter. Protect them for about one week from the hot, midday sun with some sort of shade structure to prevent sunburning the plants. Once they have adjusted to their new home, the majority like a good amount of sunshine and airy conditions. While the cacti should not be watered until they are established, the other succulents should be well watered after planting.

Because of its large size Torrey yucca can be a striking landscape feature. It needs to be located where it has plenty of room and where its form can be appreciated.

Chihuahuan Desert cacti have some of the most beautiful flowers in the plant kingdom. They will often bloom several times a season, depending upon rainfall. While the majority are hardy throughout the desert regions of the Southwest, lizard-catcher (*Mammillaria grahamii*) and golf ball cactus (*Mammillaria lasiacantha*) are somewhat tender and need protection from severe winter cold. They should probably be restricted to sites below 4,000 feet (1,200 meters) in elevation or planted in warm microclimates.

Regarding the frequent complaint that cacti and succulents are difficult to weed, this is in large part due to the opuntias. Opuntias have small, almost microscopic spines called glochids, which are actually more of a problem than the larger spines. They flake off the cactus and work their way into the skin. It's true that these make weeding and cleaning out trash from prickly pears and chollas an unpleasant task. Although other cacti and succulents also have spines, some quite sharp, they are more easily avoided than the spines of the opuntias. Many lie flat against the body of the plant or are so small that you can weed the plants or even pick them up easily. Weeds germinate best in soil that has been disturbed; therefore, to avoid the problem of weeding cacti, including opuntias, be careful when planting them to disturb the soil as little as possible.

As with any plant, careful planning and consideration are necessary in placing cacti and succulents in a garden. They are our most intriguing plants, highly prized by collectors around the world, and those who live in the Southwest deserts are indeed lucky to be able to use them in their landscapes.

Desert Wildlife and the Garden

As our cities grow, birds and other animals are finding it difficult or impossible to adjust to their new surroundings. The acres and acres of monocultural bluegrass lawns with a few exotic shrubs and trees typical of our urban landscape are unable to support those lovely creatures that used to call these places home. The sad thing is there's no reason we can't have an aesthetically pleasing landscape that's also wildlife habitat. Landscaping with native plants can provide wildlife with those elements needed for their survival: food, cover for protection, and places where they can raise a family. The addition of water in the garden in a low pool or birdbath is another key element in attracting wildlife that also adds a pleasing visual touch. Watching wildlife in the garden is great fun and

This desert garden has all of the elements necessary to attract wildlife: the birdbath furnishes water, bird feeders supply food, and the creosote bushes provide cover.

can be an educational experience for children and adults alike. It's important to remember, however, that wildlife will eat your fruits and vegetables, so you'll need to take a few precautions to protect them. Fences, screens, and mesh netting are a few of the protective materials that can be used. You might also plant native plants that bear fruits or seeds in other parts of the garden to draw wildlife away from your food-producing plants.

It's nice to note that one doesn't need a large area to create a garden for wildlife. In a very small area, you might have room for a small birdbath, a desert willow as a focal point, a clump of hedgehog cactus, and a group of two or three native shrubs. This type of planting will fulfill the needs of wildlife: water, food, and cover.

Designing a wildlife garden isn't much different from designing any other type of garden, with the exception that special attention should be given to planting species which are particularly good for food and shelter (see p. 33 for a list of plants that provide food and shelter for various types of wildlife). One important thing to keep in mind is to plant a dense cover of three- to five-feet-high shrubs somewhere on your property. These plantings should be of several species in order to provide a choice of various foods and habitat throughout the seasons and for different animals' needs. The more such plantings your property can accommodate, the more wildlife you'll be able to attract to the garden.

If you plan to supplement the food available for birds, avoid using commercial seed mixes containing sunflower seeds around plantings of any kind. Sunflower seed hulls (as well as leaves, stems, and roots) are poisonous to other plants. The toxins can leach out and build up in the surrounding soil. It is virtually impossible to get rid of the toxins once the soil is contaminated. If you want to feed the birds sunflower seeds, place your feeders near a paved area, such as a patio, where the hulls won't come into contact with the soil or plants.

When choosing plants, remember that those plants growing wild in the area are the same ones that will attract local wildlife. Don't forget the cacti and yuccas in your design. The chollas especially are very good protection for nesting birds. These plants also produce abundant quantities of fruit and seed with the least amount of rainfall, ensuring food for the wild visitors.

Water must always be available; and it is important that once it is provided to the desert creatures it not be allowed to dry up. They are likely to become dependent upon this source of water and would face hardship if it were suddenly cut off. This is especially true for those rearing young. While our local songbirds will use a birdbath, quail and some other birds prefer water closer to the ground. To attract both quail and other birds a simple solution is to place the top of a birdbath on the ground without a pedestal.

Often used by birds as nesting sites, chollas have thorny branches that offer protection from predators.

Don't be too eager to keep your garden as neat and tidy as you would with a garden that doesn't focus on wildlife. Those blossoms you would normally deadhead to produce more flowers should be left on instead to provide seeds. Similarly, dead wood can provide a home for all sorts of creatures, particularly smaller ones. In a wildlife garden the cycles of life and death are part of the garden's rhythm. A prize-winning flower is not the goal here.

Even in the larger cities it is possible to attract all sorts of desert animals to the garden. We lived in downtown Albuquerque and over the years counted numerous species of birds from hummingbirds and woodpeckers to crows and kestrels. We also saw various types of lizards and toads. Several species of butterflies, including monarchs and swallowtails, were abundant.

An important thing to remember is that insecticides, herbicides, and other chemicals should not be used in a wildlife garden if at all possible. Extreme caution should be used, particularly around water sources and food-bearing plants. For the most part, once the garden is established there's no need for them anyway. Along with the other wildlife, ladybugs, praying mantises, and predatory wasps will do the job of insect control for you.

Hummingbirds are the jewels of the bird world and among our easiest wildlife to attract to our desert gardens. If you're tired of filling hummingbird feeders and want to provide the wee ones with a natural source of food, it is nice to know that many of our most attractive wildflowers have evolved to be pollinated by these birds. These include ocotillo, red-flowered hedgehog cactus, and superb

penstemon. For information about creating a garden especially designed to attract hummingbirds, see Chapter 6.

Some of the most maligned animals around the world are snakes, even though they play an important role in our environment. People living in the Southwest have more to fear from a rodent's bite, especially those carrying the plague or Hanta virus. We would soon be overrun with mice, rats, and other rodents if it weren't for snakes and other predators. With the exception of rattlesnakes and perhaps coral snakes (our Southwest species is shy, and its mouth is quite small, making it difficult for it to bite a human), the rest of our snake species are harmless creatures. They might bite, but unless they are being harassed, this is also unlikely. Snakes which might be encountered in a garden in the Chihuahuan Desert include desert kingsnakes, gopher snakes, coachwhips, Texas long-nosed snakes, Trans-Pecos rat snakes, and western hognose snakes. Rattlesnakes do pose a dilemma. We can't live very easily with them around our homes, even if we are the ones who moved in on their territory. If you encounter a rattlesnake in the garden, try to find someone from a local herpetology group or local wildlife rescue group who can remove it (if you're afraid to do it yourself) and release it farther out in the desert, away from human habitation. As for other snakes, welcome their presence in the garden. They'll help keep the rodent population from eating your favorite plants.

The wildlife you attract to your desert garden will be an endless source of enjoyment and amusement. A pair of roadrunners nested at our home one summer. We watched with anticipation as

Blooming during the summer, New Mexico agave requires very little water and should be planted in the low-water-use area of a Xeriscape. The flowers are a favorite of bats and birds, such as hummingbirds and orioles.

Usually missing from other types of gardens, wildlife such as this roadrunner is a welcome addition to the desert garden.

LEFT
A good plant for the moderate-water-use area of a Xeriscape, tufted evening primrose scents the night air with its sweet perfume. The large white flowers attract hawk moths, which pollinate them.

RIGHT
Growing in desert washes, netleaf hackberry is a useful tree that requires little water. With pruning, it can be trained into a shade tree.

each egg was laid and each youngster appeared. With some feelings of remorse we saw our lizard population decline while mother and father fed the young. Once the young were fledged we often laughed at their antics when they roosted in our greenhouse each night and squawked harsh warnings at us each time we approached too near for comfort. As the summer passed they left us one by one until now we only see them occasionally. We know they're our babies when they visit, since they boldly walk up and chew us out for still being in their territory.

PLANTS TO ATTRACT DESERT WILDLIFE

Bat Plants

Agaves, especially Palmer agave.

Bee Plants

Acacias, agaves, Apache plume, broom dalea, cacti, creosote bush, desert senna, desert willow, honey mesquite, New Mexico buckeye, penstemons.

Berry-producing Plants for Birds and Small Mammals

Desert olive, Mexican elder, netleaf hackberry, sumacs, Texas madrone, and western soapberry.

Butterfly Plants

Apache plume, bird-of-paradise, blanketflower, desert marigold, desert senna, paperflower, penstemons, salvias, and threadleaf groundsel.

Hawkmoth Plants

Evening primroses, night-blooming cereus, and yuccas.

Hummingbird Plants

Agaves, bird-of-paradise, some cacti, desert willow, golden columbine, crimson sage, Mexican campions, ocotillos, and penstemons (especially red ones).

Seed-producing Plants for Birds and Small Mammals

Various grasses, wildflowers (especially composites), shrubs, trees, and succulents produce seeds eaten by a wide variety of wildlife.

For doves and quail: Acacias, chollas, desert senna, evening primroses, fairy duster, four-wing saltbush, honey mesquite, prickly pears, purple prairie clover, and screwbean.

Other Plants Used as Food by Wildlife

Acacia foliage and yucca leaves are sometimes eaten by jackrabbits. Agaves and opuntias are eaten by javelina. Desert willow seeds are eaten by a variety of birds. The seeds of honey mesquite are eaten by many different animals, including birds, coyotes, deer, jackrabbits, squirrels, and rodents.

CHAPTER  Desert Births: Propagation

The demand for native plants, especially native cacti and other succulents, has increased as more and more people in the Southwest are using them in their gardens. As a result it has become increasingly important to protect rare and endangered plants, which are illegal to collect in the wild. When you go to the nursery, be sure to ask if the plants sold there are wild collected or nursery propagated. Don't purchase plants from "locals" selling trees, shrubs, yuccas, and so forth out of the back of a pickup truck. Even if the plants were legally collected, their chances of survival are far less than those grown under nursery conditions. If the plant does die, you usually have no guarantee, and finding the seller will more than likely prove to be impossible.

A better way to obtain native plants for your desert garden is to grow your own plants from seeds, cuttings, offsets, and so forth. Not only is it more environmentally responsible, it also has several other advantages. Many times you will want large quantities of plants for your desert landscape design, which would be quite expensive if purchased individually. It is much more inexpensive to start the plants you need from seed, and even more so if you collect the seed yourself. By using seed, the parent plant is left to continue its life and produce seed for future generations of the species and for wildlife.

There are a limited number of natives that are available as plants in nurseries. Seeds, however, are more widely available for purchase, and your own collections might include unusual species that few others have grown, giving your garden a uniqueness (see Appendix II: Mail-order Sources for Seeds and Plants). Part of the joy of gardening is growing a plant from seed, tending to its needs from infancy to adulthood, and feeling the excitement of seeing that first blossom, perhaps of a flower you've never seen before.

Ornamental plants, including many of those natives commercially available, are most often those that are easily propagated as well as being attractive. Some of our native plants require certain strategies and treatments to get them to germinate, unlike

LEFT
Not only does it have exotic, beautiful flowers, bird-of-paradise is also easily started from seed. It grows so fast that it often blooms the first year from seed if started early in the year.

RIGHT
The bright red fruit of Engelmann prickly pear is very attractive when ripe and full of large, hard seeds in late summer and early fall.

many typical garden plants that are more than likely hybrids selected not only for aesthetic qualities but also for high germination rates and ease of growing. With the exceptions of creosote bush and the opuntias, the seeds of all the plants in the "Desert Plant Encyclopedia" can be readily germinated.

Seed Collection and Storage

Be sure to check into any laws in your area regarding seed collection before you begin, particularly on various government lands. Perhaps you have some land yourself or have a friend who has a place you can collect on. If you see some plants growing on some property and you don't know the owners, ask them for permission to collect on their land. More often than not, they won't mind as long as you are courteous and respect the property and its contents. Wild plants generally produce more seeds than necessary for germination as a protection against the elements and animals. Taking small quantities of seeds from large stands of healthy plants will have a negligible effect on the population. Never take more than you need, and leave plenty for reproduction and wildlife.

The timing of seed ripening depends largely on the blooming season of the plants you're interested in. Other than some general guidelines, observation and experience are the best guides. Seed will usually be ready a couple of months after the last flowering. The easiest way to tell a ripe fruit or seedpod is a change in color, usually from green to black, brown, tan, or red. Plants such as bird-of-paradise, agave, and penstemon have pods that split open when the seed is ripe. The entire seed heads of composites can be picked when dry. Cacti produce fleshy fruits that will detach readily when ripe. Many are covered with spines. Depending on the size of the fruit, tongs or tweezers should be used to harvest them. Cacti seeds, which are usually brownish or blackish and fairly large, benefit from a period of after-ripening; allowing the fruits to dry in a warm location is the easiest way to deal with them. After the fruit is thoroughly dry, it can be broken or smashed, and the dry seeds will spill out.

If possible to obtain, seed collected from cultivated native plants is highly desirable. Not only are the plants easier to get to, the seed is usually produced abundantly because of the extra care the plants have most likely received. More viable seed is often obtained from garden-grown plants also. One of the drawbacks to this seed is the chance of hybridization between different species of the same genera, such as some of the cacti and penstemons. Also there is less genetic variability, and the bad traits as well as the desirable ones will be passed along to future plants.

A paper bag is good for both collection and storage of seeds until they have dried. Always write the plant's name on the bag as later it may be difficult to identify the seeds or remember what plant they came from. As soon as possible after collection, clean the seeds of debris, which will lessen any chance of disease or insect larvae that may be living in the fruit. Large seeds, such as those of desert willow or Torrey yucca, are easy to remove from their pods. Other seeds require further cleaning to separate the chaff from the seeds, as in some of the composites such as desert zinnia and paperflower. Sometimes there is more than one means of cleaning seeds. For example, small quantities of penstemon capsules can be opened by splitting them in two and releasing the seeds. This is time consuming, however, and larger quantities require a different strategy. Begin by crushing the pod, seeds and all. Place the chaff and seeds in a strainer of some sort. Although sieves can be purchased for this purpose, a tea strainer or larger strainer made for kitchen use will work just fine. When shaken a little, the smaller and heavier seeds will pass through the holes, leaving most of the debris behind. A small amount will pass through with the seeds, but for the most part the seeds will be relatively clean. After the seeds have dried in the paper bag, it's a good idea to put them into jars for long-term storage so that they retain the moisture necessary to maintain their viability.

Soil Mixes for Seeds

Having cleaned and stored your seeds during the winter, when spring comes the time for sowing those seeds is at hand. Of course, with the proper storage of seeds and with the right amounts of heat and light, seeds can be started at other times of the year. The first task is to prepare a soil mix that is suitable for growing native plants. A general recipe that is good for starting almost all native desert plants, including cacti, consists of two-thirds potting soil and one-third sand. Although almost any potting soil will do, fine-grained soils that are formulated for sowing seeds are the best choice. The addition of the sand gives the mix some extra weight and the leanness desired by some of these plants. Such a soil mix also minimizes the presence of disease organisms, which is especially desirable when sowing seeds indoors, including inside greenhouses and in cold frames. For this reason avoid using garden soils, which could introduce diseases into your seed flats.

Outdoor seed beds contain a risk of disease; however, the greatest risk to seedlings, a fungal infection known as damping off, is reduced due to better air circulation than indoors. When preparing an outdoor seed bed, the addition of organic amendments such as manure, compost, and peat moss will aid in the ease of germination and growth of your seedlings. A sunken garden bed, the best means of starting yuccas from seed, works well for all desert natives except cacti. To prepare a sunken bed, begin by removing 1 foot (30 centimeters) of the topsoil layer from an area 2 to 4 feet (60 to 120 centimeters) square. Save the removed soil on a piece of plastic or in a large wheelbarrow. Then take out some soil from the next layer and place it around the perimeter of the square being dug to form a lip. Next, mix the soil that was saved with whatever organic amendments you have in a fifty-fifty ratio and return enough to fill the hole in the bed. Level the soil and it's ready for planting. The bed can be watered by flood irrigating it with a bubbler attached to the end of a hose. A seed bed such as this should be located in full sun to partial shade.

Sowing Seeds of Desert Plants

A 4- or 6- inch (10- or 15-centimeter) flat or pot can hold a large number of seedlings of many of the cacti, succulents, wildflowers, shrubs, and even some trees. Begin by filling your flat with your soil mix, tamping it so it is firm and level. Sprinkle the seeds on top, trying to keep them evenly spaced. Cover small seeds with a light layer of soil mix. Larger seeds need to be covered with soil to about three times their dimension. Very large seeds of some trees and shrubs, such as New Mexico buckeye and mesquite, can be sown directly into large containers, 1 gallon (3.8 liters) and larger, containing the leaner soil usually used for transplants. In order to prevent damping off, a fungal infection that is the main killer of young seedlings, sprinkle the flat with garlic powder (*not garlic salt—it will kill the seedlings*), which has fungicidal properties. Cacti and other succulents require an additional step. Place a thin layer of fine gravel (the type used for aquariums is good) on top of the soil and the seeds. Water the flat thoroughly either by gently sprin-

The flowers of paperflower remain on the plant long after their seeds are ripe. The seeds can be collected after the flowers have dried.

kling the top with a spray bottle or by soaking the flat in a saucer of water. Place the flat in a plastic bag to maintain a high humidity. Watch for sprouting (time varies with the species), and remove the bag after the seeds germinate. (This step is not necessary if you're starting your seeds in a greenhouse.)

To sow seeds in an outdoor seed bed, make furrows in the soil, being careful not to make them too deep for the seeds. Plant the seeds down the furrow rows and cover them with soil. Then water them thoroughly. In the Southwest a seed bed may need to be watered two to three times a day. As with seed flats, the seeds in an outdoor seed bed must be kept moist until they germinate. Many people don't realize that native seeds and seedlings need as much water as non-native plants until they germinate, and even afterwards for the first few years of their lives until they are well established.

Special Seed Treatments

If you have provided your seeds with the above conditions and they still won't germinate, they may be incapable of growing without special treatment. This is due to the timing of seed ripening in the wild. In a desert climate seeds must have a deterrent to premature germination, as they could be wiped out by drought or cold if they sprouted at the wrong time. Chemical inhibitors in the seed coat and/or hard seed coats are the primary means by which this is accomplished. Using this knowledge to our advantage, we can provide seeds with the conditions necessary for germination and get them to sprout when we want them to.

After-ripening

Some chemical inhibitors simply deteriorate over time, allowing seeds to then germinate. This is called after-ripening. Seeds needing this time period should be stored in a cool, dry location for a year or two. Some of the native seeds that do well after a period of after-ripening include the penstemons and the cacti. They can then be sown as previously discussed without any further treatments.

There are times when neither fresh nor aged seeds will germinate. If you are unsure of what to do, try the following seed treatments. Usually one or a combination of treatments will unlock the secret of getting a seed to sprout. Consult the "Desert Plant Encyclopedia" (p. 88) for germination requirements of individual species.

Stratification

In nature, including the deserts, most seeds ripen at the end of summer and/or the beginning of fall. They have inhibitors as discussed above to prevent them from germinating and being killed by winter's cold. Instead, they wait until the warmer days of spring to begin growing. During this time the embryos of some seeds finish maturing.

Over the course of winter the seeds are subjected to a cold and, hopefully, moist environment. This environment must be simulated in order to get seeds needing this treatment to germinate, a process called cold stratification. The easiest way to cold stratify seeds is to place the seeds in a sandwich bag filled with a moist potting medium (regular potting soil is fine) and put the bag in a refrigerator for a period of one to three months. Do not place the seeds in the freezer, which is too cold. It is easy to tell when certain varieties of seeds such as penstemons and some shrubs and trees are ready, since they will germinate right in the refrigerator! Check the bags every now and then after the first or second month. If the seeds have started producing small roots (radicles), it is time to start them in a seed flat following regular planting procedures. While it is generally recommended that penstemon seeds be cold stratified, and while this will aid in germinating fresh seeds, if they have been through a period of after-ripening as discussed above, cold stratification may not be necessary.

Another means of accomplishing the cold stratification of seeds is to let nature do the work for you. All you need to do is prepare an outdoor seed bed as discussed above and plant it in the fall. Remember to keep it moist over the winter.

Scarification

Scarification is a process by which the outer coat of a seed is removed to allow water to penetrate into the seed. This is done either by using chemicals such as acids or by mechanical means such as sandpaper. None of the plants mentioned in this book requires scarification with acid, and that procedure will not be described here, as it can be dangerous.

Mechanical scarification is a simple procedure requiring only a couple pieces of coarse sandpaper and a couple of wooden blocks. Glue the pieces of the sandpaper on the blocks. Then place the seed in between the two blocks and rub it with the sandpaper until the seed coat is removed. Other mechanical means of scarification involve pricking the seed coat with a pin or needle in order to allow water in. Large seeds, such as honey mesquite and Texas mountain laurel, can also be nicked with a file to accomplish the same thing. No matter what method of mechanical scarification is used, care must be taken not to injure the seed's embryo.

Another alternative to acid and mechanical scarification is known as a hot water bath or treatment. It is a particularly good treatment for the legumes and large batches of seeds. Begin by boiling some water on the stove. Place the seeds in a cup or bowl. Remove the water from the stove, allowing it to cool to 190°F to 200°F (88°C to 93°C). This is accomplished by allowing the water to stop bubbling. When this happens, take the hot water and pour it over the seeds in the container and let it cool. Allow the seeds to soak overnight, but be careful, as the seeds will "drown" if kept in oxygen-deficient water for too long. Amazingly, some seeds such as fairy duster will sprout overnight. The seeds should not be allowed to dry out. A good routine is to prepare the seeds in the evening, soak them overnight, and plant them the next morning.

Some seeds, such as the sumacs, need to be scarified first and then require a period of stratification. For many seeds it is a matter of trial and error. Try following the different treatments in the order given here. For some plants it is simply going to take some time until we can unlock the mystery of getting them to germinate for our purposes.

Whatever treatments you use be sure to label the various flats and sandwich bags with plant names and dates. Nothing is more frustrating than not knowing what plant is being treated, the date treatment was started, or when seeds need to be planted.

Seedlings

After you have planted your seeds, including those you have given special treatments to, be sure that the seedlings have the proper light. Without enough light the seedlings will become weak and spindly. Artificial lights can help when growing them indoors. Otherwise, they can be started outdoors in a cold frame or in a greenhouse. Waiting until there is enough natural light outdoors will eliminate this problem.

The timing of planting outdoors is also determined by the various temperature requirements of each particular species. Artemesias and columbines prefer cool temperatures and can be planted as early as February in many areas of the Southwest. A broad range of species such as superb penstemon, Apache plume, and desert olive can be planted from March to May. Cacti, succulents, mesquites, desert willow, and many other plants prefer very warm temperatures and can be sown from mid-May to mid-September.

Transplanting Seedlings

Once the seedlings are up and growing, keep them moist. Although they need a good amount of light, also be aware that they can sunburn. Cacti and succulent seedlings prefer being somewhat crowded and resent transplanting too early and too often. While they grow slowly at first, from their second year on they grow fairly rapidly.

When the seedlings of other native desert plants develop their first set of true leaves, they are ready to be transplanted. When transplanting seedlings, use a leaner soil mix than that which was used in the germination flat or pot. A good soil mix for all of our Chihuahuan Desert plants should be well draining and somewhat lean (that is, not too rich in nutrients). A combination of good soil such as that used by professional growers (available at many garden centers and greenhouse supply stores) or regular potting soil and one-third to two-thirds sand or scoria (crushed volcanic rock)

Mexican elder is an attractive, small- to medium-sized tree. It is easily propagated from seeds or cuttings and is one of the most popular native plants offered by nurseries.

The largest native prickly pear in the Southwest, Engelmann prickly pear is easily propagated from cuttings of its pads.

works well. The different ratios vary with the different species' needs, although the two-thirds mix is a good general mix for most species.

To transplant the seedlings, remove them from the pot or flat with a spoon or knife. Lift the seedling gently by the leaves and place it in the new pot. Never lift the seedling by the stem because it will usually die if damaged. After firming the soil around the seedling, water it thoroughly.

Different species of desert plants grow at different rates. Some, such as honey mesquite, grow astonishingly fast and are ready to plant outdoors in late summer. Many will be ready for planting by the fall. Still others, such as the small cacti and many succulents, won't be ready until the second year after being started.

Other Methods of Propagating Chihuahuan Desert Plants

There are various ways of propagating native desert plants besides seeds, including cuttings, divisions, and offsets. This section discusses the advantages to these methods, also known as asexual reproduction. For some plants, such as prickly pears and chollas, it may be difficult to get seeds to germinate but easy to start them from a cutting. Others may take a long time to grow from seeds, and cuttings or offsets may produce larger plants more quickly. Another reason plants are often produced asexually is to propagate a particularly nice horticultural specimen.

Cuttings

There are several different types of cuttings, including hardwood and softwood cuttings. While several of the plants listed in this book can be propagated by these methods, all of the plants listed are easily grown from seed, with the exception of creosote bush and the opuntias. While creosote bush remains a difficult plant to propagate, opuntias are easy to grow from cuttings. Other plants that are easy to propagate from cuttings include crimson sage, desert willow, Fendler penstemon, hedgehog cacti, mealycup sage, Mexican elder, and superb penstemon.

To start opuntia cuttings, cut a pad or joint from the parent plant. Allow the cut end to callous over, that is, to dry out for three or four days. After this has been done, take the pad or joint and pot it up in a container. Water it lightly to stimulate root production.

For further information on taking cuttings of other native plants, consult a book that specializes in plant propagation.

Easily reproduced from cuttings, crimson sage has bright red flowers that are favored by hummingbirds.

Division

Many native perennials can be propagated by dividing the parent plant into several new, smaller individual plants. Begin by digging up the parent plant and cutting it up into sections with a knife or pulling it apart into separate sections. These can then be directly planted into the garden or potted up for further growth. In either case be sure to water them well. Many times, division of the parent plant stimulates new growth and rejuvenates an otherwise declining plant. Some of the plants in this book that can be propagated by this method are blanketflower, chocolate flower, penstemons, hedgehog cacti, and verbenas.

Offsets

Actually a form of division, offsets are young clones formed at the base of the parent plant that can be removed and planted. Begin by digging around the base of the mother plant to further expose the offset and as much root as possible. Cut off the young shoot with a knife. Replant the offset in the ground or in a container for further growth as with other divisions. This is a quick means of reproducing some natives such as yuccas and agaves that would take awhile if grown from seed.

Propagating plants of the Chihuahuan Desert is a rewarding experience. There is a tremendous sense of satisfaction in seeing wildflowers, native shrubs, or cacti you have raised thrive and bloom for the first time. From then on you can look forward to future years of enjoyment from your green success. Economically,

This large Parry agave has a number of offsets surrounding it. Such offsets can be dug up and transplanted elsewhere in the garden or in containers.

propagating your own plants makes it possible to have a garden rich in plant species and numbers without great expense. Environmentally, it helps restore a balance of nature to our man-made environment, providing food and shelter for wildlife.

CHAPTER 4 Care of Desert Plants

A garden of native desert plants in the Southwest is by its very nature a low-maintenance landscape, but it is not a no-maintenance landscape! Many people have the mistaken idea that native plants can simply be planted and left to fend for themselves. Initially, native plants need the same care as non-native plants to survive the desert environment. For example, until they have established their root systems, native plants (except for cacti) need to be regularly watered.

Because native plants are low maintenance, they are ideal replacements for the water and energy inefficient landscapes that often surround commercial and industrial buildings. Too often we see small median strips planted with bluegrass. Not only is it a thirsty planting, it is difficult to mow and maintain. Bluegrass is also very much out of character with the surrounding natural landscape. With native plants such as low-growing shrubs and wildflowers, less water and fertilizers are required and the flavor of the region is retained.

Many people are interested in native plants but are unsure of the correct means of taking care of them. The following information on native plants will provide a basic knowledge of some of the requirements for growing and maintaining these desert denizens.

Desert Soils

There are several types of soils in the deserts of the Southwest. Near mountain foothills, they often consist of decomposed granite. The flat plains of the desert grasslands and the desert itself often have sandy or gravelly soils. Riparian areas and their associated floodplains may also contain sandy areas as well as heavy clay soils deposited in years past when periodic floods were common.

The various soil types can pose different problems when we attempt to garden in them. Trying to amend the soils with various things, including sand or organic matter such as compost, is probably a waste of time except in small planting beds. While clay soils hold lots of water and sandy soils lose water rapidly, it is more beneficial (and far less expensive) to mulch than try to change their structure, especially when dealing with large areas. Soil amendments in most desert soils usually break down so rapidly that they are of little value. Exceptions to this are special areas, such as vegetable gardens, orchards, and non-native plantings.

The easiest way to deal with our soils is not to deal with them at all! There's no need to if you plant native plants already adapted to our desert region's high-alkaline, nutrient-deficient soils.

Planting

There are preferred times to plant various desert species and a recommended method of planting. By planting one- to three-year-old nursery-propagated plants, you can get a jump on plants you start from seed.

Fall is a good time to plant many trees, shrubs, and wildflowers. The cooler autumn days and warm soil temperatures promote good root development without hot weather stressing the plant. In cooler areas of the desert region, such as Albuquerque, certain exceptions (including desert willow, yellow bird-of-paradise, and leguminous trees and shrubs) should be planted in late spring or early summer after the danger of spring frosts is past. Otherwise, these plants might not be established enough to survive the cold winter.

Another good time to plant many of our desert plants is during the summer rainy season. Temperatures are warm, and the higher humidity combined with the increased rainfall makes it much easier to keep new plantings adequately moist.

Cacti and succulents like to be planted in the heat of summer. An ideal time to plant them is late spring or early summer after the danger of late spring frosts is past. If they haven't established their roots before winter, they will die during the cold weather.

The following method of planting should be followed for all of our native plants except cacti. Dig a hole that is at least twice as wide and twice as deep as the root ball. When removing the plant from the container, check for roots that may be circling around the root ball. If you find any, carefully loosen and spread out these roots or they will continue to grow in a spiral manner and will eventually choke the plant to death. Otherwise, try to keep the root ball intact with as little disturbance as possible. Many native plants resent transplanting due to any root damage that may occur. This is especially true of legumes, which may even defoliate when transplanted; keep them adequately watered and they will eventually come back. Don't give up on newly transplanted material, particularly if it was dormant and leafless when planted. Some plants take a long time to bounce back.

Backfill the hole with some of the soil removed from the hole so that the soil level at the top of the container or root ball is just below the level of the surrounding soil when the plant is placed in the hole. Then backfill the hole with the soil that was removed. To get rid of any air pockets, tamp the soil lightly around the plant. In order to water, build an earthen well of soil around the perimeter of the newly planted tree, shrub, or wildflower. A perforated device called a bubbler can be attached to a hose and laid inside the well. A bubbler allows a slower penetration of water with very little disturbance of the soil surrounding the plant.

When planting cacti, follow the above procedures with the exception of the planting well. Simply give the newly planted cactus a good drink and forget about it for a while until it has established itself somewhat.

There are always exceptions to rules, and one is when you are planting deeply rooted plants such as honey mesquite in hardpan or, as it is known in the Southwest, caliche. The procedure to follow in this case is to first soften the hardpan with water then try breaking through it with a pick, shovel, auger, or whatever it takes to reach a sandier subsoil. Then follow the above procedure with this exception: add fine gravel or sand to your backfill. This is one of the few times that soil amendments can make a difference in dealing with the desert soils.

Watering

Watering is the most difficult aspect of caring for plants in the desert. In order to water efficiently, both from the standpoint of water conservation and from the plants' needs, it is important that you know something about the water-holding capacity of your soil structure. With this information and a knowledge of the plants themselves, you can begin to make decisions regarding the amount and frequency of water to be applied.

With desert plants a self-sufficient landscape can be established if desired. Three years is generally the amount of time it takes for the larger plants, trees such as catclaw acacia, desert willow, and honey mesquite, and most shrubs, including Apache plume, creosote bush, and shrubby senna, to become self-sufficient. Cacti and perennials will often be established in one or two seasons. Establishment can take a shorter or longer period depending on other conditions such as soil structure and weather.

As mentioned, desert plants are unable to survive on their own until establishment. Given time to establish their root systems, they will develop the drought-tolerant characteristics we desire in our gardens. With ample watering at the start, supplemental watering becomes less necessary. Use a method that gives the plants a deep, penetrating watering; you will not have to water them as often. Excessive watering encourages rank growth that requires more pruning, is more tempting to damaging insects, and can

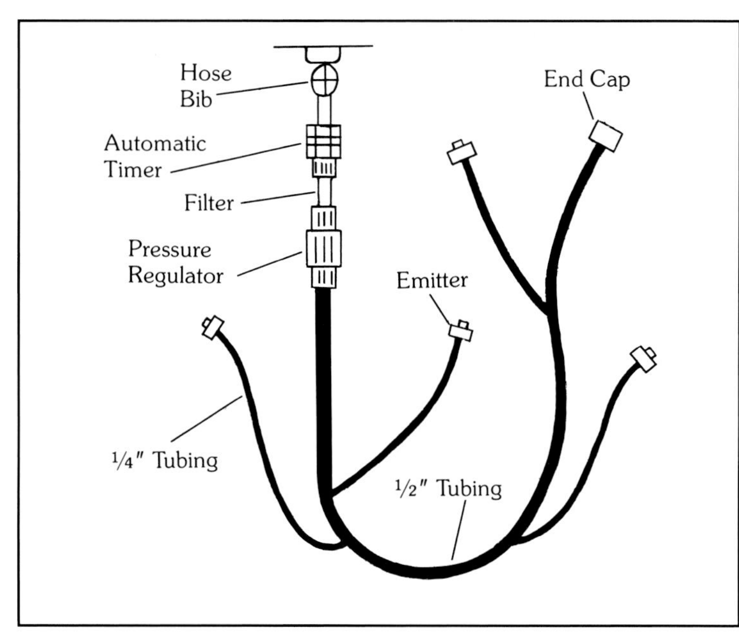

SIMPLE DRIP IRRIGATION INSTALLATION
(other components such as a fertilizer injector can be added)

cause an increase in disease. Drip irrigation is a very good tool to establish plants in the landscape.

The drip irrigation installation can be removed or used periodically once the plants have been weaned to less frequent irrigations. A bubbler device that fits on the end of a hose is another method that is economical to use. While watering by hand is time consuming, it is also relaxing and a good time for observation of any problems the plants may be having.

Watering is an art more than a science. It's impossible to tell someone how and when to water, except in general terms. You must learn the needs of the plants involved, observe the weather, and

LEFT
Once established, shrubby senna will be covered during the summer with bright yellow flowers.

RIGHT
Although it is the most common plant of the North American deserts, creosote bush is one of the most difficult to propagate and to transplant.

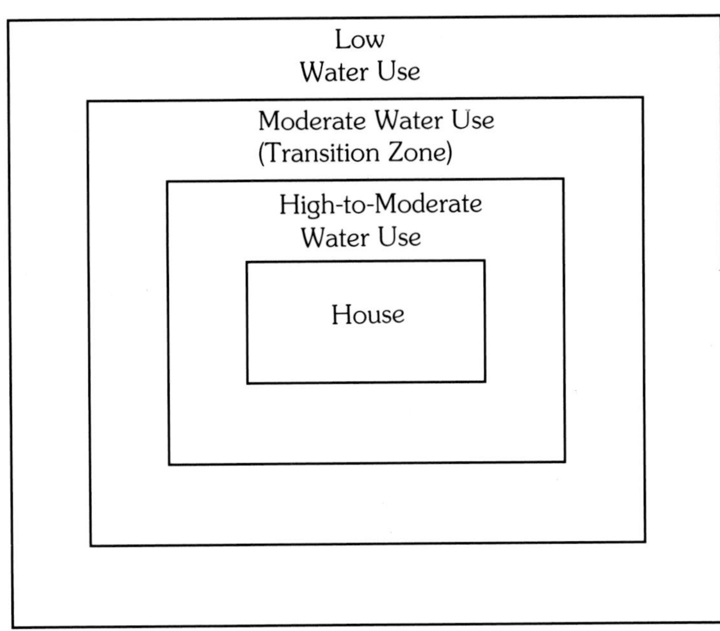

It's easy to meet each species's needs and to make decisions about irrigation system types if you zone your landscape according to water use.

know the way water flows through your soil. Many people want their watering to be a push-button experience like so many things in our technological society. While this may have its place for those who must be away from their homes a lot, there is nothing more infuriating to the water-wise gardener than seeing automatically-timed sprinklers running during a heavy downpour. Sprinklers should only be used for lawns or large areas anyway.

Because of excessive evaporation during the heat of the day, it is best to water during the early morning hours. Evening hours are also acceptable. During the summer avoid watering between the hours of 10:00 A.M. and 5:00 P.M. to save water. Don't forget to water

Among the easiest native plants to grow, desert willow has beautiful, orchidlike flowers.

occasionally during the winter, as it can be quite dry during this time of year. Pick a day that's going to be sunny and warm followed by a forecast of warm, dry days.

Mulching

There are several reasons mulches are used, including weed control, moderating soil temperatures, preventing evaporation of soil moisture, and eliminating soil crustation. Mulches should be applied 2 to 3 inches (5 to 8 centimeters) thick. If mulches are applied any thicker, the surface roots may grow too shallow, even up into the mulch itself.

There are several materials that can be used for mulches. In the desert garden two of the best are bark and crusher fines. Shredded bark has the advantages of being attractive, inexpensive, and remaining dry, especially on the surface. As bark mulches decompose, they will use up nitrogen. Keep an eye on your plants, and fertilize them with nitrogen if necessary.

Crusher fines (also arroyo gravel, decomposed granite, and other fine gravels) make a very good mulch for desert plants, especially around cacti and succulents. Such gravels have a very natural appearance while maintaining proper soil moisture. Other advantages of crusher fines are their low cost and their ability to suppress weeds, making weeding those that do appear an easier task. On top of clay soils, crusher fines also prevent the crusting and cracking so common to these soils as they dry out. This helps to prevent the tendency to overwater an already water-holding soil and enables the gardener with a clay soil to grow better plants without adding soil amendments. Crusher fines compact with age and the addition of water. A good sprinkling with the hose and a few rainfalls are all that is necessary. Crusher fines can also be used to expand outdoor living areas such as patios, sitting areas, and paths throughout the desert garden.

Other mulches available include larger gravels, cobblestones, grass clippings, hay, and straw. The practice of putting down black plastic, covering it with gravel, and planting a few very tough and hardy plants in this bleakness continues by some landscape contractors in the Southwest. This creates a hot surface that can raise air temperatures surrounding a home, making it very uncomfortable during the summer months. It also results in a waste of energy since more air conditioning is required to cool down the interior of the house or building. With time, the black plastic underneath deteriorates and starts coming up through the gravel, creating a litter mess. Instead, gravel and cobblestone should be applied sparingly and in an attractive manner, such as creating a dry wash through the landscape or in low areas where water collects after a rainstorm. Appropriate species can then be planted along the perimeter of the wash, creating a natural look, and the plants will be able to take advantage of the moisture beneath the stone mulch.

Mulches of grass, hay, and straw are very inexpensive and easily applied. Be aware, however, of weed and grass seeds that may come up. One way of preventing this problem is to put down a layer of newspaper or cardboard before applying the mulching materials. The paper will allow air and water to penetrate, eventually decomposing along with the mulch.

In the heat of summer, soil temperatures can reach high extremes of 120°F (49°C) plus. This can kill surface roots and scald the bark of trees and shrubs due to reflected heat. Mulches will prevent this by keeping the soil temperatures cool.

Fertilizers

Native plants require very little in the way of fertilizers, an advantage to those who want a low-maintenance landscape. Adapted to desert soils, native plants will often do very well on the nutrients that are naturally there. As with non-native plants, however, there are times when a deficiency of nutrients requires the addition of fertilizers.

When purchasing a general purpose fertilizer, check the label and you will see three numbers, such as 2-1-1 up to much higher numbers, such as a very popular brand with the numbers 15-30-15. These numbers are the ratio of nitrogen to phosphorus to potassium—three elements known as macronutrients. Additionally, there are micronutrients required by plants, and these are sometimes included with the macronutrients. These elements are listed in percentages. Additional percentages consist of inert fillers. For native plants choose one of the low-numbered fertilizers. A good choice is fish emulsion fertilizer; one brand that has proven to be very effective has a ratio of 5-2-2.

In our alkaline soils, iron is often locked up in the soil and unavailable for use by the plants. Yellowing leaves in which the veins remain green is symptomatic of iron chlorosis. To counter this micro-nutrient deficiency, there are products available called iron chelates. As with all fertilizers and garden products, follow the directions on the label of the particular brand you are using.

Applications of general or complete fertilizers should be made when it appears that the plant needs an additional boost. This might be in the form of a "spring tonic," applied after the leaves have emerged on deciduous plants. Fertilizer can be applied sparingly during the growing season until midsummer. Do not apply after this period, as new fall growth could be significantly damaged by frost. Be careful not to overfertilize, as excessive growth is more susceptible to insect damage and requires extra watering. Do not fertilize new plantings until they have been in the ground for several months.

Seedlings benefit from light applications of general fertilizers. Liquid seaweed has a very low ratio of nitrogen, phosphorous, and potassium and is ideal for young plants.

Pruning

Pruning is another area where natives are truly low maintenance. Allow your desert shrubs and trees to develop a natural growth form and appearance. The reasons for pruning include to remove dead or damaged wood due to disease, frost, or insects; to eliminate rubbing or crossing branches; to remove suckers; and to maintain the plant's natural shape.

To avoid a later problem, be sure that you know the ultimate size of a tree or shrub before you plant it. Pruning a plant to try to fit it into a space that was too small for it to begin with is a frequent landscaping mistake. If this occurs, it's best to remove the problem plant and replace it with an appropriate-sized tree or shrub.

After a cold winter wait until new growth has started in the spring before pruning away dead wood so you don't damage living tissue. Prune back to the first sprouting bud on the stem, cutting right above the bud. Additional pruning may be required in order to restore the plant's shape.

The time to prune a plant usually depends on the time the plant blooms. Summer-, fall-, and ever-blooming plants such as bird-of-paradise and desert willow should be pruned in late winter or early spring, as most bloom on the season's new growth. Spring-blooming plants, such as Texas mountain laurel, flower on the previous season's growth and should be pruned after blooming. Otherwise, you'll cut off the current season's flowers.

Use the proper tools to make pruning cuts. Prune smaller stems with pruning shears and larger limbs with loppers. When pruning for appearance, you may want a shrub to have either a bushy or a more open appearance. To encourage bushiness, you can pinch the growing tips, thereby forcing more growth from lower down on the stems. If the shrub would look better with a more open form, then thinning the stems by removing crossing branches, rank growth, and suckers will enhance its appearance. For a more formal appearance, which may be your preference or a necessity dictated by your local neighborhood, some shrubs such as desert olive and four-wing saltbush can be sheared into hedges or shapes normally associated with non-native plants such as privet.

Trees are often incorrectly pruned by a manner known as topping. This very harmful practice consists of cutting off the top of the main trunk and/or lateral branches. It forces a flush of weak growth that is more susceptible to disease and insect damage. Also the tree is unable to close its wounds properly, adding to the possibility of disease. The correct way to prune a tree is to remove dead wood,

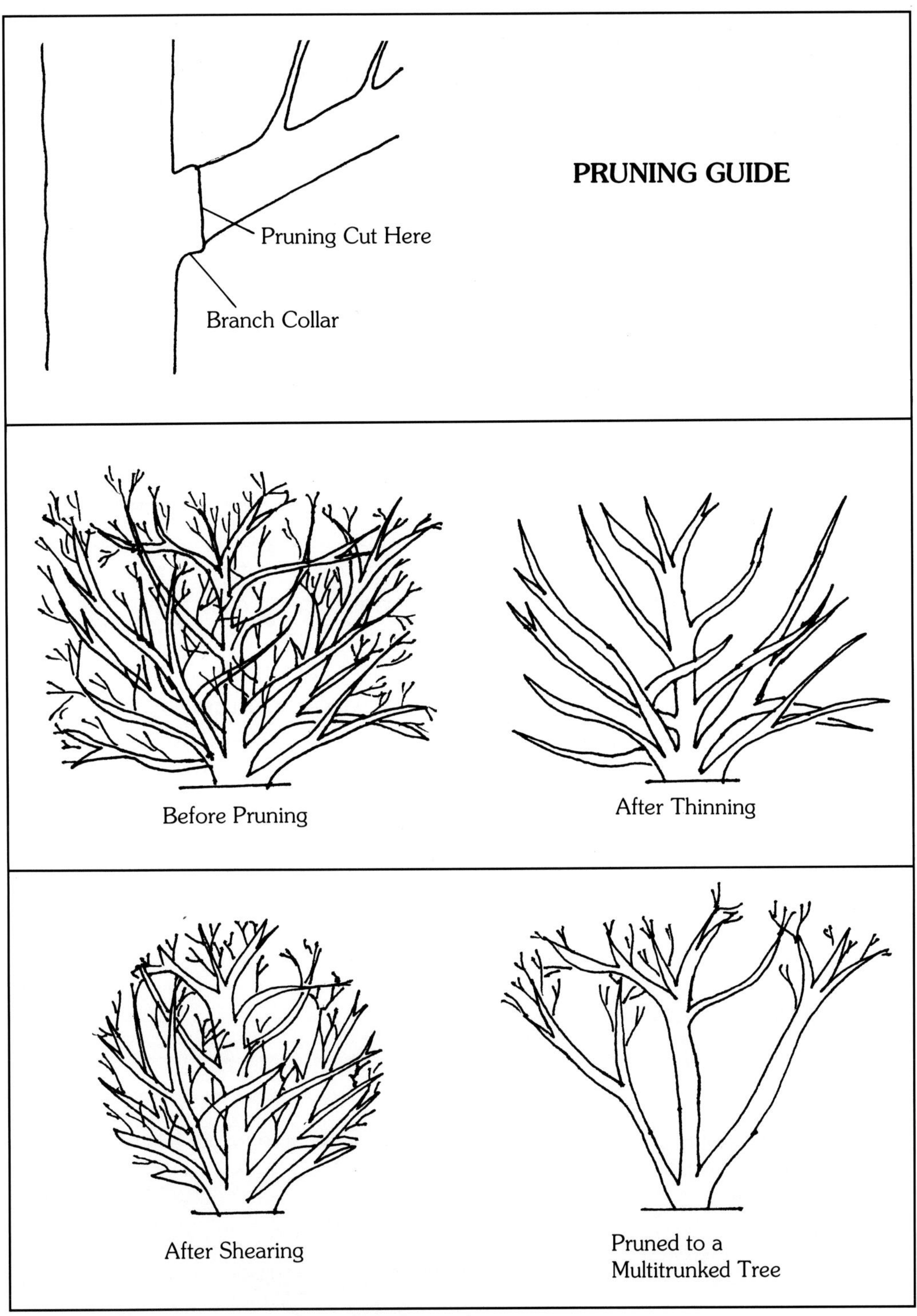

limbs that pose a danger if they were to fall, and crossing limbs. Another good reason to prune is to train young trees to a particular shape. Most desert trees, including mesquite, desert willow, and desert olive are normally multitrunked and should be pruned to the desired number of trunks. When pruning trees, make your cuts at the collar at the base of the limb. This will allow the tree to heal itself naturally by callousing over the wound. Don't cut the limb flush with the trunk, as it will cause damage to the tree.

Special Care of Cacti and Succulents

For truly low-maintenance plants, there aren't many that can fit the bill as well as cacti and succulents. They do, however, have their special requirements.

As previously mentioned, the bad reputation cacti have regarding weeding is primarily due to some of the very spiny prickly pears. Keep this in mind when planning your garden and plant smaller and less spiny plants nearer walkways and the spiny, larger plants away from paths. Avoid planting prickly pears where they will receive excessive amounts of water, which will encourage weeds. Another problem with the prickly pears is the accumulation of wind-blown trash in between the pads. To remove the trash, use tongs or some type of pointed tool.

When planting cacti and succulents, remember the old adage "Cacti and succulents require good drainage." While they will grow in almost any soil with the exception of heavy clay, cacti and succulents will appreciate the extra drainage created by raised areas such as mounded island beds or slopes. These also have microclimates that can be used to advantage. Keeping cacti dry is very important, even more so than with other succulents. Most of our soils in the Southwest are acceptable for growing these plants, and amendments can be added to soils if necessary. If the soil has a lot of clay, for example, the addition of soil amendments such as sand, scoria, or pumice to the mound will help. Special raised beds called sand beds used in wetter, non-desert climates are a good alternative for people with heavy soils (see Chapter 5 for construction details).

One of the few large cacti that can tolerate the cold and snow of winter is the tree cholla.

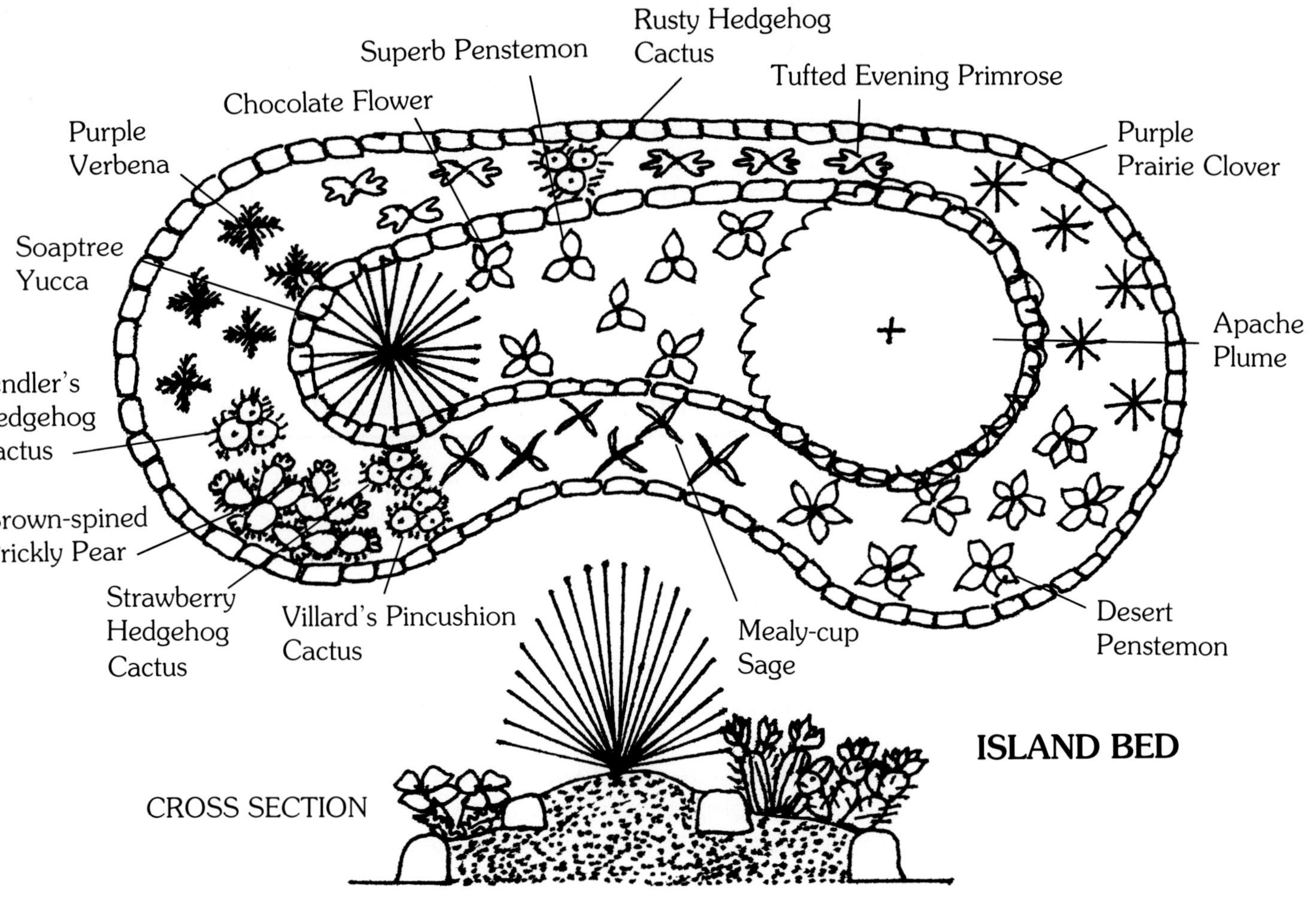

ISLAND BED

While some cacti do grow in sandy soils, they do not grow in a sterile environment. They need the nutrients required by all plants for good growth. The addition of organic matter in small amounts to the planting area will supply their needs. During the growing season of spring and summer, cacti and succulents can be given regular doses of low-numbered fertilizers. They can also take more water at this time of year. Stop giving cacti and succulents any additional water or fertilizer when fall arrives. In particular, avoid giving them any water during the cold winter months. Chihuahuan Desert cacti and succulents are among the most winter hardy of this type of plant, but they can't take frozen water around their bases and roots. Their natural dormancy reduces their need for water, and the use of a gravel mulch will help keep them dry.

Provided with the above conditions, cacti and succulents will thrive, and your garden will have a unique character. They make a definite statement: Southwest!

Insects, Rodents, and Other Pests

The best means of preventing damage to native plants, especially from insects, is to maintain your plants in a healthy condition. Avoid overwatering, which will cause juicy, rank growth that is particularly attractive to destructive insects such as aphids. Now that you have planted a desert garden with an emphasis on the natural environment, it is no longer desirable or necessary to use dangerous, toxic insecticides. There are many products on the market now that are safe for people, pets, wildlife, and the overall environment. Look for those that are labeled or sold as organic. Also remember that not all insects are enemies. Many are helpful in controlling other insects by predation such as ladybugs and lacewings. Known collectively as beneficial insects, these are the "good guys" in the garden that feed on bugs such as aphids, which we want to keep under control. Remember also that a garden is not a work of perfection. By its very nature, it is in constant change. Learn to live with a few holes in a leaf, a little damage to a plant.

Aphids

These are small, soft-bodied insects with long antennae and pear-shaped bodies. There are a number of species in a variety of colors: yellow, green, black, and so forth. Aphids live by sucking the sap from a plant. This causes the leaves to wilt, resulting in a less healthy plant. Aphids also transmit diseases from one plant to another. They are particularly fond of soft, juicy plant stems and can be a problem on desert willow and penstemons.

Controls: Luckily, aphids are one of the easiest pests to get rid of. They can be knocked off the plant with a hard stream of water. For bad infestations, spraying with insecticidal soap works well. Beneficial insects, including ladybugs and lacewings, are voracious predators of aphids.

Cactus Borers

Members of the genus *Monilaema*, cactus borers can be a real problem, especially in rural areas where there are wild populations of cacti nearby. The large, black adults with long antennae feed on the outside of the body of the cactus, usually only causing cosmetic damage. The real problem is with the larvae, which begin life as eggs laid at the base of the cactus then hatch and eat out the inside of the cactus. The problem usually goes undetected until the final stages of both the cactus borers' youthful existence and the cactus plant's life. What is left of the cactus at the end is a shell of the last living tissue of the plant. Unfortunately, at this point there is nothing that can be done to save the cactus. Cactus borers are particularly fond of hedgehog cacti and opuntias.

Controls: While there may be some systemic insecticides that will kill the larvae, cacti are not usually prone to take them up in sufficient quantities to kill the parasites. Additionally, systemic insecticides are usually very dangerous chemicals, and their use is probably unwarranted in this situation. The best way to try and keep the problem under control is to destroy the adult beetles whenever possible. They are usually active during the early morning and late evening hours or on cloudy days when they can avoid the midday heat. Knock them off the cactus and dispose of them as you wish.

Cochineal

These scale insects are relatives of the cochineal of the Aztecs, used in making a bright red dye. The female produces a cottony material on the surface of the prickly pear pads on which she feeds. Not only is it unsightly, but it can cause considerable damage to the pads.

Controls: Insecticidal soap may eliminate the insects. Cochineal can be washed off the pads with a strong stream of water, a process you may need to repeat at several different intervals to get the problem under control.

Cutworms

Cutworms are the larvae of various moths. Emerging at night and on cloudy days, they feed on the stems of young plants, cutting them off at ground level. Cutworms are most often a problem when setting out seedlings or small plants.

Controls: The easiest way to control cutworms is to make a cardboard collar and place it around the young plant to prevent the larvae from getting to new transplants. It should be stuck into the ground 1 inch (2.5 centimeters) below the soil level, and it should stick up 2 inches (5 centimeters) above. You can also go out at night with a flashlight and pick the cutworms off the plants on which they're feeding. Sometimes other wildlife will come to your aid. At one time a family of starlings nesting in a tree in our yard fed upon cutworms, keeping them under control.

Leaf-cutting Bees

If one day you're looking at the leaves on your desert olive, Mexican buckeye, mesquite, or some other plant and you notice neatly cut circles, it is probably the handiwork of leaf-cutting bees. While they may make some leaves look unsightly, the damage they cause is relatively minor.

Controls: There are no effective controls for leaf-cutting bees. Keep in mind that they are also beneficial pollinators of flowering plants. Allowing them the little pieces of leaves they use to line their nests is a small price to pay for their services.

Mealybugs

If you have ever grown cacti or other succulents indoors or in a greenhouse, it is likely that you have encountered these little, cottony white pests. They love to feed on the soft, juicy bodies as well as on the roots of plants. Mealybugs will often cause the death of cacti after feeding on the roots. This causes problems with rot due to the inability of the plant to properly absorb water.

Controls: For small infestations, simply smear the insect with a cotton swab soaked in rubbing alcohol. For a severe problem, spraying with insecticidal soap, pyrethrum, rotenone, or the use of beneficial insects is necessary. Ladybugs, lacewings, and Cryptolaemus beetle larvae are effective controls.

Mexican Steel Blue Flea Beetles

These insects are very small and get their name from hopping around like fleas when bothered. Mexican steel blue flea beetles are a problem on evening primroses (*Oenothera* species); they descend on these plants in hordes, eat many tiny holes in the leaves, and then depart. Other than leaving raggedy-looking plants, flea beetles are not a serious pest.

Controls: A spray made from garlic and water is reportedly effective in repelling flea beetles. Insecticidal soap should work as well.

Spider Mites

Spider mites, usually red ones, can be a problem on some natives, including cacti, penstemons, and Apache plume. They look like tiny specks on the underside of plant leaves or in the crevices of the body of a cactus. The easiest way to see them is with a magnifying glass. By holding a piece of white paper under the plant and shaking the branch, some will fall off onto the paper, and you can see these tiny bugs moving around. Sometimes the mites will build fine webs on the leaves. Another sign of spider mite damage is a yellow stippling on the surface of the leaves.

Controls: Spider mites are especially a problem during hot, dry weather. They do not like moisture. A spraying of water with the hose will wash them off infested plants. For bad infestations, insecticidal soap works well. Beneficial predators include green lacewing larvae.

Longhorned Beetles

Longhorned beetles of the family Cerambicydae and the genus *Oncideres* are pests of mesquite and other desert trees. While the females have antennae that are just a little shorter than their bodies, the males have antennae that are almost twice as long as their bodies. After they mate in the spring, the female girdles the stem of a branch. She then goes to the tip of the branch and lays an egg or two. Active at night, the adult beetles go about their business of eating and mating. Once the eggs hatch out, the cylindrical larvae eat the pith of the twigs. This is very evident as the leaves at the tips turn brown and die. Reaching maturity, the larvae drop from the branch tips to the ground, where they pupate into adults at the end of the growing season or at the beginning of the next.

Controls: Because of the longhorned beetles' interesting life cycle, there is really no good time for applications of insecticides. The best control is to simply cut off the affected twigs as the damage appears. Fortunately, the damage is often minimal. The cycles of the beetle infestations also vary from year to year, and severe problems only occur periodically.

Rodents

When growing native plants, native rodents often come along for the dinner. From small amounts of damage, such as bites out of leaves, to total destruction of a plant by eating it, rodents can be a very difficult problem. Gophers, ground squirrels, and various species of desert rats and mice will eat cacti, wildflowers, and young trees and shrubs.

Controls: Trapping and removing rodents to another location is a humane solution to the problem. Call your county extension agent for details on trapping procedures and the availability of traps, often free as a government service. Also remember that predators such as snakes and raptors are nature's control, and they should be protected and encouraged.

Rabbits and Hares

Desert cottontails and jackrabbits (actually hares) are often very destructive to native plants. They seem particularly fond of new, succulent, tender growth at the end of trees and shrubs. More than likely they are seeking the moisture contained within the plant's tissues.

Controls: The same controls as mentioned for rodents are an effective way to deal with rabbits and hares. Also, if a source of water, such as the top of a birdbath, is placed on the ground where they can get a drink, this will often help cut down on the damage.

Quail

Many people are surprised that these cute little birds can actually be destructive to garden plants. They are particularly fond of new growth on desert wildflowers and eat the leaves.

Controls: Wire cages placed around the plants will discourage quail (and rabbits) from such activity.

Remember that no matter what pests appear in your garden, Mother Nature usually keeps them under control by one means or another. By encouraging native predators, providing water, and simply letting nature take its course, you can help establish a balance.

Diseases

Healthy native plants are rarely bothered by disease. It is the overwatered, overfertilized plants that are more susceptible. Prevention is always better than trying to cure a disease once it becomes prevalent. Although it is often easier to remove an infected plant rather than allow it to spread the disease to others, a rare or prized specimen may be worth fighting for.

Powdery Mildew

This is a fungus that appears as powdery-looking gray or white patches on the surfaces of leaves. Spreading rapidly, it is a problem on plants grown in shady conditions. It is fond of warm days and cool nights, typical of desert climates. Penstemons are a native plant on which this mildew frequently appears.

Controls: Removal of infected plants and/or infected individual plant parts is one control. In the past there were fungicides available to deal with the problem, but they were very toxic to the environment. There are now organic fungicides on the market that are safe to use for this and other fungus problems.

Rots

Various disease organisms, including bacteria, viruses, and fungi will attack the roots of plants, causing them and eventually the whole plant to die. This is almost always a sign of overwatering, often combined with high soil temperatures.

Controls: The use of mulches is perhaps the best and often the only means of dealing with this problem. Knowing the cultural requirements of the plants involved is a must in order to provide the correct amount of water to supply the plants' needs.

Rusts

This is another group of fungi that likes desert conditions, warm days and cool nights combined with moisture—such as rain or overhead watering. Each rust is specific to a particular type of plant. Cacti rusts, for example, only attack cacti. Rusts are easy to recognize, as they usually live up to their name and look like the infected plant is covered with rust. Overhead watering from sprinklers is responsible for much of this problem in the Southwest.

Controls: One solution is to irrigate by another means such as drip irrigation (see p. 48). The organic fungicides are very effective at eliminating rusts and keeping them under control. As with all chemicals, always remember to read and follow the label so as not to harm yourself, other people, or even the plants themselves.

CHAPTER 5 Growing Desert Plants under Non-desert Conditions

A planting of Chihuahuan Desert plants will create a truly distinctive landscape, no matter if you live in the Southwest or elsewhere. These plants are easily grown outside their native home if given conditions to their liking. The following information will help you in growing these plants under your specific conditions, whether it is in a greenhouse, on a windowsill, in a pot, or outdoors.

Greenhouse Growing

A greenhouse is a controlled environment in which plants can be given their ideal growing conditions. With less stress from wind, temperatures, predation, and drought, your plants can put their energy into growth. Many will thank you with flowers.

There are many types of greenhouses available today for both home and commercial growers. They are made of many different materials, including wood and metal frames, and glass, fiberglass, and plastic coverings (also known as glazing). Fiberglass or a similar material is a good choice, as it is more resistant to the high winds and hail common in the Southwest. Shade cloth or other shading is a mandatory item as it helps cut down on heat buildup in the greenhouse and will prevent the plants from sunburning. Even the cacti and succulents need protection from our intense sunlight.

In northern climates greenhouses are usually sited on an east-west axis to take advantage of solar gain during the winter. In the Southwest greenhouses are often sited on a north-south axis so that during the growing season of spring and summer, light is more evenly distributed across the greenhouse as the sun passes from east to west. Better plant growth is the result. Heating in winter is not as much of a concern as in a more northerly climate. All of the Chihuahuan Desert plants in this book can take temperatures well below freezing. In fact, the native cacti require cool winter temperatures in order to maintain their overall health and to stimulate bud formation and flower production in spring. The cacti and succulents of the Chihuahuan Desert are among the best natives for greenhouse growing, as they are very adaptable to the temperature swings of an unheated greenhouse. Other native plants do well in greenhouses, including wildflowers, shrubs, and trees, until they grow too tall for the greenhouse. Some plants that are especially good for containers are bird-of-paradise, blackfoot daisy, crimson sage, desert olive, desert senna, Mexican campion, and Mexican elder.

Heating or cooling may be required in climates that are different from the Chihuahuan Desert region. A minimum-maximum thermometer that gives the highest and lowest temperatures within the last twenty-four hours can help you make the necessary cooling and heating adjustments. Ideal winter temperatures should be in the 40°F (4°C) range at the coldest, although most native plants will survive periods of cold in the single digits (Fahrenheit).

Summer heat is not too much of a problem if the greenhouse is covered with shade cloth. Desert plants are used to growing in very hot situations. The key is to provide adequate ventilation with vents, fans, or a combination of the two. Even more important than heating or cooling, good air circulation will discourage fungi, such as damping off, and insects, such as spider mites.

Just as zoning is a concept used in landscaping, it can be used as a means of organizing greenhouse space. Group your tropical and other temperate plants separately from your desert plants. They have different watering and light requirements, and using the correct plant in the correct location will utilize your space more efficiently. For example, cacti can be placed on top of the greenhouse bench, where they will receive more sunshine and dry out faster. Leafy plants can be placed under the bench, where they will be shaded and retain moisture for a longer period of time. When the weather warms up in the spring, you can take many of the plants outdoors. They will appreciate the fresh air and sunshine almost as much as you do. Be sure to put them in a shady spot at first, as they might burn if placed out in direct sun. In climates outside the Southwest, you may want to put them under a porch, patio roof, or tree to prevent plants accustomed to the desert's limited moisture from getting overwatered.

A Desert on the Windowsill

Many of our desert plants are more than willing to grow under the dry conditions of a sunny window that would kill more tender houseplants from a tropical climate. Once again the small cacti make excellent specimens due to their adaptable nature. Button cactus, catclaw cactus, and even barrel cactus are a few of the cacti that can be grown in pots.

The two-thirds mix used for growing plants discussed in the chapter "Desert Births: Propagation" (see p. 34) is good for pots indoors. The plants will need to be watered regularly during the growing seasons of spring and summer, just as if they were outside. It is critical that they not be given too much water during the fall and winter months. If possible, they should be moved to a cool room, perhaps one that is unheated. The plants require a dormant period in order to bloom the following spring.

Windowsill plants will need to be given a low-numbered fertilizer on a regular basis during the growing season. They will also need as much light as possible at this time. Desert cacti and succulents are very good choices for south-facing windows. East- and west-facing windows are acceptable second alternatives. It is usually impossible to provide enough light for these plants with a north-facing window. Additional light such as that provided by fluorescents made for growing plants indoors may be required.

Even if you live in an apartment, you can grow these interesting desert plants. Many are small and will grow happily confined in a pot for years. I know a woman in Fairbanks who says that cacti and succulents are the perfect houseplants for Alaska. They go dormant during the long, dark winters and tolerate the dry conditions of a heated home. She grows them on windowsills where they get cool enough to go through the cold period necessary to trigger blooming in the spring.

Desert Plants in Containers

No matter where you live, if you use containers you can grow desert plants indoors or out. Once again, the cacti and succulents are the star performers here. Their sculptural shapes and rugged character are ideally suited to container culture. Yuccas and agaves make outstanding plants in large pots. Even though they will grow quite big in nature, in a container they will adapt to the size of the pot. Limiting their growth like goldfish in a bowl, they practically stop growing when they have filled out the pot.

The various types of clay pottery from Mexico and the Southwest look good as pots for individual plants or when plants are grouped together in container gardens. On a patio, porch, balcony, or indoors, these container plants are very decorative. The plants can be moved around the garden at will for instant effects. In colder areas, pots can be taken outdoors and sunken into the ground and top-dressed with gravel so no one will know the plants are not actually planted in the ground.

Using soil mixes suitable for various plants, containers can be planted with all types of natives. Only the size of the containers limit the plants that can be used. Dish gardens can be created using several different types of plants. Once again, cacti and succulents are excellent for this purpose. Allow for future growth of the plants and don't overcrowd them. A top-dressing of gravel will help tie the "garden" together. In a large container, you can include desert wildflowers with the cacti and succulents. In very large containers such as half whiskey barrels, trees and shrubs such as desert willow and bird-of-paradise are striking specimens.

Plants in containers need to be given more water and fertilizer than those planted in the ground. With proper care they can survive for years of enjoyment.

Growing Desert Plants Outside in Non-desert Climates

It comes as a big surprise to many people that cacti and other desert plants can be grown in climates with much more moisture than the Southwest. I've seen full-grown chollas (*Opuntia imbricata*) growing in a central Pennsylvania garden and pictures of agaves, cacti, and yuccas in gardens in Washington, D.C., and Florida. These are areas of high rainfall and, in the case of Pennsylvania, an area with wet, cold winters.

How have these gardeners done it? By constructing what is known as a dry sand bed. The main problem with growing plants from an area like the Chihuahuan Desert in non-desert climates is excess moisture. This causes the plants to rot and encourages diseases. A dry sand bed is a very simple solution. A layer of sand between 6 and 10 inches (15 and 25 centimeters) deep is spread over ordinary garden soil. The dry, nutrient-deficient sand helps deter the rot-causing organisms. As a result, native plants of the Chihuahuan Desert and other arid regions of the world can be grown almost anywhere outside. After spreading out the sand, it is simply a matter of planting the plants directly into the bed. These beds can be small or as large as a front or backyard. Site them in as much full sun as possible. At this point you can landscape with these plants in the same manner as previously described. The majority of the plants in this book are hardy in U.S.D.A. hardiness zones 7 and above (see discussion on p. 88). Others are hardy as far down as zone 4. When planning a garden or sand bed in a colder zone, the following list is useful for choosing which plants are hardy in your zone. Plants from a zone numbered lower than your own will usually be hardy in your zone. Consult the "Desert Plant Encyclopedia" (p. 88) for detailed information about specific plants.

Engelmann prickly pear has found a home in this Virginia landscape, where it is mulched with oyster shells, a local product.

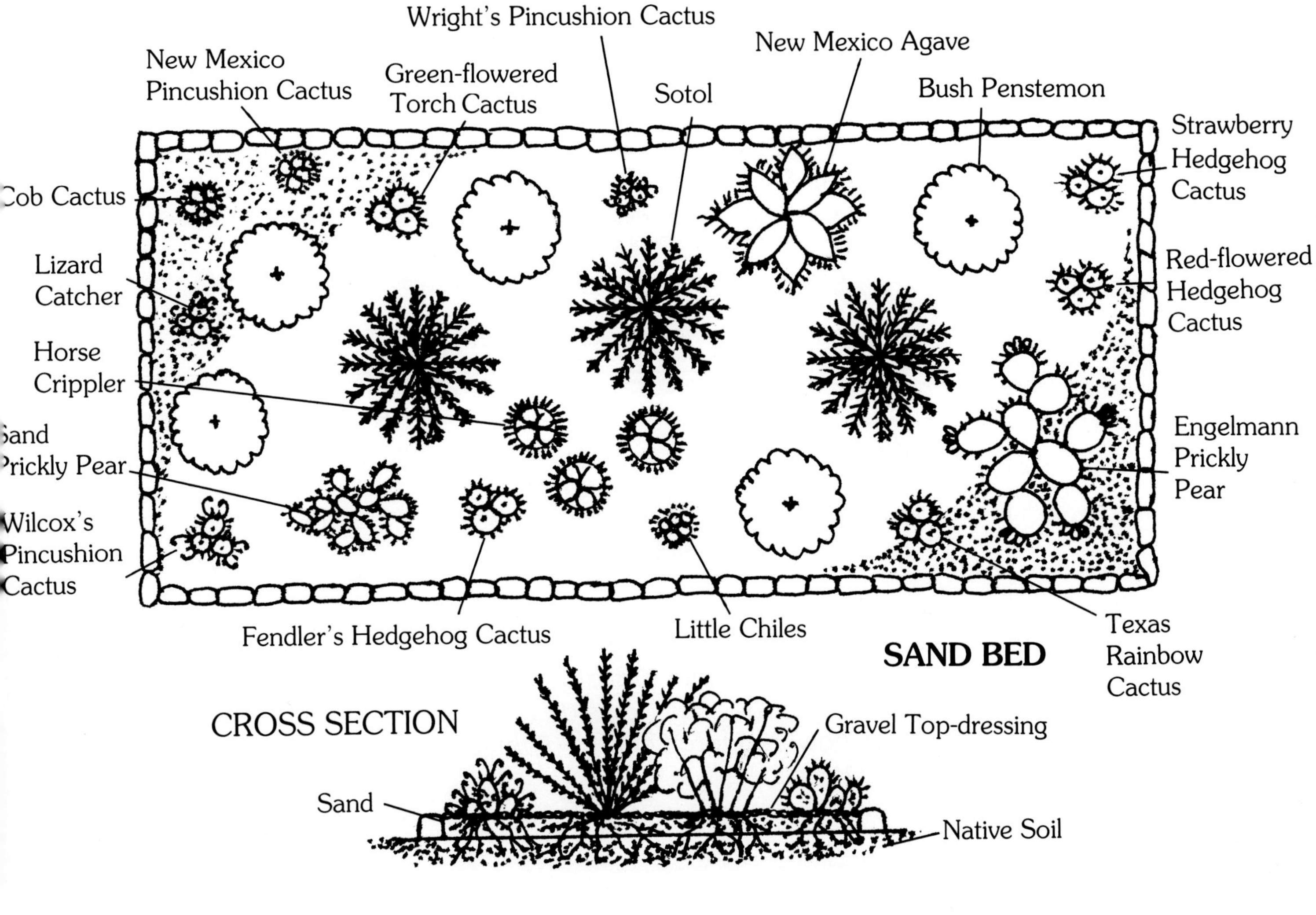

Wright's Pincushion Cactus
New Mexico Agave
New Mexico Pincushion Cactus
Green-flowered Torch Cactus
Sotol
Bush Penstemon
Strawberry Hedgehog Cactus
Cob Cactus
Lizard Catcher
Red-flowered Hedgehog Cactus
Horse Crippler
Sand Prickly Pear
Engelmann Prickly Pear
Wilcox's Pincushion Cactus
Fendler's Hedgehog Cactus
Little Chiles
Texas Rainbow Cactus

SAND BED

CROSS SECTION
Gravel Top-dressing
Sand
Native Soil

HARDINESS ZONE PLANT LIST

Zone 4:

Wildflowers:

Blackfoot daisy (*Melampodium leucanthum*)
Chocolate flower (*Berlandiera lyrata*)
Desert zinnia (*Zinnia grandiflora*)
Purple verbena (*Glandularia wrightii*)
Threadleaf groundsel (*Senecio douglasii* var. *longilobus*)
Tufted evening primrose (*Oenothera caespitosus*)

Cacti:

Claret-cup hedgehog cactus (*Echinocereus triglochidiatus*)
Grasslands prickly pear (*Opuntia pottsii*)
New Mexico pincushion cactus (*Escobaria vivipara* var. *neomexicana*)
Plains prickly pear (*Opuntia polyacantha*)
Red-flowered hedgehog cactus (*Echinocereus coccineus*)

Shrubs:

Apache plume (*Fallugia paradoxa*)
Cliff fendlerbush (*Fendlera rupicola*)
Four-wing saltbush (*Atriplex canescens*)
Indigo bush (*Amorpha fruticosa*)
Three-leaf sumac (*Rhus trilobata*)

Trees:

Desert olive (*Forestiera neomexicana*)

Zone 5:

Wildflowers:

Bush penstemon (*Penstemon ambiguus*)
Desert penstemon (*Penstemon pseudospectabilis*)
Paperflower (*Psilostrophe tagetina*)

Cacti and Succulents:

Brown-spined prickly pear (*Opuntia phaeacantha*)
Club cholla (*Opuntia clavata*)
Fendler's hedgehog cactus (*Echinocereus fendleri*)
Green-flowered torch cactus (*Echinocereus chloranthus* var. *cylindricus*)
Koenig's pincushion cactus (*Escobaria orcuttii* var. *koenigii*)

Little chiles (*Mammillaria meiacantha*)
New Mexico agave (*Agave neomexicana*)
Rusty hedgehog cactus (*Echinocereus russanthus*)
Sand prickly pear (*Opuntia arenaria*)
Tree cholla (*Opuntia imbricata*)

Trees:
Fragrant ash (*Fraxinus cuspidata*)

Zone 6:

Wildflowers:
Autumn sage (*Salvia greggii*)
Blue stars (*Amsonia hirtella*)
Fendler penstemon (*Penstemon fendleri*)
Golden columbine (*Aquilegia chrysantha*)
Havard penstemon (*Penstemon havardii*)
Mexican campion (*Silene laciniata*)
Superb penstemon (*Penstemon superbus*)
Thurber Penstemon (*Penstemon thurberi*)
White sand stars (*Amsonia arenaria*)

Cacti and Succulents:
Beargrass (*Nolina texana*)
Desert Christmas cactus (*Opuntia leptocaulis*)
Early bloomer (*Echinomastus intertextus*)
Klein cholla (*Opuntia kleiniae*)
New Mexico rainbow cactus (*Echinocereus chloranthus* var. *chloranthus*)
Orcutt's pincushion cactus (*Escobaria orcuttii* var. *orcuttii*)
Purple prickly pear (*Opuntia macrocentra*)
Scheer's pincushion cactus (*Corypantha scheeri*)
Soaptree yucca (*Yucca elata*)
Texas rainbow cactus (*Echinocereus pectinatus* var. *dasyacanthus*)
Wright's pincushion cactus (*Mammillaria wrightii* var. *wrightii*)

Trees:
Honey mesquite (*Prosopis glandulosa*)
Netleaf hackberry (*Celtis reticulata*)
Screwbean (*Prosopis pubescens*)
Western soapberry (*Sapindus saponaria* var. *drummondii*)

A pink-flowered form of plains prickly pear is a lovely addition to the winter-hardy cactus garden.

The snow on these soaptree yuccas highlights their forms beautifully. Soaptree yucca is one of the hardiest trunk-forming yuccas.

It is evident from the preceding list that there are a lot of choices for gardeners living in cold, temperate climates. In the arid regions of the western United States north of the Chihuahuan Desert, these plants are useful for adding a touch of the warmth and drama associated with the Southwest. In other arid regions of the world, these plants can be used for landscaping—with caution. When moving plants from one region to another, it is important to remember that a potential problem always exists when plants adapt too successfully to their new home and become invasive. For example, prickly pears can be invasive when grown in the absence of natural predators. In Australia they have colonized acres of land, becoming a nuisance. In other areas, such as the Mediterranean region, desert plants have been used in gardens for so long that they are now part of the overall landscape.

In wetter regions of the world, there is little chance that desert plants will escape cultivation. Keeping in mind that these plants have evolved to live in some of the driest country on earth, they are unlikely to survive without being given special attention, for example, protection from too much moisture as in the sand bed previously discussed. If you're aware of your environment, it can be great fun to grow plants from other areas of the world, especially from a place as exotic as the Chihuahuan Desert.

CHAPTER 6 Pleasure Gardens

In courtyards and other outdoor areas, fountains introduce the soothing effect of water into the desert environment.

Designing a garden of one's own is an act of personal creation. While a book such as this can present the procedures to follow, the ultimate design should be yours. The garden will be one you will be living and working with. This chapter is intended to give you some ideas on using desert plants and to encourage you to use your imagination to create your own garden design.

The following gardens are meant to be both lovely to look at and easy to maintain. That is the pleasure in using plants from the Chihuahuan Desert. With their beautiful flowers, forms, and foliage, and their tough characters, they are well adapted to surviving under conditions that would kill many other plants while providing the desert gardener with a wide choice of ornamentals.

Have fun with these landscaping ideas. Most of all, have fun in your own garden. Celebrate the desert!

Small Spaces

In developing an area that is pleasing to the senses, patios, courtyards, and other small areas where people congregate require careful placement of plants and other elements. Plants that have pretty flowers and fragrance are especially appreciated here.

Because these spaces are usually close to living areas, plants that use more water can be planted in them. Small trees are in keeping with the scale of these situations. Fragrant ash is an ideal tree for use here, as it has beautiful, fragrant flowers and nice green foliage. Desert willow is another small tree well suited to these areas. Its colorful, orchidlike flowers have a long season of bloom that is advantageous where space is limited and only one or a few trees can be planted. Also desert willow will not tear up sidewalks, patios, or foundations like many other trees.

Avoid using plants with thorns or spines in these locations unless they can be planted away from places where they might injure someone. Chihuahuan whitethorn is a perfect example of

Bird-of-paradise requires very little water and fertilizers; it has lovely blossoms that attract hummingbirds and humans alike.

Chocolate flower is an ideal plant for chocolate lovers. Plant it near walkways and patios where its fragrance can be appreciated.

a plant that is desirable for its sweet fragrance but has thorns.

Some of the wildflowers have pleasant fragrances and are good for containers and flower beds alongside patios and in courtyards. Chocolate flower will bring an aroma of milk chocolate to your morning walks. Blue stars and white sand stars are sweetly fragrant and also very pretty to look at. Tufted evening primrose will fill the night air with its perfume.

A patio or courtyard is also the place for water—not necessarily for the plants but for the enjoyment of people passing by. A small pool or fountain in a desert setting evokes the feeling of an oasis. Although this is an old idea that goes back to the Moors and the Egyptians, among others, it is still a good idea.

There are many hard surfaces in a courtyard or patio area, and often there is little room for plants. One solution is to use containers in these locations. They can decorate what might otherwise be a drab area. Small cacti and succulents, with their colorful flowers and sculptural forms, are good choices. It is often difficult to keep other plants in containers wet enough in desert areas, but cacti such as pincushions and hedgehogs will thrive in pots.

In these areas it is important to remember a few tips for successful gardening. First, use plants that add something decorative, such as pretty flowers, lush foliage, or sculptural forms. Second, use plants that scent the air nearby. Finally, think small; smaller plants will not overwhelm what are normally tight areas.

With a host of desirable qualities, desert willow can be used in many areas which are not suitable for other trees.

When in full bloom, the striking red flowers of claret-cup hedgehog cactus will be sure to entice hummingbirds into your garden.

The Hummingbird Garden

I don't know of anyone who doesn't like hummingbirds. Planting a garden to attract these wonderful creatures is how I first became interested in gardening with native plants.

One of the nice things about a hummingbird garden is that it can be as small as a single red-flowered plant in a pot, which they will visit occasionally, or as large a garden as you wish to plant. Regardless, the key factor in drawing hummingbirds into the garden is red flowers, although they will also go to flowers of other colors (especially yellow) if the flowers produce nectar they like.

In the Southwest hummingbirds return in early spring and stay throughout the summer into fall before heading south to Mexico and Central America for the winter. Some, such as the rufous hummingbird, pass through the Southwest on their migration to and from areas further north, stopping to feed for a while. To attract these lovely and entertaining birds during their stay in the Southwest, plant a garden using those flowers whose blooming coincides with the time the hummingbirds are here. Crimson sage, golden columbine, and superb penstemon begin blooming at about the time these tiny birds arrive in early spring. These are followed in late spring and summer by agaves, bird-of-paradise, claret-cup hedgehog cactus, desert willow, Mexican campion, ocotillo, and red-flowered hedgehog. Bird-of-paradise, desert willow, Mexican campion, and superb penstemon will

LEFT
Blooming from April through September, superb penstemon will keep the hummingbirds happy in the desert garden the whole season long.

RIGHT
During their spring migration north, many hummingbirds take advantage of bright red ocotillo flowers full of nectar.

continue blooming into late summer and fall, providing food for the rest of the season.

Golden columbine and Mexican campion should be planted with other flowers where they can be given the extra water they require. The others listed are all low-water-use plants and require full sun to look their best. Combine these plants with a few additional ones such as desert olive, fragrant ash, and little-leaf sumac, which have nice green foliage that will serve as a background for the other plants. The olive, ash, and sumac have minute, cream-colored flowers which are attractive but not flashy and won't detract from the bright-colored hummingbird flowers. They will also provide perches for these tiny birds. Keep in mind the ultimate height of these plants so one doesn't get hidden behind another where you can't see the hummingbirds feeding.

A hummingbird garden is for bright-colored birds that feed on bright-colored flowers that can be appreciated by bright-spirited people.

The Cactus Garden

When most people think of a cactus garden, they picture a collection of prickly plants, perhaps some rocks, and lots of gravel. While cacti will grow under such conditions and some actually like it, overall it's not particularly appealing to most people's sense of beauty. This has caused some people not to use cacti in their gardens, but, as previously discussed, it's a matter of using cacti in the right places

HUMMINGBIRD PLANTS

Name	Flower Color	Ultimate Height	Main Season of Bloom
Alamo penstemon (*Penstemon alamosensis*)	red	28 in. (71 cm.)	spring
Bird-of-paradise (*Caesalpinia gilliesii*)	yellow and red	15 ft. (450 cm.)	summer fall
Claret-cup hedgehog cactus (*Echinocereus triglochidiatus*)	red	1 ft. (30 cm.)	spring
Crimson sage (*Salvia henryi*)	red	2 ft. (60 cm.)	spring
Desert penstemon (*Penstemon pseudospectabilis*)	pink	4 ft. (120 cm.)	spring summer
Desert willow (*Chilopsis linearis*)	pink, white purple, burgundy	25 ft. (750 cm.)	spring summer, fall
Golden columbine (*Aquilegia chrysantha*)	yellow	3 ft. (90 cm.)	spring
Mexican campion (*Silene laciniata*)	red	2 ft. (60 cm.)	summer fall
New Mexico agave (*Agave neomexicana*)	yellow	15 ft. (450 cm.)	spring summer
Ocotillo (*Fouquieria splendens*)	red	20 ft. (600 cm.)	spring
Palmer agave (*Agave palmeri*)	yellow	18 ft. (540 cm.)	summer
Red-flowered hedgehog cactus (*Echinocereus coccineus*)	red	14 in. (36 cm.)	spring
Superb penstemon (*Penstemon superbus*)	red	4 ft. (120 cm.)	spring summer, fall

The tubular red flowers of a penstemon are favorites of hummingbirds as well as gardeners.

Wildflowers, creosote bush, and small soaptree yuccas complement the cacti, forming a natural-looking desert garden scene.

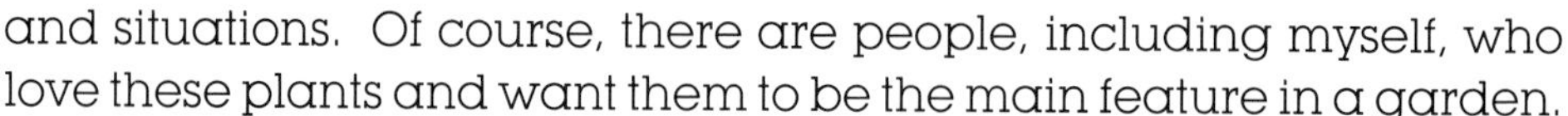

and situations. Of course, there are people, including myself, who love these plants and want them to be the main feature in a garden.

In emphasizing cacti and other succulents, little needs to be done, as their forms lend themselves to being noticed. Some of the miniatures, such as button cactus, golf ball cactus, and Sneed's pincushion cactus, need to be placed in the front of the garden where they can be seen. Plant them in groups of three or more and they will be less likely to get lost in the landscape. All cacti will look good if planted in such groups. Since most members of a species tend to bloom at the same time, the resulting show of flowers can be very spectacular when these plants are placed near one another.

The large, reddish purple flowers of Fendler's hedgehog cactus are sure to be admired in a desert garden.

When preparing an area for cacti, it must be in full sun, and the soil must be well draining. Keeping this in mind, other plants intended for use in this garden should be able to withstand the dry conditions cacti prefer. It's important to use other plants along with the cacti, as they will give this type of garden a more natural look. In nature cacti don't grow alone; they always have companions growing with them in the desert. Wildflowers such as chocolate flower, desert marigold, desert zinnia, tufted evening primrose, and verbenas are a few which will be happy in this garden. Small shrubs such as bush penstemon and fairy duster will give the garden a little height and add a different texture to the garden in contrast to the cacti. Remember to plant these shrubs in odd-numbered groups for a natural effect.

Larger cacti, including the opuntias and barrel cacti, should be used in the center or background. They can be placed as accent plants to highlight their forms or as backdrops for other plants.

Useful as a background or accent plant, Klein cholla has pretty, apple-blossom pink flowers in late spring or early summer.

As the cacti of the Chihuahuan Desert are among the hardiest in the world, there are a good number of them that can be grown in diverse conditions. Whether in the desert or elsewhere, they are a cactus collector's delight, as they can be grown outdoors under conditions which would kill cacti from the nearby Sonoran Desert, for example. Cold extremes can kill them, however, especially if the soil is wet. Under these conditions, cacti and succulents will simply rot. To prevent this, a mulch of crusher fines or small gravel will keep the surface dry near the base of the plants. These materials also absorb heat during the day and may help keep the soil warmer during the night.

A cactus garden is one way to grow some of the world's most unusual and intriguing plants that will be a source of enjoyment for years.

Rocks and cacti are a natural combination. Here cob cactus seems to be rising right out of the rock.

The Sand Box Many people have sand for their gardening pleasure, although most probably regard it as more of a problem than an asset. Gardeners everywhere need to learn to work with their particular environmental conditions. This is especially true in the Southwest, where all of the growing factors (sun, wind, poor soil, little rain) contribute to the need for one item in desert gardening—water. Sandy soils which drain well (too well for many gardeners and many plants) require more water than other soils unless you work with them by looking to nature for your examples.

Some of the plants in the "Desert Plant Encyclopedia" thrive in sandy soil. Using them a whole landscape can be planned that

Bush penstemon cascades over rocks in this garden. Its delicate appearance is deceptive since it thrives in hot, dry locations.

When broom dalea is in bloom, this normally unobtrusive shrub suddenly gets lots of attention from people who would like to have it in their gardens. But it will only grow in gardens with sandy soil.

Wildflower meadows are a colorful way to cover large areas.

will not require soil amendments and excessive watering. Plants which prefer sandy soils include bush penstemon, white sand stars, sand prickly pear, soaptree yucca, and broom dalea. Others that often grow in sand but also grow in other soils include blue stars, chocolate flower, paperflower, threadleaf groundsel, desert zinnia, Scheer's pincushion cactus, horse crippler, Fendler's hedgehog cactus, early bloomer, club cholla, tree cholla, desert Christmas cactus, Engelmann prickly pear, purple prickly pear, brown-spined prickly pear, plains prickly pear, grasslands prickly pear, plains yucca, four-wing saltbush, bird-of-paradise, Apache plume, creosote bush, little-leaf sumac, desert willow, and honey mesquite.

Most of the other plants listed in this book will also grow in sandy soils without a lot of work, although they may need to be watered and fertilized more often. A mulch such as crusher fines or bark will help keep the soil moist longer between waterings.

Clearly, there is a long list of plants for a sandy garden. Some, such as bush penstemon and broom dalea, are coveted by other gardeners, but without sandy conditions these plants are difficult to grow.

In designing a sand garden, use plants in groups of three, five, or more and limit the choice of species. Natural sandy areas tend to have large numbers of individuals. Avoid one-of-a-kind, collector-type gardens with these plants. When installing the garden, it is important to keep the plants well watered, as they will not have developed the fibrous root systems and/or taproots necessary for their survival in these soils. Once they have established themselves (one to three years, depending upon the plant), these plants will help stabilize the soil and provide pleasure for years to come with very little effort on the part of the gardener.

Wildflower Meadows Wildflower meadows have at times been regarded as a nuisance where weed ordinances fail to recognize the difference between environmentally sensitive meadow planting and vacant lots full of weeds. This hasn't been much of a problem in the Southwest so far, where more and more people and local governments are becoming aware of the necessity for water-conserving landscapes. In planting a meadow the procedure for sowing native grasses is followed (see p. 22), with the addition of wildflower seeds to the grass seed mix. However, since meadows can be difficult to establish by seed, an easier method is to directly plant small wildflowers in your garden area. Of course, only desert and drought-tolerant species should be planted in order to conserve water and lessen maintenance. Desert wildflowers often occur in naturally large expanses of colorful displays, and this should be imitated when considering a meadow.

The following desert plants are good candidates for wildflower meadows in the Southwest: blackfoot daisy, blue stars, chocolate flower, desert marigold, desert senna, desert zinnia, mealy-cup sage, Mexican evening primrose, paperflower, penstemons, purple prairie clover, threadleaf groundsel, tufted evening primrose, verbenas, and white sand stars.

To create your meadow, first till the area to be planted. It may be helpful to water it in order to germinate any weed seed that is lying dormant in the soil. After the weeds have sprouted, till them under and you're ready to plant. During the summer rainy season and into the fall is the best time to plant in the Southwest because of monsoon moisture, higher humidity, and cooler temperatures, all of which help the plants survive the shock of transplanting. It's easier to use transplants than trying to keep seed wet enough to germinate in our dry climate. Use the wildflowers listed above along with pots of native grasses, and plant in random groups in the area. Water them until they are well established. After that, they will only need an occasional watering during long dry periods to keep the meadow looking good. Hand weeding will be necessary to prevent weeds such as tumbleweeds and kochia from taking over.

By choosing a variety of wildflowers, a desert meadow can be in bloom from spring through fall. On the other hand, you can select plants which are predominantly spring-, summer-, or fall-blooming if you want to have a big splash of color at a particular time of year. Look at the chart below for blooming periods and consult the "Desert Plant Encyclopedia" for information on how to grow meadow wildflowers.

Wildflower Bloom Chart

	February	March	April	May	June	July	August	September	October	November
Meadow Wildflowers										
Blackfoot daisy (*Melampodium leucanthum*)		X	X	X	X	X	X	X	X	X
Blue stars (*Amsonia hirtella*)		X	X	X	X					
Bush penstemon (*Penstemon ambiguus*)				X	X					
Chocolate flower (*Berlandiera lyrata*)					X	X	X	X	X	
Desert marigold (*Baileya multiradiata*)					X	X	X	X	X	
Desert penstemon (*Penstemon pseudospectabilis*)			X	X	X					
Desert senna (*Senna covesii*)			X	X	X	X	X	X		
Desert zinnia (*Zinnia grandiflora*)				X	X	X	X	X	X	
Fendler penstemon (*Penstemon fendleri*)			X	X	X	X	X			
Mealy-cup sage (*Salvia farinacea*)			X	X	X	X	X	X	X	
Mexican evening primrose (*Oenothera speciosa*)			X	X	X	X	X	X		
Paperflower (*Psilostrophe tagetina*)	X	X	X	X	X	X	X	X	X	
Purple prairie clover (*Petalostemum purpureum*)						X	X	X		
Purple verbena (*Glandularia wrightii*)			X	X	X	X	X	X		
Threadleaf groundsel (*Senecio douglasii*)			X	X	X	X	X	X	X	X
Tufted evening primrose (*Oenothera caespitosa*)			X	X	X	X	X			
White sand stars (*Amsonia arenaria*)			X	X	X					

U.S.D.A. PLANT HARDINESS ZONE MAP

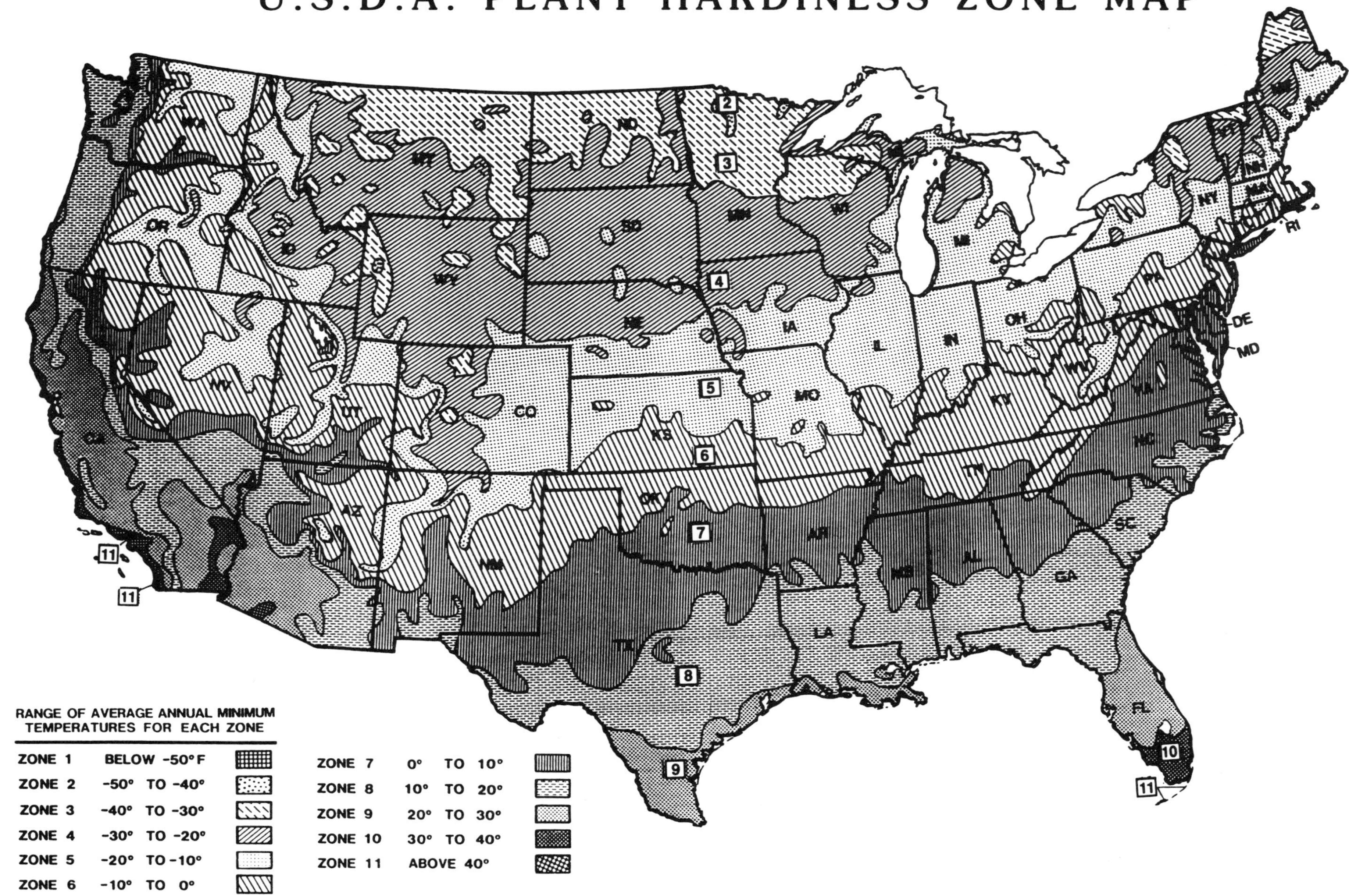

COMMON NAME CROSS-REFERENCE GUIDE

Common Name	Species Name	Plant Type	Page
agrillo	*Rhus trilobata*	desert shrub	175
agritos	*Rhus microphylla*	desert shrub	175
Alamo penstemon	*Penstemon alamosensis*	wildflower	100
American agave	*Agave americana*	succulent	159
amole	*Yucca elata*	succulent	162
Apache plume	*Fallugia paradoxa*	desert shrub	171
autumn sage	*Salvia greggii*	wildflower	107
barometer bush	*Leucophyllum* (see *Penstemon superbus*)	desert shrub	104
barrel cactus	*Ferocactus wislizenii*	cactus	134
beargrass	*Nolina texana*	succulent	160
big nipple corycactus	*Coryphantha macromeris*	cactus	112
bird-of-paradise	*Caesalpinia gilliesii*	desert shrub	168
bisnaga	*Ferocactus wislizenii*	cactus	134
bisnagre	*Echinocactus horizonthalonius* var. *horizonthalonius*	cactus	115
biznaga de chilitos	*Mammillaria heyderi* var. *heyderi*	cactus	137
——	*Mammillaria heyderi* var. *bullingtoniana*	cactus	139
——	*Mammillaria meiacantha*	cactus	140
blackfoot daisy	*Melampodium leucanthum*	wildflower	98
black-spined prickly pear	*Opuntia macrocentra*	cactus	149
blue barrel	*Echinocactus horizonthalonius*	cactus	115
blue stars	*Amsonia hirtella*	wildflower	91
broom dalea	*Dalea scoparia*	desert shrub	174
——	*Psorothamnus scoparia*	desert shrub	174
brown-flowered cactus	*Echinocereus chloranthus* var. *chloranthus*	cactus	117
brown-flowered hedgehog	*Glandulicactus wrightii*	cactus	136
brown-spined prickly pear	*Opuntia phaeacantha*	cactus	151
brown spine hedgehog	*Echinocereus chloranthus* var. *chloranthus*	cactus	117
——	*Echinocereus chloranthus* var. *cylindricus*	cactus	117
bush penstemon	*Penstemon ambiguus*	wildflower	101
button cactus	*Epithelantha micromeris*	cactus	126
button mammillaria	*Mammillaria lasiacantha*	cactus	139
candle cholla	*Opuntia kleiniae*	cactus	146
candy barrel	*Ferocactus wislizenii*	cactus	134
cane cholla	*Opuntia imbricata*	cactus	145
catchfly	*Silene laciniata*	wildflower	110
catclaw acacia	*Acacia greggii*	desert tree	179
catclaw cactus	*Glandulicactus wrightii*	cactus	136
cenizio	*Leucophyllum* (see *Penstemon superbus*)	desert shrub	104

century plant	*Agave neomexicana*	succulent	157
——	*Agave palmeri*	succulent	159
chamiso	*Atriplex canescens*	desert shrub	167
chaparral	*Larrea tridentata*	desert shrub	173
Chihuahuan whitethorn	*Acacia neovernicosa*	desert shrub	164
chilitos	*Mammillaria lasiacantha*	cactus	139
chocolate flower	*Berlandiera lyrata*	wildflower	95
claret-cup cactus	*Echinocereus coccineus* var. *gurneyi*	cactus	118
claret-cup hedgehog cactus	*Echinocereus triglochidiatus*	cactus	120
cliff fendlerbush	*Fendlera rupicola*	desert shrub	173
club cholla	*Opuntia clavata*	cactus	143
coachwhip	*Fouquieria splendens*	succulent	160
cob cactus	*Escobaria dasyacantha*	cactus	127
——	*Escobaria tuberculosa*	cactus	132
coral penstemon	*Penstemon superbus*	wildflower	103
creosote bush	*Larrea tridentata*	desert shrub	173
crimson sage	*Salvia henryi*	wildflower	106
dagger cholla	*Opuntia clavata*	cactus	143
datil yucca	*Yucca baccata*	succulent	163
desert agave	*Agave deserti*	succulent	157
desert beardtongue	*Penstemon pseudospectabilis*	wildflower	103
desert candle	*Dasylirion wheeleri*	succulent	159
desert catalpa	*Chilopsis linearis*	desert tree	184
desert Christmas cactus	*Opuntia leptocaulis*	cactus	146
desert daisy	*Melampodium leucanthum*	wildflower	98
desert elderberry	*Sambucus mexicana*	desert tree	194
desert marigold	*Baileya multiradiata*	wildflower	93
desert olive	*Forestiera neomexicana*	desert tree	185
desert penstemon	*Penstemon pseudospectabilis*	wildflower	103
desert senna	*Senna covesii (Cassia covesii)*	wildflower	108
desert sotol	*Dasylirion wheeleri*	succulent	159
desert spoon	*Dasylirion wheeleri*	succulent	159
desert sumac	*Rhus microphylla*	desert shrub	175
desert willow	*Chilopsis linearis*	desert tree	184
desert zinnia	*Zinnia grandiflora*	wildflower	110
——	*Zinnia acerosa*	wildflower	111
devil's claw	*Echinocactus texensis*	cactus	115
devil's head	*Echinocactus horizonthalonius* var. *horizonthalonius*	cactus	115
dog cholla	*Opuntia grahamii*	cactus	144
Doña Ana cactus	*Coryphantha macromeris*	cactus	112
Duncan's cactus	*Escobaria duncanii*	cactus	128
Duncan's pincushion cactus	*Escobaria duncanii*	cactus	128
dwarf cholla	*Opuntia grahamii*	cactus	144
eagle's claw	*Echinocactus horizonthalonius* var. *horizonthalonius*	cactus	115
——	*Echinocactus texensis*	cactus	115

early bloomer	*Echinomastus intertextus* var. *intertextus*	cactus	125
——	*Echinomastus intertextus* var. *dasyacanthus*	cactus	125
Englemann prickly pear	*Opuntia englemanii*	cactus	148
estria del tarde	*Escobaria vivipara* var. *neomexicana*	cactus	133
evergreen sumac	*Rhus virens*	desert shrub	177
fairy duster	*Calliandra eriophylla*	desert shrub	170
false mesquite	*Calliandra eriophylla*	desert shrub	170
Fendler penstemon	*Penstemon fendleri*	wildflower	102
Fendler's cactus	*Echinocereus fendleri*	cactus	121
Fendler's hedgehog cactus	*Echinocereus fendleri* var. *rectispinus*	cactus	121
——	*Echinocereus fendleri* var. *fendleri*	cactus	121
fishhook barrel cactus	*Ferocactus wislizenii*	cactus	134
fishhook cactus	*Mammillaria grahamii*	cactus	136
flor de mimbre	*Chilopsis linearis*	desert tree	184
flor sauco	*Sambucus mexicana*	desert tree	194
four-wing saltbush	*Atriplex canescens*	desert shrub	167
fragrant ash	*Fraxinus cuspidata*	desert tree	187
fresno	*Fraxinus cuspidata*	desert tree	187
frijolillo	*Sophora secundiflora*	desert shrub	178
giant fishhook cactus	*Ferocactus hamatacanthus*	cactus	134
giant palm yucca	*Yucca faxoniana*	succulent	163
gilia penstemon	*Penstemon ambiguus*	wildflower	101
gobernadora	*Larrea tridentata*	desert shrub	173
gold cholla	*Opuntia davisii*	cactus	144
goldenball leadtree	*Leucanea retusa*	desert tree	187
golden columbine	*Aquilegia chrysantha*	wildflower	91
golden rainbow cactus	*Echinocereus pectinatus* var. *dasyacanthus*	cactus	121
golf ball cactus	*Mammillaria lasiacantha*	cactus	139
Graham dog cactus	*Opuntia grahamii*	cactus	144
Graham's cactus	*Opuntia grahamii*	cactus	144
grasslands prickly pear	*Opuntia pottsii*	cactus	152
greasewood	*Larrea tridentata*	desert shrub	173
green-flowered hedgehog	*Echinocereus chloranthus* var. *chloranthus*	cactus	117
——	*Echinocereus chloranthus* var. *cylindricus*	cactus	117
green-flowered pitaya	*Echinocereus chloranthus* var. *cylindricus*	cactus	117
green-flowered torch cactus	*Echinocereus chloranthus* var. *cylindricus*	cactus	117
hairy senna	*Senna covesii (Cassia covesii)*	wildflower	108
Havard penstemon	*Penstemon havardii*	wildflower	104
hediondilla	*Larrea tridentata*	desert shrub	173

Henry's sage	*Salvia henryi*	wildflower	106
honey mesquite	*Prosopis glandulosa*	desert tree	190
horse crippler	*Echinocactus texensis*	cactus	115
huajillo	*Calliandra eriophylla*	desert shrub	170
Indian pink	*Silene laciniata*	wildflower	110
indigo bush	*Amorpha fruticosa*	desert shrub	166
jaboncillo	*Sapindus saponaria* var. *drummondii*	desert tree	194
Klein cholla	*Opuntia kleiniae*	cactus	146
Koenig's pincushion cactus	*Escobaria orcuttii* var. *koenigii*	cactus	130
largoncillo	*Acacia constricta*	desert shrub	165
lechuguilla	*Agave lechuguilla*	succulent	155
Lee's pincushion cactus	*Escobaria leei*	cactus	128
little chiles	*Mammillaria heyderi* var. *heyderi*	cactus	137
——	*Mammillaria heyderi* var. *bullingtoniana*	cactus	139
——	*Mammillaria meiacantha*	cactus	140
little green eyes	*Berlandiera lyrata*	wildflower	95
little-leaf sumac	*Rhus microphylla*	desert shrub	175
lizard-catcher	*Mammillaria grahamii*	cactus	136
long-flowered amsonia	*Amsonia longiflora*	wildflower	91
long mama	*Coryphantha macromeris*	cactus	112
long nipple cactus	*Coryphantha scheeri* var. *valida*	cactus	114
long-tubercled coryphantha	*Coryphantha scheeri* var. *scheeri*	cactus	113
——	*Coryphantha scheeri* var. *valida*	cactus	114
madrono	*Arbutus texana*	desert tree	181
mealy blue sage	*Salvia farinacea*	wildflower	106
mealy-cup sage	*Salvia farinacea*	wildflower	106
mealy sage	*Salvia farinacea*	wildflower	106
mescal	*Agave neomexicana*	succulent	157
——	*Agave palmeri*	succulent	159
mescal bean	*Sophora secundiflora*	desert shrub	178
mescat acacia	*Acacia constricta*	desert shrub	165
mesquite	*Prosopis glandulosa*	desert tree	190
Mexican buckeye	*Ungnadia speciosa*	desert tree	197
Mexican campion	*Silene laciniata*	wildflower	110
Mexican elder	*Sambucus mexicana*	desert tree	194
Mexican evening primrose	*Oenothera speciosa*	wildflower	100
mezquite	*Prosopis glandulosa*	desert tree	190
mimbre	*Chilopsis linearis*	desert tree	184
monillo	*Ungnadia speciosa*	desert tree	197
mounded dwarf cholla	*Opuntia grahamii*	cactus	144
mountain cob cactus	*Escobaria dasyacantha*	cactus	127
mulato	*Epithelantha micromeris*	cactus	126
mulee	*Coryphantha scheeri* var. *scheeri*	cactus	113
——	*Coryphantha scheeri* var. *valida*	cactus	114

needle mulee	*Coryphantha scheeri* var. *scheeri*	cactus	113
——	*Coryphantha scheeri* var. *valida*	cactus	114
netleaf hackberry	*Celtis reticulata*	desert tree	182
New Mexico agave	*Agave neomexicana*	succulent	157
New Mexico buckeye	*Ungnadia speciosa*	desert tree	197
New Mexico coryphantha	*Escobaria vivipara* var. *neomexicana*	cactus	133
New Mexico olive	*Forestiera neomexicana*	desert tree	185
New Mexico pincushion cactus	*Escobaria vivipara* var. *neomexicana*	cactus	133
New Mexico prickly pear	*Opuntia phaeacantha*	cactus	151
New Mexico privet	*Forestiera neomexicana*	desert tree	185
New Mexico rainbow cactus	*Echinocereus chloranthus* var. *chloranthus*	cactus	117
——	*Echinocereus pectinatus* var. *dasyacanthus*	cactus	121
night-blooming cereus	*Peniocereus greggii*	cactus	152
nipple beehive	*Coryphantha macromeris*	cactus	112
nipple cactus	*Mammillaria heyderi* var. *heyderi*	cactus	137
——	*Mammillaria heyderi* var. *bullingtoniana*	cactus	139
——	*Mammillaria meiacantha*	cactus	140
nopal	*Opuntia englemanii*	cactus	148
ocotillo	*Fouquieria splendens*	succulent	160
Orcutt's pincushion cactus	*Escobaria orcuttii* var. *orcuttii*	cactus	129
palma	*Yucca torreyi*	succulent	163
Palmer agave	*Agave palmeri*	succulent	159
Palmer penstemon	*Penstemon palmeri*	wildflower	104
palmilla	*Yucca elata*	succulent	162
palm yucca	*Yucca torreyi*	succulent	163
palo blanco	*Celtis reticulata*	desert tree	182
——	*Forestiera neomexicana*	desert tree	185
——	*Sapindus saponaria* var. *drummondii*	desert tree	194
paperflower	*Psilostrophe tagetina*	wildflower	105
paradise poinciana	*Caesalpinia gilliesii*	desert shrub	168
Parry agave	*Agave parryi*	succulent	157
Parry penstemon	*Penstemon parryi*	wildflower	104
pencil cholla	*Opuntia leptocaulis*	cactus	146
phlox penstemon	*Penstemon ambiguus*	wildflower	101
pincushion cactus	*Mammillaria grahamii*	cactus	136
——	*Mammillaria heyderi* var. *heyderi*	cactus	137
pitaya	*Echinocereus enneacanthus* var. *brevispinus*	cactus	120
——	*Echinocereus stramineus*	cactus	124
plains penstemon	*Penstemon fendleri*	wildflower	102
plains prickly pear	*Opuntia polyacantha*	cactus	151
——	*Opuntia pottsii*	cactus	152
plains yucca	*Yucca glauca*	succulent	163
ponil	*Fallugia paradoxa*	desert shrub	171

prairie flame-leaf sumac	*Rhus lanceolata*	desert shrub	177
prairie zinnia	*Zinnia grandiflora*	wildflower	110
purple prairie clover	*Petalostemum purpureum*	wildflower	105
purple prickly pear	*Opuntia macrocentra*	cactus	149
purple sage	*Psorothamnus scoparia*	desert shrub	174
purple verbena	*Glandularia wrightii (verbena wrightii)*	wildflower	97
queen-of-the-night	*Peniocereus greggii*	cactus	152
rainbow hedgehog	*Echinocereus pectinatus* var. *dasyacanthus*	cactus	121
rattlebox	*Senna covesii (Cassia covesii)*	wildflower	108
red-flowered hedgehog cactus	*Echinocereus coccineus* var. *gurneyi*	cactus	118
——	*Echinocereus coccineus* var. *coccineus*	cactus	120
red sage	*Salvia henryi*	wildflower	106
reina-de-la-noche	*Peniocereus greggii*	cactus	152
Rocky Mountain zinnia	*Zinnia grandiflora*	wildflower	110
rusty hedgehog cactus	*Echinocereus russanthus*	cactus	123
sacahuista	*Nolina texana*	succulent	160
Sandberg's pincushion cactus	*Escobaria sandbergii*	cactus	130
sand penstemon	*Penstemon ambiguus*	wildflower	101
sand prickly pear	*Opuntia arenaria*	cactus	147
scarlet bugler	*Penstemon barbatus*	wildflower	104
Scheer's pincushion cactus	*Coryphantha scheeri* var. *scheeri*	cactus	113
——	*Coryphantha scheeri* var. *valida*	cactus	114
Schott's mountain yucca	*Yucca schottii*	succulent	163
screwbean	*Prosopis pubescens*	desert tree	192
screw-pod mesquite	*Prosopis pubescens*	desert tree	192
shindagger	*Agave schottii*	succulent	157
shrubby senna	*Senna wislizenii*	desert shrub	177
slender stem cactus	*Opuntia leptocaulis*	cactus	146
soaptree yucca	*Yucca elata*	succulent	162
soapweed yucca	*Yucca angustissima*	succulent	162
sotol	*Dasylirion wheeleri*	succulent	159
——	*Dasylirion leiophyllum*	succulent	160
Spanish bayonet	*Yucca torreyi*	succulent	163
Spanish dagger	*Yucca torreyi*	succulent	163
Sneed's pincushion cactus	*Escobaria sneedii*	cactus	131
stemless evening primrose	*Oenthera caespitosa*	wildflower	98
strawberry cactus	*Echinocereus enneacanthus* var. *brevispinus*	cactus	120
——	*Echinocereus stramineus*	cactus	124
strawberry hedgehog cactus	*Echinocereus enneacanthus* var. *brevispinus*	cactus	120
——	*Echinocereus fendleri* var. *rectispinus*	cactus	121
sunset cactus	*Mammillaria grahamii*	cactus	136
superb penstemon	*Penstemon superbus*	wildflower	103

tasajillo	*Opuntia leptocaulis*	cactus	146
te de senna	*Senna covesii (Cassia covesii)*	wildflower	108
Texas barrel cactus	*Ferocactus hamatacanthus*	cactus	134
Texas buckeye	*Ungnadia speciosa*	desert tree	197
Texas madrone	*Arbutus texana*	desert tree	181
Texas mountain laurel	*Sophora secundiflora*	desert shrub	178
Texas rainbow cactus	*Echinocereus pectinatus* var. *dasyacanthus*	cactus	121
Texas ranger	*Leucophyllum* (see *Penstemon superbus*)	desert shrub	104
Texas silverleaf	*Leucophyllum* (see *Penstemon superbus*)	desert shrub	104
threadleaf groundsel	*Senecio douglasii* var. *longilobus*	wildflower	108
three-leaf sumac	*Rhus trilobata*	desert shrub	175
Thurber penstemon	*Penstemon thurberi*	wildflower	104
torch cactus	*Echinocereus fendleri* var. *rectispinus*	cactus	121
tornadora	*Tecoma stan* var. *angustata*	desert shrub	185
tornillo	*Prosopis pubescenes*	desert tree	192
Torrey yucca	*Yucca torreyi*	succulent	163
tree cholla	*Opuntia imbricata*	cactus	145
tufted evening primrose	*Oenothera caespitosa*	wildflower	98
Turk's head	*Echinocactus horizonthalonius* var. *horizonthalonius*	cactus	115
——	*Ferocactus hamatacanthas*	cactus	134
twisted bean	*Prosopis pubescens*	desert tree	192
una de gato	*Acacia greggii*	desert tree	179
Utah agave	*Agave utahensis*	succulent	159
Villard's pincushion cactus	*Escobaria villardii*	cactus	132
viscid acacia	*Acacia neovernicosa*	desert shrub	164
visnaga	*Ferocactus hamatacanthus*	cactus	134
viznaga	*Echinocactus texensis*	cactus	115
western honey mesquite	*Prosopis glandulosa* var. *torreyana*	desert tree	190
western soapberry	*Sapindus saponaria* var. *drummondii*	desert tree	194
white-flowered visnagita	*Echinomastus intertextus* var. *intertextus*	cactus	125
——	*Echinomastus intertextus* var. *dasyacanthus*	cactus	125
whitethorn acacia	*Acacia constricta*	desert shrub	165
white sand stars	*Amsonia arenaria*	wildflower	91
Wilcox's pincushion cactus	*Mammillaria wrightii* var. *wilcoxii*	cactus	141
woven spine pineapple cactus	*Echinomastus intertextus* var. *intertextus*	cactus	125
——	*Echinomastus intertextus* var. *dasyacanthus*	cactus	125
Wright's pincushion cactus	*Mammillaria wrightii* var. *wrightii*	cactus	141
yellow bells	*Tecoma stans* var. *angustata*	desert shrub	185
yellow-flowered pitaya	*Echinocereus pectinatus* var. *dasyacanthus*	cactus	121
zumaque	*Rhus virens*	desert shrub	177

CHAPTER 7 Desert Plant Encyclopedia

The following plants of the Chihuahuan Desert are the perfect solution to gardening in the Southwest. They are well adapted to the harsh elements our climate can present at times. And many have colorful flowers that will brighten your home landscape just as they do the desert wildlands.

This encyclopedia is divided into the following sections: wildflowers, cacti, succulents, shrubs, and trees. The entry for each individual plant contains a description of the plant, information on its range and location in the wild, and instructions on how to plant and care for it, as well as remarks concerning its uses in landscaping.

The hardiness zones listed are based on the current United States Department of Agriculture zone map (see p. 80). Zones in this case refer to regions of temperature hardiness as opposed to the zones of water usage around a house or building. Hardiness is an indication of minimum winter temperatures in a particular zone. The lower the number, the hardier the plant. Zones above that number are usually okay for growing a plant from a lower numbered zone. Most of the Chihuahuan Desert in the United States lies in U.S.D.A. zones 7 and 8. Looking at the map, it is obvious that a variety of climates exist within zones 7 and 8, which extend across the United States from the West Coast south and east to the Atlantic Ocean. Zone 8 in South Carolina is vastly different from zone 8 in New Mexico when the amounts of rainfall are compared. The South Carolina areas can typically receive up to 49 inches (125 centimeters) of precipitation in a year as compared to an average of 8 inches (20 centimeters) per year in New Mexico. A transplanted palmetto from South Carolina wouldn't freeze in New Mexico, but without extra watering it would die of thirst. Conversely, a barrel cactus from New Mexico would rot in South Carolina if it were not provided with some means of repelling excess moisture.

Moisture content also makes a difference in the winter. Low

temperatures may only last for brief periods during the night in the Chihuahuan Desert. Because of this and a lack of moisture in the soil, the ground does not often freeze, which could damage a plant's roots. As such, often the tops of desert plants will die back to the ground but will recover quickly in spring from the undamaged roots. The key to growing desert plants in a cold climate is keeping the roots dry. If they can be kept dry, such as in a sand bed or container, they can be grown in an otherwise hostile (to the plants) climate.

Before obtaining any of the following plants, be sure to check the source of your potential purchases. There are laws protecting native plants at the federal and state levels in the United States. Both the United States and Mexico are signees of the Convention on International Trade in Endangered Species (CITES) agreement. This treaty prohibits the trade of cacti, for example, without the proper permits. Other plant laws, such as those in Arizona and New Mexico, have permit systems for collecting native plants. Plants should never be removed without the proper permits, especially from public lands. On private lands, the owner's and sometimes the state's permission must be obtained. Otherwise, you could be charged with trespassing and theft as well as violation of native plant protection laws.

The survival rate of desert plants is always better if they are purchased as nursery-propagated plants or if you start them yourself from seeds or cuttings. It is important that plants not be purchased from collected sources (except for plants that have been rescued from habitat destruction, such as highway and building construction). First, they will likely not survive the transplanting since the plants will have lost their life-sustaining root systems no matter how carefully they were treated. Second, from an environmental standpoint, removing plants from the wild can quickly deplete native populations important for the reproduction of the species.

Desert Wildflowers

In spring the desert can be a tapestry of wildflowers if we've been lucky enough to receive the winter moisture necessary to produce them. The real flower show in the Chihuahuan Desert occurs later, however, during our "second spring," with the arrival of the summer monsoon season from July through September. These rains are the most reliable moisture this desert receives. In response to this phenomenon, many of the region's wildflowers put on most of their growth and flowers at this time.

Planning a garden with these plants will provide not only spring beauty but also a spectacular fall display. Because most of the cacti bloom in the spring and early summer months, planting wildflowers that bloom in the fall can liven up an area that might otherwise be somewhat dull at that time of year. Mexican evening primrose and desert zinnia, for example, are colorful companions to prickly pears that are no longer in flower.

Once planted, desert wildflowers need very little attention other than an occasional watering to keep them looking good and in flower. They appreciate a fertilizing with a low-numbered fertilizer, such as fish emulsion, when they renew growth in the spring. Most have the same requirements as other desert plants, that is, full sun and good drainage.

The following wildflowers were chosen with a number of attributes in mind: showy flowers, hardiness, drought tolerance, and the ability to attract wildlife; they are all perennials. Some of these plants are fairly easy to find in nurseries throughout the Southwest. To obtain others, you will need to find a source for seed and grow them yourself. Either way, the wildflowers of the Chihuahuan Desert will bring a flourish of color to your garden.

WILDFLOWERS

Species Name: *Amsonia hirtella*

Family: Apocynaceae (Dogbane)

Common Name(s): BLUE STARS

Description: *Amsonia hirtella* is an herbaceous perennial with numerous leafy, erect stems that grow up to 20 inches (51 centimeters) tall.

Leaves: The leaves are linear-lanceolate or ovate-lanceolate and appear to be whorled at the top of the plant.

Flowers: *Amsonia hirtella* has a dense, many-flowered inflorescence of lavender-blue, starlike flowers. Blue stars flower from March to June.

Fruit: The numerous slender brown seeds are cylinder shaped.

Range and Habitat: Found in southwestern New Mexico, Trans-Pecos Texas, southeast Arizona, and northern Mexico from 1,500 to 5,500 feet (450 to 1,650 meters) on rocky slopes and canyons in the Chihuahuan Desert and desert grassland.

Hardiness: Zone 6

Planting and Care: Seeds of blue stars are sometimes available from Southwest seed companies. They require no special treatment and can be started any time in spring or summer.

Remarks: Blue stars is a drought-resistant perennial member of a mainly tropical family that includes the well-known oleander. It forms large clumps over time that add an unusual touch of blue to the desert garden, where most colors are yellows and reds.

Related Species: *Amsonia arenaria*, white sand stars, has clusters of white flowers on 10-inch (25-centimeter) stems. This sand-loving perennial is very arid adapted. White sand stars is native to the Chihuahuan Desert of southern New Mexico, Trans-Pecos Texas, and Chihuahua, Mexico. Hardiness: Zone 6.

Amsonia longiflora, long-flowered amsonia, is a 2-foot-(60-centimeter-) tall perennial covered with tubular, pale blue flowers. It is native to the Chihuahuan Desert of New Mexico, Texas, and Mexico. Hardiness: Zone 7.

Species Name: *Aquilegia chrysantha*

Family: Ranunculaceae (Buttercup)

Common Name(s): GOLDEN COLUMBINE

Description: *Aquilegia chrysantha* has bright yellow flowers and pretty green, lacy foliage. It is a tall perennial, reaching a height of about 3 feet (90 centimeters).

Leaves: The medium-green leaves grow up to 1¾ inches (4 centimeters) wide and long. They are divided into two or three small leaflets.

Flowers: The large, golden yellow flowers are 2 to 3 inches (5 to 8 centimeters) wide. There are five petals, each with a long spur that grows up to 2¾ inches (7 centimeters) long. Golden columbine blooms from April to June.

Fruit: The fruit is a simple, slender, podlike structure that splits open when dry to release the tiny black seeds.

Range and Habitat: Found in New Mexico, Trans-Pecos Texas, Arizona, southern Colorado, and northern Mexico from 3,500 to 9,500 feet (1,050 to 2,850 meters) on moist soils in the canyons and mountains of the Chihuahuan Desert and other regions of the Southwest.

Hardiness: Zone 6

Planting and Care: Seeds and plants are readily available at nurseries in the Southwest and through the mail-order sources in Appendix II of this book. Golden columbine is easily grown

Amsonia hirtella • *page 92* ▶

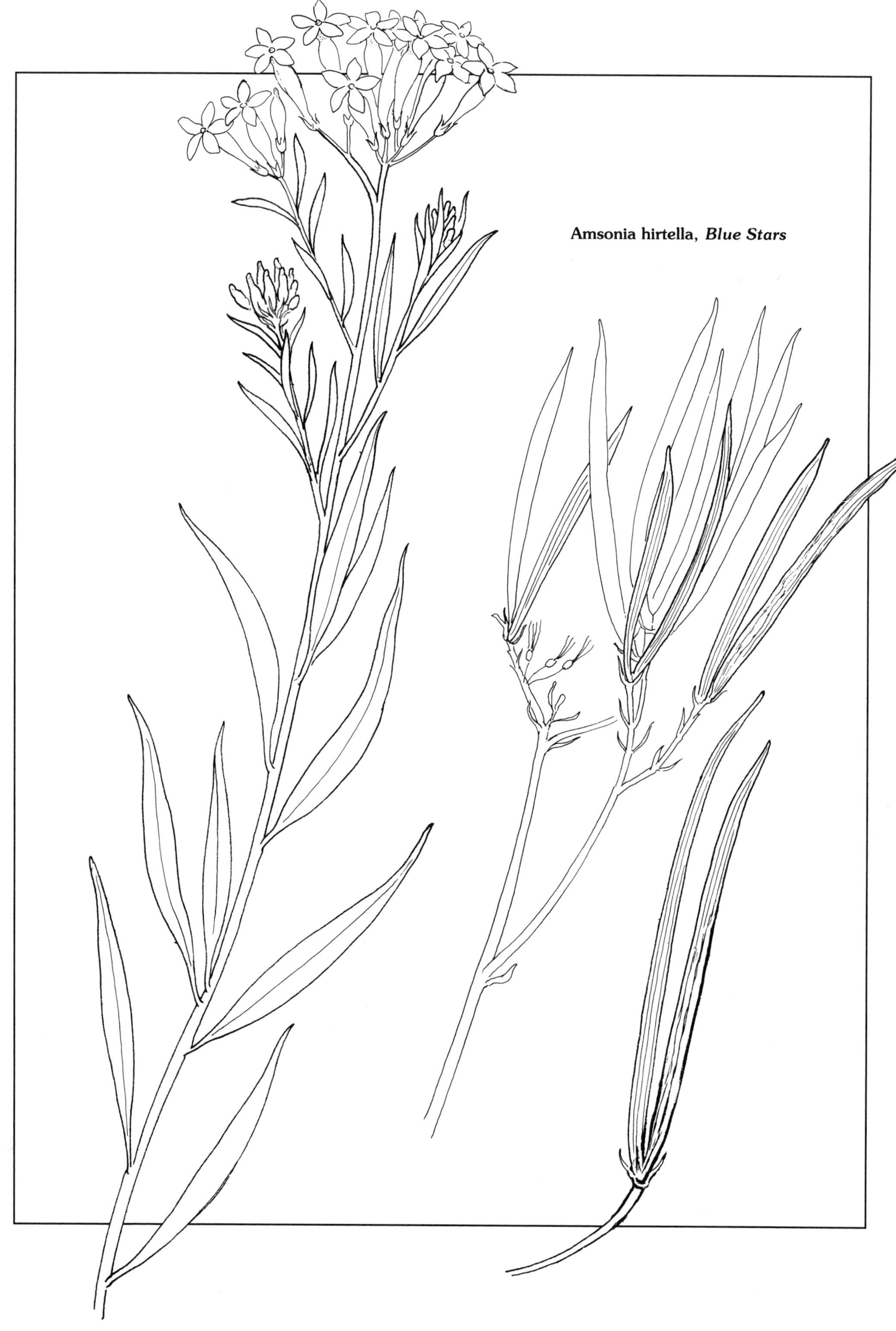
Amsonia hirtella, *Blue Stars*

from seeds, which require no pretreatment if sown during the cooler times of the year, such as in January, in cool greenhouses and cold frames. Otherwise, they should be sown in the fall outdoors or cold stratified for thirty days. Plants take two years before blooming, but the bright yellow flowers are well worth the wait. They should be planted in light shade in arid areas, such as near a northern or eastern exposure of a house. While golden columbine tolerates drier conditions and more heat than most columbines, it needs extra watering in the desert garden.

Remarks: Golden columbine is one of our showiest natives. In Dog Canyon at Oliver Lee State Park near Alamogordo, New Mexico, it is quite beautiful in spring. It is especially abundant there, growing in association with ferns along the canyon stream. As a landscape plant, it blends in well in perennial borders and other areas that are regularly watered. Otherwise, it will go dormant in the summer heat or may even die from drought.

The large flowers of golden columbine were crossed with European columbines to give us the hybrids common in our gardens today. Plant breeders wanted a flower with the long spurs of the golden columbine and the various colors of the European columbines.

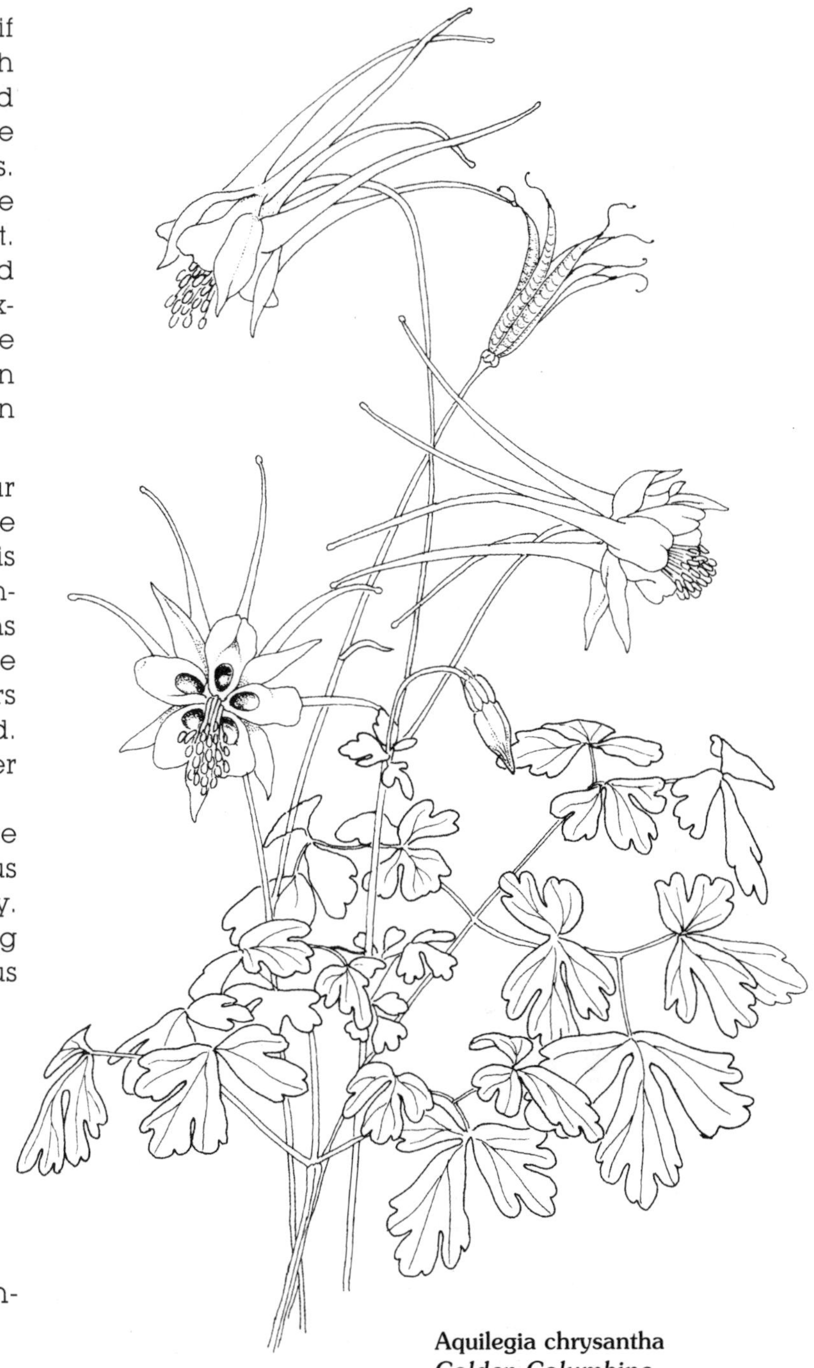

Aquilegia chrysantha
Golden Columbine

Species Name: *Baileya multiradiata*

Family: Asteraceae (Compositae) (Sunflower)

Common Name(s): DESERT MARIGOLD

Description: *Baileya multiradiata* is a wildflower of the southwestern deserts that grows 1 to $1^1/_2$ feet (30 to 45 centimeters) tall. It has gray, woolly leaves and bright yellow flowers.

Leaves: The grayish green leaves are usually described as woolly. They form a rosette from which the flower stems grow. A few leaves are found on the lower parts of the flower stems. The larger leaves are about $1^1/_2$ inches (4 centimeters) long.

Flowers: The yellow daisies are about $1^1/_2$ inches (4 centimeters) across. They have a long period of bloom, from early summer up to frost.

Fruit: The seeds are somewhat angled and white with faint stripes.

Baileya multiradiata • *page 94* ▶

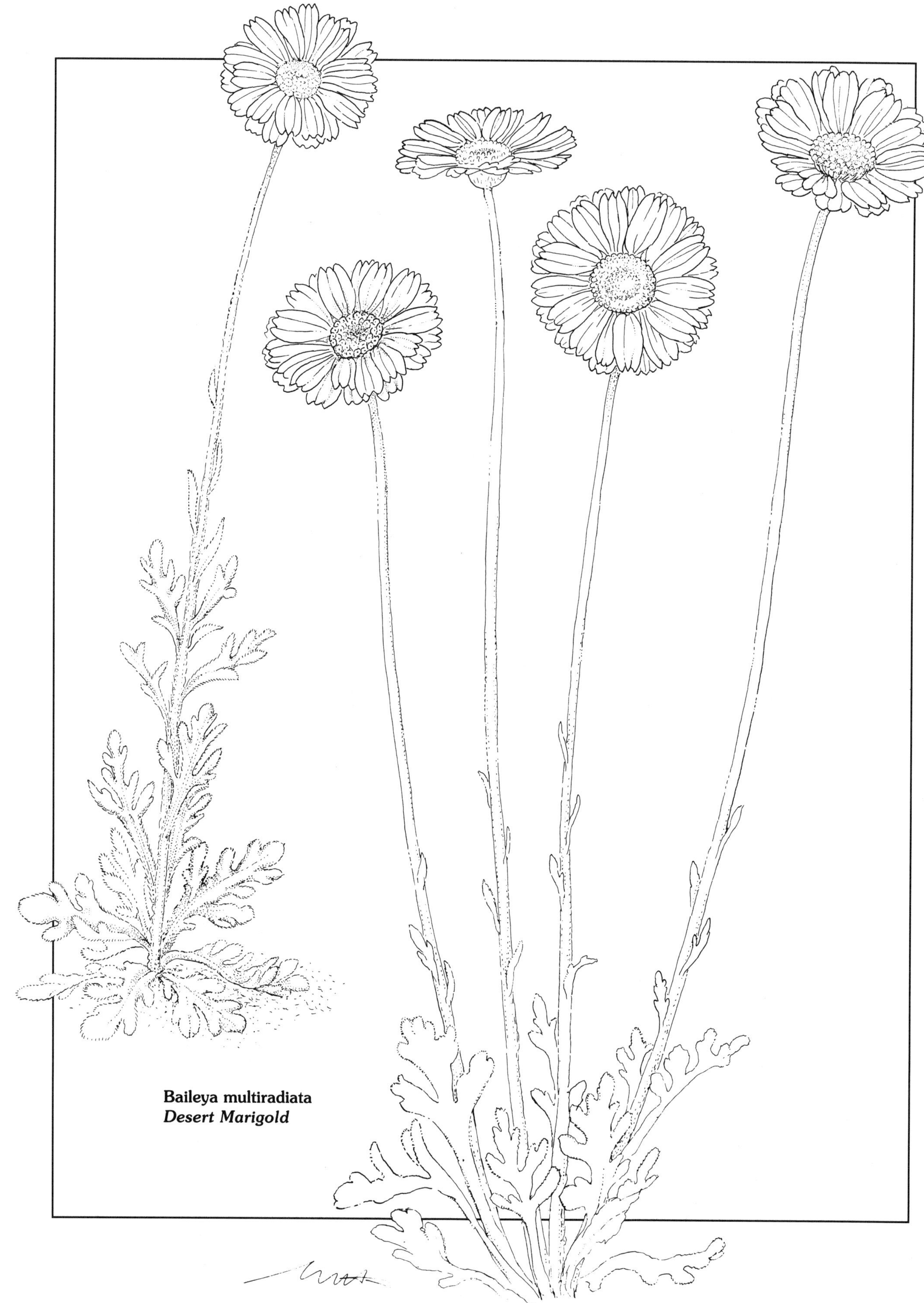

Baileya multiradiata
Desert Marigold

Range and Habitat: Found in New Mexico, western Texas, Arizona, southeastern California, southern Nevada, southern Utah, and Chihuahua, Coahuila, Sonora, and Baja California in Mexico from 3,500 to 6,000 feet (1,050 to 1,800 meters) on gravelly or sandy soils in the Chihuahuan and Sonoran deserts and the desert grassland.

Hardiness: Zone 7

Planting and Care: Seeds are available at nurseries and through mail-order sources. Plant the seeds in the fall, directly in the area where they are to grow. Be sure the soil is well drained, that is, sandy or gravelly. Although considered a perennial, desert marigold often acts more like a biennial, sending up a rosette of gray-green leaves in the fall, then flowering throughout spring, summer, and fall of the following year. A little extra water will encourage more flowering, but be sure not to overwater or it will shorten the life of the plant.

Remarks: Desert marigold is a short-lived yellow daisy. It reseeds itself freely, popping up here and there in the garden; however, desert marigold is not an invasive plant. Its cheerful flowers are among the desert's most showy.

Its pollen is a favorite of bees, especially during the late summer monsoon season.

Species Name: *Berlandiera lyrata*

Family: Asteraceae (Compositae) (Sunflower)

Common Name(s): CHOCOLATE FLOWER, LITTLE GREEN EYES

Description: *Berlandiera lyrata* is a woolly perennial that grows up to 1½ feet (45 centimeters) tall and wide. It is a morning flower, closing in the heat of the afternoon. The fragrance of its flowers gives chocolate flower one of its common names.

Leaves: The pale green leaves grow up to 5½ inches (14 centimeters) long. They grow in a basal rosette around the stem and on the stem itself. Some leaves are deeply cut with rounded lobes.

Flowers: The yellow daisy flowers are ¾ to 1¼ inches (2 to 3 centimeters) wide with eight yellow ray flowers (the "petals" of the daisy) and maroon-colored disk flowers in the center. They bloom from June through October.

Fruit: The seeds are flat achenes with fine hairs.

Range and Habitat: Found in New Mexico and from Arkansas and Louisiana to Arizona and Mexico from 4,000 to 7,000 feet (1,200 to 2,100 meters) on limestone soils of dry plains and hills in the Chihuahuan Desert, the desert grassland, and a wide variety of other habitats.

Hardiness: Zone 4

Planting and Care: Seeds and plants of chocolate flower are readily available at nurseries and through mail-order sources in the Southwest. Chocolate flower is easily started from seeds without any special treatment. It self-sows in the garden, and these plants can be transplanted to desirable locations.

Remarks: Chocolate flower is used for dried flower arrangements, as the green, flat bracts beneath the blossom are exposed when the ray flowers drop. When this happens, the center disk also turns green with the demise of the disk flowers, giving the flower another of its common names, little green eyes.

Chocolate flower is a good example of looking to nature for inspiration in designing with and combining native plants in the landscape. Along the roadsides in central New Mexico, chocolate flower grows in association with Apache plume (*Fallugia paradoxa*) and bush penstemon (*Penstemon ambiguus*), all of which bloom at the same time, creating a colorful display. This same combination in the desert garden is both beautiful to look at and very drought tolerant. Chocolate flower will quickly become one of your favorite plants, delighting children and adults alike.

Berlandiera lyrata • *page 96* ▶

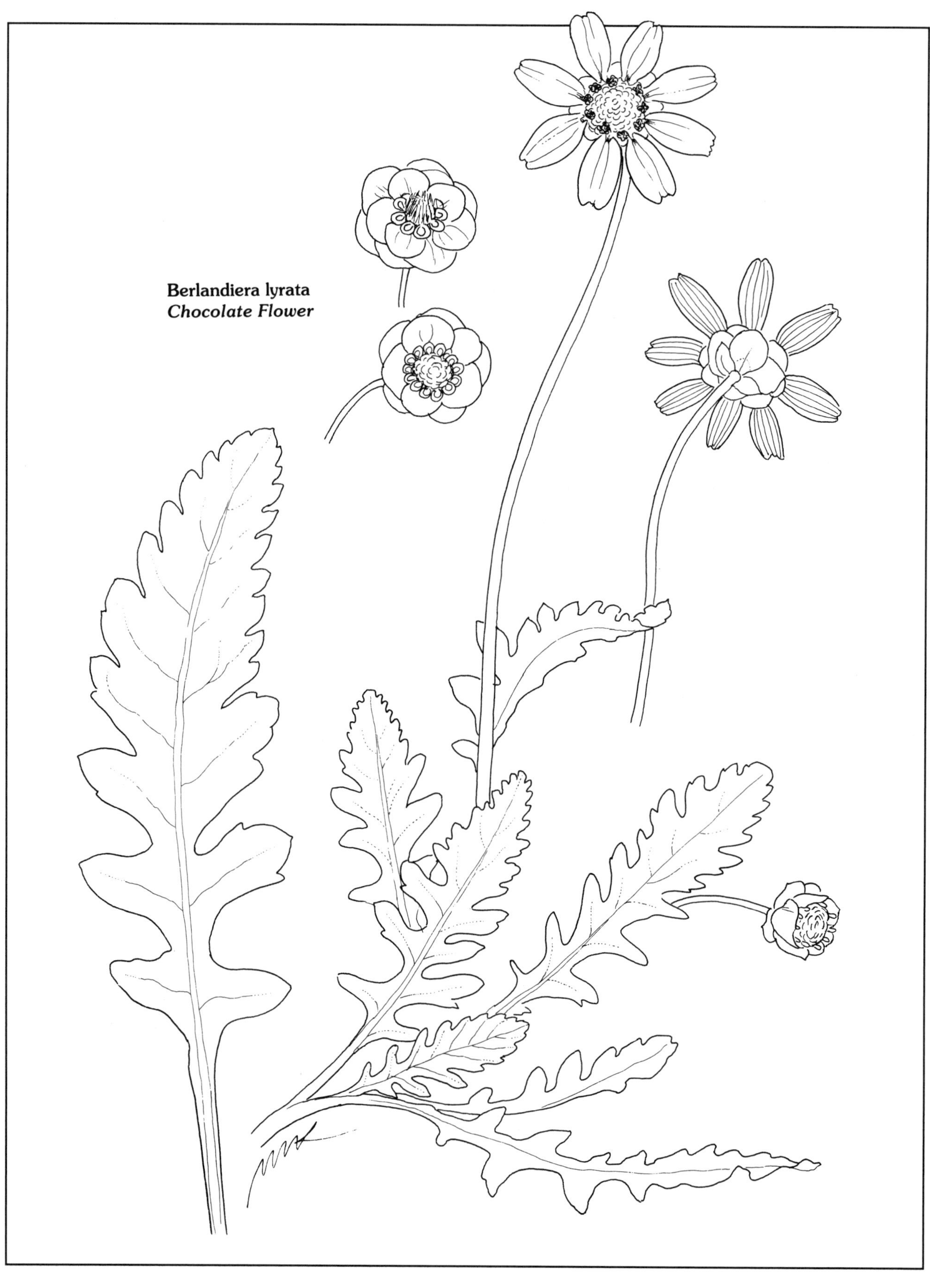
Berlandiera lyrata
Chocolate Flower

Glandularia wrightii
Purple Verbena

Species Name: *Glandularia wrightii (Verbena wrightii)*

Family: Verbenaceae (Vervain)

Common Name(s): PURPLE VERBENA

Description: *Glandularia wrightii* is a low-mounding plant with masses of purple flowers in the spring and summer. The mounds are 6 to 20 inches (15 to 50 centimeters) high and up to 2 feet (60 centimeters) across.

Leaves: The green leaves are $1\frac{1}{2}$ inches (4 centimeters) long and are finely divided.

Flowers: The rose-purple flowers are grouped together in umbels up to 1 inch (2.5 centimeters) across. Purple verbena blooms from May to October.

Fruit: The fruit and seed are very tiny.

Range and Habitat: Found in New Mexico, Kansas, Oklahoma, Colorado, Texas, Arizona, and northern Mexico from 4,500 to 8,000 feet (1,350 to 2,400 meters) on limestone soils on gravelly plains and slopes in the Chihuahuan Desert, desert grassland, and other habitats.

Hardiness: Zone 5

Planting and Care: Seeds and plants are available from a few sources in the Southwest. Seeds should be sown in a sunny location during spring and summer, or they can be started in containers and then transplanted into the garden. The seeds don't require any pretreatment. All they need is sunlight and regular watering until germination. After they are planted outside, give them regular waterings until the plants are established. They are very drought tolerant after that.

Remarks: Purple verbena is a short-lived perennial that will often reseed itself in the garden. It makes a good ground cover for hot, dry places. By itself or in combination with plants such as California poppy and Mexican evening primrose, purple verbena is a wonderful plant for large containers such as half whiskey barrels.

Purple verbena is an excellent choice for erosion control. When my parents moved into a recently cleared subdivision in New Mexico, purple verbena was one of the first native plants to reappear.

Species Name: *Melampodium leucanthum*

Family: Asteraceae (Compositae) (Sunflower)

Common Name(s): BLACKFOOT DAISY, DESERT DAISY

Description: *Melampodium leucanthum* is a widespread daisy that forms a round mound of showy white flowers with yellow centers.

Leaves: The gray-green leaves are small, 1/8 inch (3 millimeters) wide by 1 inch (2.5 centimeters) long.

Flowers: The pretty white daisies are 3/4 inch to 1 inch (2 to 2.5 centimeters) across. They typically bloom from May to October but can bloom as long as from mid-March to December in the warmer areas of the plant's range.

Fruit: The black seeds are surrounded by a black, papery husk. This black husk is foot shaped, giving blackfoot daisy its common name.

Range and Habitat: Found in New Mexico, West Texas, Kansas, Oklahoma, Colorado, Arizona, and Chihuahua and Sonora, Mexico, from 2,000 to 6,500 feet (600 to 1,950 meters) on dry, rocky slopes, usually limestone, in the Chihuahuan Desert, the desert grassland, oak woodland, and other habitats.

Hardiness: Zone 4

Planting and Care: Seeds and plants are widely available in the Southwest. Seeds should be sown as soon as possible after ripening; otherwise, getting the seeds to germinate can be difficult. Fresh seeds germinate best. Blackfoot daisy can be grown from cuttings treated with a rooting hormone. Cuttings should be taken from stems that are somewhat woody.

Blackfoot daisy is very drought tolerant once established. An extra watering now and then will promote extra flowering; however, avoid overwatering, which will cause the plant to become scraggly looking and shorten the life of the plant.

Remarks: Blackfoot daisy's tolerance of hot, dry sites lends itself to many uses in a desert garden. It can be planted in dry-country rock gardens, in the foreground of borders, and among cacti and succulents. Massed, blackfoot daisy makes a good ground cover. It is useful for erosion control in dry, hot areas, especially in difficult places such as slopes. In the garden blackfoot daisy's white flowers combine well with other colors of desert plants. This showy plant also does well in containers.

Species Name: *Oenothera caespitosa*

Family: Onagraceae (Evening primrose)

Common Name(s): TUFTED EVENING PRIMROSE, STEMLESS EVENING PRIMROSE

Description: *Oenothera caespitosa* is a low, ground-hugging plant that grows to 8 inches (20 centimeters) tall and 1 to 2 feet (30 to 60 centimeters) wide.

Leaves: The gray-green, fuzzy leaves form a basal rosette, sometimes forming a cluster of several rosettes. The leaves, which grow 1 1/4 to 4 inches (4 to 10 centimeters) long, are lobed or sometimes toothed.

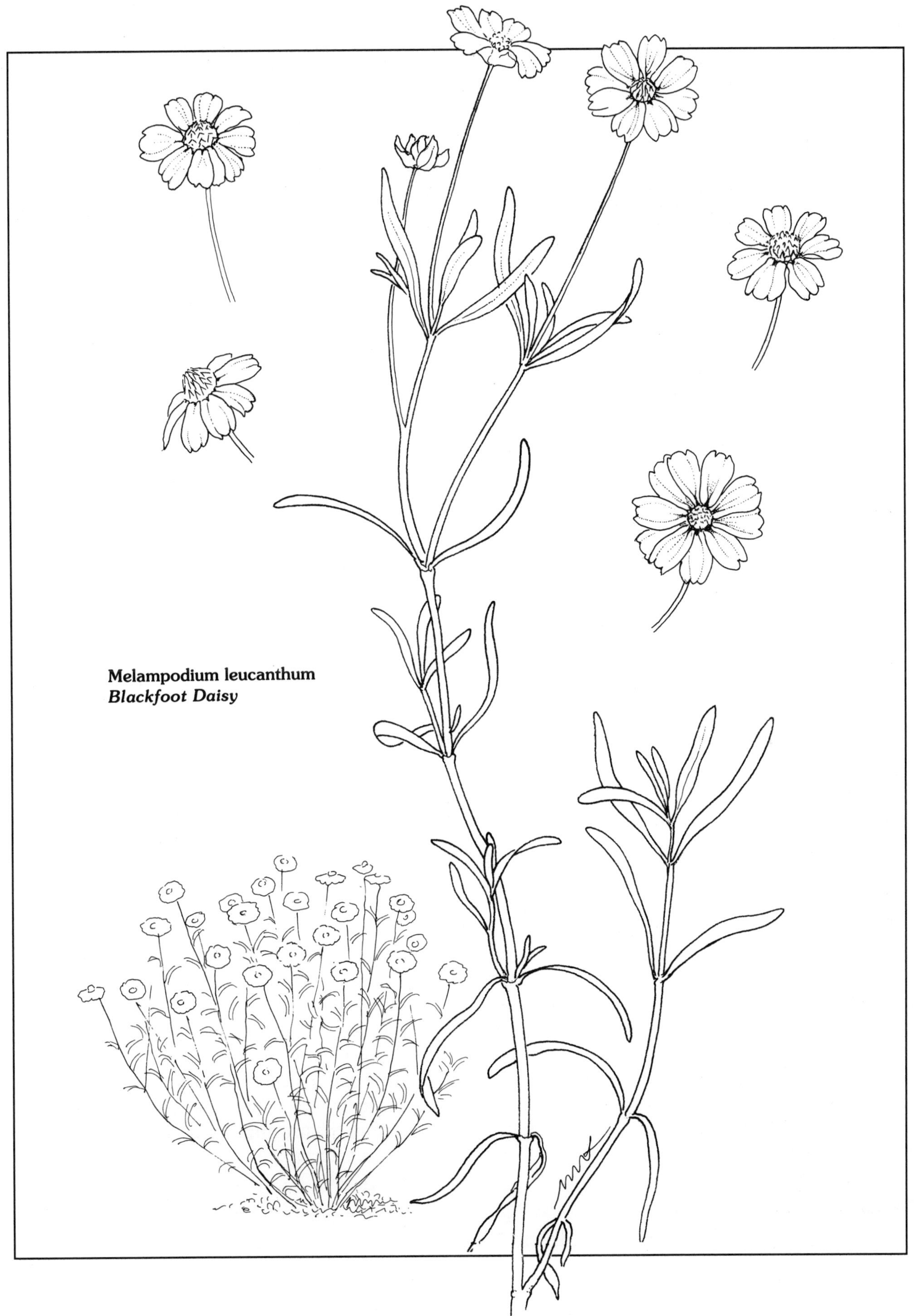
Melampodium leucanthum
Blackfoot Daisy

Oenothera caespitosa, *Tufted Evening Primrose*

Flowers: The large, white flowers, 3 to 4 inches (8 to 10 centimeters) wide, open in the evening and close the following morning. The four petals sit on top of a long, slender floral tube that contains the nectar. Hawkmoths have evolved long tongues with which they can obtain this nectar while pollinating the primrose at the same time. Tufted evening primrose blooms from April through August.

Fruit: The long, green seed capsules mature into woody, light brown capsules.

Range and Habitat: Found in New Mexico and from Minnesota to Washington State south to Mexico from 4,000 to 7,500 feet (1,200 to 2,250 meters) on dry, rocky slopes in the Chihuahuan Desert, the desert grassland, and a wide variety of other habitats.

Hardiness: Zone 4

Planting and Care: Seeds and plants of tufted evening primrose are readily available at nurseries and through mail-order sources in the Southwest. The seeds are slow to sprout, and germination is erratic. The best germination is achieved at cool temperatures. Tufted evening primrose dies back to the ground in the fall and regrows in early spring.

Remarks: Tufted evening primrose is a very drought-tolerant plant, is good in the foreground of the desert garden, and is an excellent companion plant for small cacti. It is fun to go out at sunset, sit, and watch the flowers open. They open quickly, but it is reminiscent of a slow-motion film.

Related Species: Mexican evening primrose (*Oenothera speciosa*) has bright pink flowers, $1^1/_2$ inches (4 centimeters) wide, that bloom all summer long. This perennial dies back to the ground each winter. It spreads by rhizomes and makes an excellent ground cover. They look especially nice planted around large prickly pear cactus. Mexican evening primrose is not hardy above 6,000 feet (1,800 meters) in the Southwest. Hardiness: Zone 5.

Species Name: *Penstemon alamosensis*

Family: Scrophulariaceae (Figwort)

Common Name(s): ALAMO PENSTEMON

Description: *Penstemon alamosensis* is a rare plant that is endemic to the Chihuahuan Desert region. It grows 12 to 28 inches (30 to 71 centimeters) tall with many flowering stems per plant arising from a basal rosette of leaves.

Leaves: The blue-gray basal leaves are elliptic or broadly lance shaped and crinkled. They grow up to 6 inches (15 centimeters) long. The much smaller stem leaves are green or grayish green and lance shaped. They graduate from 6 inches (15 centimeters) long at the base to $1^1/_2$ inches (1.5 centimeters) at the top.

Flowers: The bright coral red, tubular flowers grow from $^1/_2$ to 1 inch (1 to 2.5 centimeters) wide with five petals that flare out to create an almost symmetrical face. Alamo penstemon blooms in May and June, with occasional bloom through fall.

Fruit: The seed capsule is typical of this genus. See *Penstemon ambiguus* for a description.

Range and Habitat: Found in southwestern New Mexico and possibly adjacent Texas from 4,500 to 5,000 feet (1,350 to 1,500 meters) on rocky limestone ridges in dry washes, canyon bottoms, and crevices of the west slope of the Sacramento Mountains in the Chihuahuan Desert.

Hardiness: Zone 7

Planting and Care: Seeds and plants of Alamo penstemon are sometimes available from seed sources in the Southwest. It is easy to start from seeds, which should be cold stratified for one to three months.

Remarks: Alamo penstemon is a good plant for the front of a flower garden. It combines well with other low-growing desert plants such as tufted evening primrose and small cacti in a dry-country rock garden. If purchasing plants, be sure to buy them from a nursery-propagated source, as Alamo penstemon is threatened by livestock grazing and overcollection. Alamo penstemon's pretty blossoms are a favorite of hummingbirds.

Species Name: *Penstemon ambiguus*

Family: Scrophulariaceae (Figwort)

Common Name(s): BUSH PENSTEMON, SAND PENSTEMON, PHLOX PENSTEMON, GILIA PENSTEMON

Description: *Penstemon ambiguus* is a many-branched, twiggy shrub that grows up to 2 feet (60 centimeters) tall and is completely covered with flowers in spring and after summer rains.

> ***Leaves:*** Bush penstemon has very narrow, bright green, grasslike leaves, which grow from $^3/_8$ to $^1/_2$ inch (1 centimeter) long.
>
> ***Flowers:*** The tubular, white to pink flowers are borne in loose panicles and look more like phlox than a typical penstemon. The flowers are $^3/_5$ to 1 inch ($1^1/_2$ to $2^1/_2$ centimeters) long. Bush penstemon blooms from late May through mid-autumn.

Penstemon ambiguus
Bush Penstemon

> ***Fruit:*** The small brown seedpods are ovoid capsules with sharp points. They contain numerous, angular seeds.

Range and Habitat: Found in New Mexico, West Texas, Colorado, Utah, north to Kansas and west to California at 4,000 to 6,500 feet (1,200 to 1,950 meters) in dry washes, on sandy mesas, and grasslands in the Chihuahuan Desert, desert grassland, Great Plains grassland, and other habitats.

Hardiness: Zone 5

Planting and Care: Seeds and plants of bush penstemon are usually available at nurseries and through mail-order sources in the Southwest. Seeds are also produced abundantly on plants, which tend to grow along roadsides. The seeds do not need cold stratifying as with many other penstemons. Older seeds germinate better, as bush penstemon, like several other family members, prefers an after-ripening period of the seeds. Bush penstemon requires a dry, well-drained, sandy soil. Overwatering will cause it to become leggy and will eventually kill it. In containers bush penstemon can look quite lanky, almost sickly, but once planted in the ground it will quickly grow into its normal, almost perfectly symmetrical shape.

Penstemon fendleri
Fendler Penstemon

Remarks: Bush penstemon is a long-lived, heat- and drought-tolerant plant. It combines well with Apache plume and chocolate flower to provide a long season of color without much water.

Species Name: *Penstemon fendleri*

Family: Scrophulariaceae (Figwort)

Common Name(s): FENDLER PENSTEMON, PLAINS PENSTEMON

Description: *Penstemon fendleri* is a small, erect perennial that grows 8 to 20 inches (20 to 50 centimeters) tall with violet to blue flowers in whorls around the stems.

Leaves: The gray-green basal leaves are lance to oval shaped, while the stem leaves, 2 inches (5 centimeters) long, are usually sharp pointed and lance shaped.

Flowers: The violet to blue flowers are $^5/_8$ to 1 inch (2 to 2.5 centimeters) long with dark violet-purple guidelines. The staminode is bearded. Fendler penstemon blooms from April to August.

Fruit: The seed capsule is typical of this genus. See *Penstemon ambiguus* for a description.

Range and Habitat: Found in central and southern New Mexico, Oklahoma, and Texas to southwestern Arizona and Chihuahua, Mexico, from 5,000 to 8,000 feet (1,500 to 2,400 meters) on sandy or gravelly hills and plains in the Chihuahuan Desert, the desert grassland, and other habitats.

Hardiness: Zone 6

Planting and Care: Seeds are sometimes available by mail order. More than likely, you'll need to collect the seeds yourself. The seeds need to be cold stratified in order to germinate. The seed flat should be drenched with a fungicide, as Fendler penstemon seedlings are prone to damping off.

Remarks: Fendler penstemon is a small, delicate-looking perennial that is very well suited to growing in the dry conditions of the desert garden or dry-country rock garden. Once it's up and growing Fendler penstemon will add a touch of blue to the landscape.

Species Name: *Penstemon pseudospectabilis*

Family: Scrophulariaceae (Figwort)

Common Name(s): DESERT PENSTEMON, DESERT BEARDTONGUE

Description: *Penstemon pseudospectabilis* is a very attractive plant with fine-toothed, blue-green foliage and large, lovely rose-purple flowers. Desert penstemon grows 2 to 4 feet (6 to 120 centimeters) tall.

> ***Leaves:*** The blue-green, triangular leaves are sharply toothed and encircle the stem. They grow to about 3 inches (8 centimeters) long and a little more than 1 inch (2.5 centimeters) wide.
>
> ***Flowers:*** The funnel-shaped flowers have been described as shocking pink. They are about 1 inch (2.5 centimeters) long. Desert penstemon blooms from April to July.
>
> ***Fruit:*** The seed capsule is typical of the genus. See *Penstemon ambiguus* for a description.

Range and Habitat: Found in southwestern New Mexico to southeastern California below 6,000 feet (1,800 meters) on mesa slopes and in mountain canyons, occasionally in the Chihuahuan and Sonoran deserts, among other habitats.

Hardiness: Zone 5

Planting and Care: Desert penstemon is widely available in Southwest nurseries and by mail order as both plants and seeds. It is easy to grow from seeds, which need to be cold stratified. Desert penstemon is one of the most drought-tolerant penstemons. As such, be careful not to overwater or the stems will get floppy.

Remarks: Desert penstemon's large, bright pink flowers attract hummingbirds. With its large, showy leaves and flowers, desert penstemon makes a good accent plant. It works well placed in the middleground of a native landscape.

Species Name: *Penstemon superbus*

Family: Scrophulariaceae (Figwort)

Common Name(s): SUPERB PENSTEMON, CORAL PENSTEMON

Description: *Penstemon superbus* has large, rather thick, blue-green leaves that are particularly attractive in winter when the undersides turn purplish. The large rosettes look like giant hens and chickens.

> ***Leaves:*** The leaves form a rosette 12 inches (30 centimeters) across or more. The bases of the leaves clasp the stem.
>
> ***Flowers:*** The coral red flowers are funnel shaped and grow profusely on stems that are 3 to 4 feet (90 to 120 centimeters) long. The sterile stamen is bearded near the tip. Superb penstemon blooms in April and May and occasionally throughout the summer.
>
> ***Fruit:*** The seed capsule is typical of the genus. See *Penstemon ambiguus* for a description.

Range and Habitat: Found in southwestern New Mexico, southeastern Arizona, and adjacent Mexico from 4,500 to 6,000 feet (1,350 to 1,800 meters) in canyons and gravelly washes of the Chihuahuan Desert and desert grassland.

Hardiness: Zone 6

Planting and Care: Superb penstemon is sometimes available as plants in Southwest nurseries, and seeds are available through mail order. Fresh seeds need to be cold stratified for one to three months. Better results can be achieved by using seeds that are one or more years old. They germinate well without being cold stratified or treated any other way, especially when sown during the cooler spring months.

Remarks: Superb penstemon is an extremely showy plant with its abundant flower stalks and large flowers. Hummingbirds love this plant.

Related Species: There are many southwestern penstemons suitable for desert gardeners, including red-flowered *Penstemon barbatus* (scarlet bugler), which blooms from June until frost, hardiness: Zone 3; red-flowered *Penstemon havardii* (Havard penstemon), which blooms from June to August, hardiness: Zone 6; pink-flowered *Penstemon palmeri* (Palmer penstemon), which blooms from June to July, hardiness: Zone 4; pink-flowered *Penstemon parryi* (Parry penstemon), which blooms in March and April, hardiness: Zone 7; and pink-to blue-flowered *Penstemon thurberi* (Thurber penstemon), which blooms from April to August, hardiness: Zone 6.

Leucophyllum species, known as Texas ranger, cenizio, and Texas silverleaf, are beautifully flowered shrubs from the Chihuahuan Desert. The showy blooms, which appear from June to October, range in color from pink to pale violet to purple. *Leucophyllums* are also called barometer bushes because they bloom shortly after it rains. Several cultivated varieties are widely available at nurseries in desert

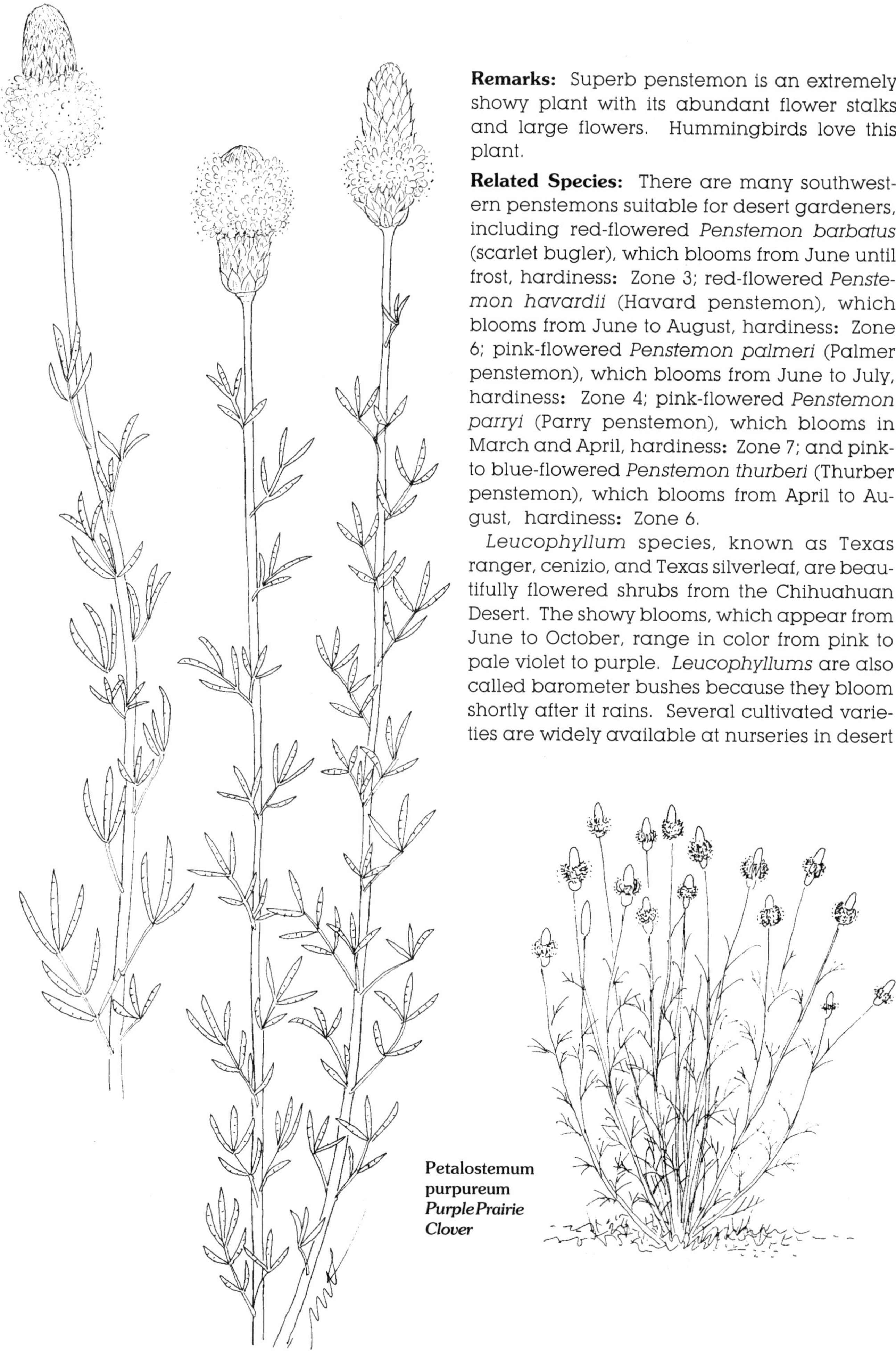

Petalostemum purpureum
Purple Prairie Clover

regions. Unfortunately, these penstemon relatives aren't hardy below zone 8.

Species Name: *Petalostemum purpureum*

Family: Fabaceae (leguminosae) (Pea); Subfamily: Faboideae (Bean)

Common Name(s): PURPLE PRAIRIE CLOVER

Description: *Petalostemum purpureum* is a prairie plant with bright violet to crimson flowers. It is a deep-rooted plant that grows to 2 feet (60 centimeters) tall.

> ***Leaves:*** The leaves are short, finely cut, and compound, with three to five linear leaflets 1/3 to 3/4 inch (3 millimeters to 2 centimeters) long.
>
> ***Flowers:*** The rose-purple, 2-inch (5-centimeter)-long flower spikes open from the base of the stem upward. They have bright orange anthers that contrast with the purplish petals. Purple prairie clover blooms from July to September.
>
> ***Fruit:*** The seeds form on a cone left after flowering.

Range and Habitat: Found in New Mexico, Arizona, Indiana to Saskatchewan, south to Texas from 3,500 to 7,000 feet (1,050 to 2,100 meters) on plains and prairies in the Great Plains grasslands and on the edges of the desert grassland.

Hardiness: Zone 4

Planting and Care: Plants and seeds are available at nurseries specializing in native plants of the Southwest and through mail order. The seeds need a hot water treatment in order to germinate. Purple prairie clover is a nitrogen-fixing legume and requires little or no fertilizing in the garden. In the desert garden it requires supplemental watering to look its best. It will bloom again if cut back after flowering.

Remarks: Purple prairie clover is very drought tolerant and adapts well to gardens throughout the Southwest, including the desert areas. It is especially striking when planted in masses as a ground cover or in a meadow.

Species Name: *Psilostrophe tagetina*

Family: Asteraceae (Compositae) (Sunflower)

Common Name(s): PAPERFLOWER

Description: *Psilostrophe tagetina* is named for its dried flowers, which feel like paper. This bushy perennial grows up to 20 inches (50 centimeters) tall.

> ***Leaves:*** The gray-green basal leaves grow up to 4 inches (10 centimeters) long. The smaller, upper leaves grow from 1/5 to 2/5 inch (.5 to 1 centimeter) long. Both are covered with fine hairs.
>
> ***Flowers:*** The bright yellow flowers are 1 inch (2.5 centimeters) wide. They bloom in clusters from February to October, depending upon location and weather conditions.
>
> ***Fruit:*** The seed is an achene—a dry, one-seeded fruit with the outer shell separate from the seed.

Range and Habitat: Found in New Mexico, Arizona, Texas, Utah, and Mexico from 4,000 to 7,000 feet (1,200 to 2,100 meters) on dry plains, hills, and mesas of the Chihuahuan Desert and desert grassland up into the Southwest woodlands.

Hardiness: Zone 5

Planting and Care: Plants and seeds are available through several mail-order sources. The seeds require no special treatment and grow rapidly. These fast-growing plants are very drought tolerant, and overwatering will cause them to grow long and lanky or even kill them.

Remarks: Paperflower is a mounded mass of yellow daisies before drying. It is a good companion plant with large prickly pears and/or bush penstemon, especially in sandy soils.

Psilostrophe tagetina • *page 106* ▶

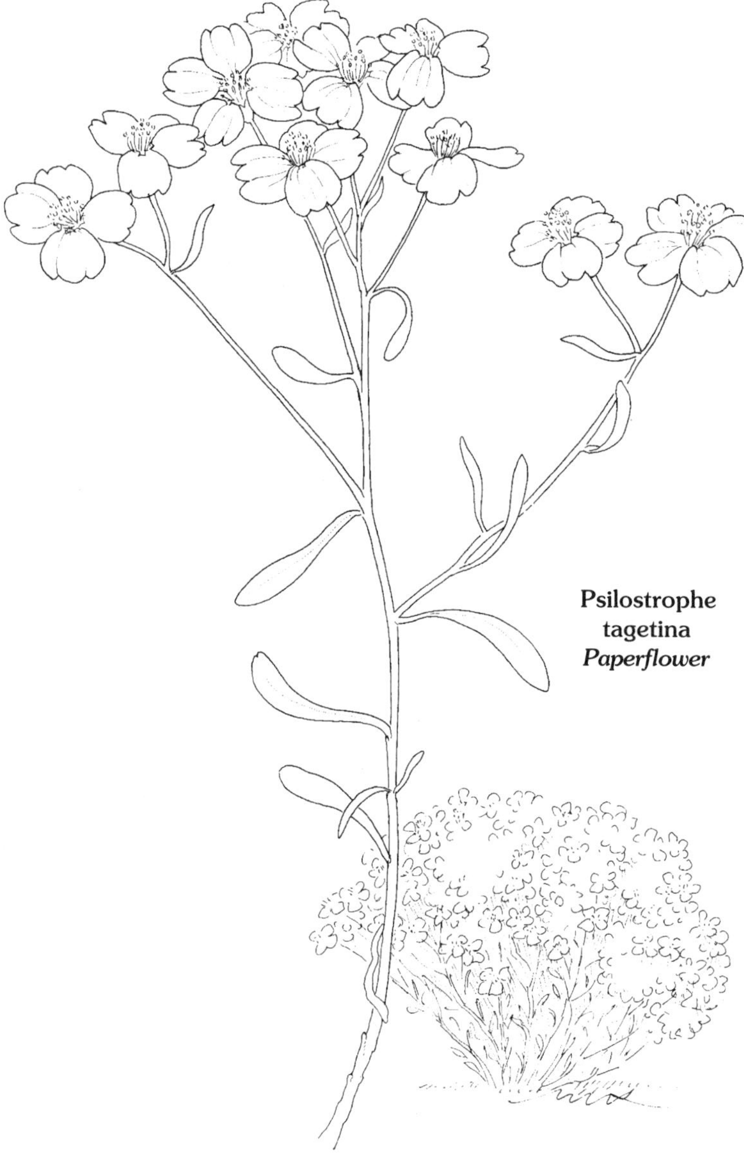

Psilostrophe tagetina
Paperflower

Species Name: *Salvia farinacea*

Family: Lamiaceae (Labiatae) (Mint)

Common Name(s): MEALY-CUP SAGE, MEALY SAGE, MEALY BLUE SAGE

Description: *Salvia farinacea* is a perennial sage that grows 2 to 3 feet (60 to 90 centimeters) tall. It grows in relatively moist spots in the Southwest, such as canyon bottoms.

Leaves: The linear leaves, which are 1 to 3 inches (2.5 to 8 centimeters) long and 1/4 to 1/2 inch (.6 to 1 centimeter) wide, are fuzzy and silvery or whitish in color; hence the common names.

Flowers: The blue to purple flowers, which are 1/2 to 1 inch (1 to 2.5 centimeters) long, are typical sage flowers borne on stalks 12 to 16 inches (30 to 41 centimeters) tall. Mealy-cup sage blooms from mid-spring to frost.

Fruit: The small brown seeds ripen throughout the season of bloom.

Range and Habitat: Found in southern New Mexico and Texas from 3,500 to 6,000 feet (1,050 to 1,800 meters) on limestone soils of plains, low hills, and canyons of the Chihuahuan Desert, desert grassland, and other habitats.

Hardiness: Zone 7, annual in lower zones

Planting and Care: The cultivated forms of mealy-cup sage are widely available in nurseries. For the wild variety, you'll need to collect the seeds yourself. Mealy-cup sage is easy to grow from seeds, needing no special treatment. Cuttings are also an easy means of starting new plants. It grows fast in the garden, where it can be planted in full sun to partial shade. In the desert garden extra watering is a definite requirement.

Remarks: Mealy-cup sage is the best-known and most widely-used plant native to the Chihuahuan Desert. It is a popular garden ornamental grown throughout the United States and elsewhere. Several cultivated varieties (cultivars) are available, including the blue-purple "Victoria" and pure white "Alba" forms. In northern climates, mealy-cup sage is usually grown as an annual, as it is not reliably hardy north of its native range. Most people, including those living in the Southwest, are unaware that these beautiful plants are a native plant of the region. Mealy-cup sage is representative of the future garden potential inherent in our Chihuahuan Desert plants.

Species Name: *Salvia henryi*

Family: Lamiaceae (Labiatae) (Mint)

Common Name(s): CRIMSON SAGE, RED SAGE, HENRY'S SAGE

Salvia farinacea
Mealy-cup Sage

Description: *Salvia henryi* grows to about 2 feet (60 centimeters) tall in arid habitats. It is especially pretty at Valley of Fires State Park in south-central New Mexico, where the red flowers contrast sharply with the black lava rock.

Leaves: The grayish green leaves, 1 to 2½ inches (2.5 to 5 centimeters) long, are deeply toothed or lobed, with the end segment being the largest.

Flowers: The brilliant crimson flowers, which are 1½ inches (4 centimeters) long, are bilaterally symmetrical and occur in pairs on a four-sided stem. Crimson sage flowers from April through September.

Fruit: The tiny, round black seeds form at the back of the flower.

Range and Habitat: Found in southern New Mexico, western Texas, southern Arizona, and northern Mexico from 4,500 to 7,000 feet (1,350 to 2,100 meters) on dry hills, rocky slopes, and in canyons in the Chihuahuan Desert and other habitats.

Hardiness: Zone 7

Planting and Care: Seeds and plants of crimson sage are occasionally available through mail-order sources in the Southwest. Germination of the seeds, which need no special treatment, is erratic and can take from one week to two months. Excess water will produce leggy plants, as is true of many of our native plants.

Remarks: Crimson sage is a very pretty perennial that does well in the desert garden, tolerating heat and drought. It is a hummingbird favorite. Plant it near walkways and in foregrounds, as crimson sage is a small but showy wildflower.

Related Species: Autumn sage (*Salvia greggii*), a Texas native, is a small shrubby sage with red, violet, pink, or white flowers which bloom from spring until frost. It is very ornamental and widely available. In areas where it goes below 15°F (9°C), it may freeze back to the ground but recovers quickly in the spring. Autumn sage requires extra water in desert areas. Hardiness: Zone 6.

Species Name: *Senecio douglasii* var. *longilobus*

Family: Asteraceae (Compositae) (Sunflower)

Common Name(s): THREADLEAF GROUNDSEL

Description: *Senecio douglasii* var. *longilobus* is a large, shrubby perennial covered with bright yellow daisies in late summer through fall. Its silver-gray foliage provides an interesting contrast when planted with green-foliaged plants.

> ***Leaves:*** The 3-inch- (8-centimeter-) long, succulent leaves are finely divided into smaller leaflets that are 1 inch (2.5 centimeters) long and 1/16 inch (2 millimeters) wide.
>
> ***Flowers:*** The large, yellow daisylike flowers are 1 inch (2.5 centimeters) wide with slender petals. Threadleaf groundsel blooms from April to November.
>
> ***Fruit:*** The dry seeds appear grayish or whitish. They have "hairs" which aid in dispersal of the seeds by the wind.

Range and Habitat: Found in New Mexico, western Texas, Arizona, southern Colorado, southern Utah, and northern Mexico from 2,500 to 7,500 feet (750 to 2,250 meters) on dry, gravelly slopes and stream beds, sandy washes, and disturbed areas in the Chihuahuan Desert, the desert grassland, pinyon-juniper woodland, and other habitats.

Hardiness: Zone 4

Planting and Care: The seeds germinate readily without any pretreatment. The plants grow quickly. Be careful about giving this plant too much attention, as it can tend to become invasive with extra watering. Also avoid overwatering to prevent rangy, weedy-looking growth. Seeds and plants are sometimes available through mail-order sources and at nurseries.

Remarks: Threadleaf groundsel is a widespread sub-shrub that grows 1 1/2 to 3 feet (45 to 90 centimeters) tall by 2 feet (60 centimeters) wide. Its large size lends itself well to the informal look of a naturalistic desert garden. Threadleaf groundsel is very drought tolerant, making it a good choice for areas that are difficult to water. Massed, it can be used as an accent or as a large ground cover. Because it is very winter hardy, threadleaf groundsel is useful in gardens outside of the Chihuahuan Desert region.

Species Name: *Senna covesii* (*Cassia covesii*)

Family: Fabaceae (Pea); Subfamily: Caesalpinoideae (Bird-of-Paradise)

Common Name(s): DESERT SENNA, HAIRY SENNA, RATTLEBOX, TE DE SENA

Description: *Senna covesii* is a somewhat shrubby perennial of the southwestern deserts with bright yellow flowers 2 inches (5 centimeters) wide. Its small size, up to 2 feet (60 centimeters) tall, makes it a good plant for desert gardens. The stems are covered with white hairs, the source of the common name hairy senna.

> ***Leaves:*** The silvery-colored foliage consists of four to six oblong leaflets per leaf that grow from 3/8 to 1 3/16 inches (1 to 3 centimeters) long.
>
> ***Flowers:*** The five-petaled yellow flowers, 2 inches (5 centimeters) wide, bloom all summer from April to October. Desert senna has no nectar, only pollen to attract bees. In order to obtain the pollen, bees have to use their flight muscles to shake the pollen free from the anthers in a technique called buzz-pollinating.
>
> ***Fruit:*** The fruit is a long, hair-covered pod that is 3/4 to 1 3/16 inches (2 to 3 centimeters) in length.

Range and Habitat: Found in southwestern New Mexico, Arizona, southern California, southern Nevada, and northwestern Mexico up to 4,500 feet (1,350 meters) on dry, rocky slopes and mesas in the Chihuahuan and Sonoran deserts.

Hardiness: Zone 8

Planting and Care: Seeds are sometimes available from mail-order sources in the Southwest.

Senecio longilobus
Threadleaf Groundsel

The seeds need a hot water treatment to germinate. Desert senna is a bright, cheery wildflower that is very drought tolerant and nitrogen fixing. It requires full sun in the garden. Desert senna is not hardy above 4,500 feet (1,350 meters) in the Southwest. Plant it in May in order to get it established before winter.

Remarks: In nature desert senna blooms after periods of rainfall. The seeds rattle in the dry seedpods when shaken, startling those who brush up against them and think they have stumbled upon a rattlesnake, a characteristic that accounts for the common name rattlebox.

Species Name: *Silene laciniata*

Family: Caryophyllaceae (Pink)

Common Name(s): MEXICAN CAMPION, INDIAN PINK, CATCHFLY

Description: *Silene laciniata* is native to the foothills and riparian areas of the region. Mexican campion grows 1 to 2 feet (30 to 60 centimeters) tall.

> ***Leaves:*** The medium-green, lance-shaped leaves grow up to 1 to 4 inches (3 to 10 centimeters) long.
>
> ***Flowers:*** The sepals of the flower are united, forming a 1-inch (2.5-centimeter) tube from which the showy red-orange, fringed, petal-like lobes project.
>
> ***Fruit:*** The oblong seed capsules contain lots of tiny brown seeds.

Range and Habitat: Found in New Mexico, Trans-Pecos Texas, Arizona, southern California, and northern Mexico from 4,500 to 10,000 feet (1,350 to 3,000 meters) in woodlands and along riparian areas in the mountains of the Chihuahuan and Sonoran desert regions.

Hardiness: Zone 6

Planting and Care: Seeds and plants are sometimes available through mail-order sources and nurseries. The seeds germinate readily without any pretreatment. Mexican campion prefers a semishaded location, although it will grow in full sun. In the desert garden it needs extra water.

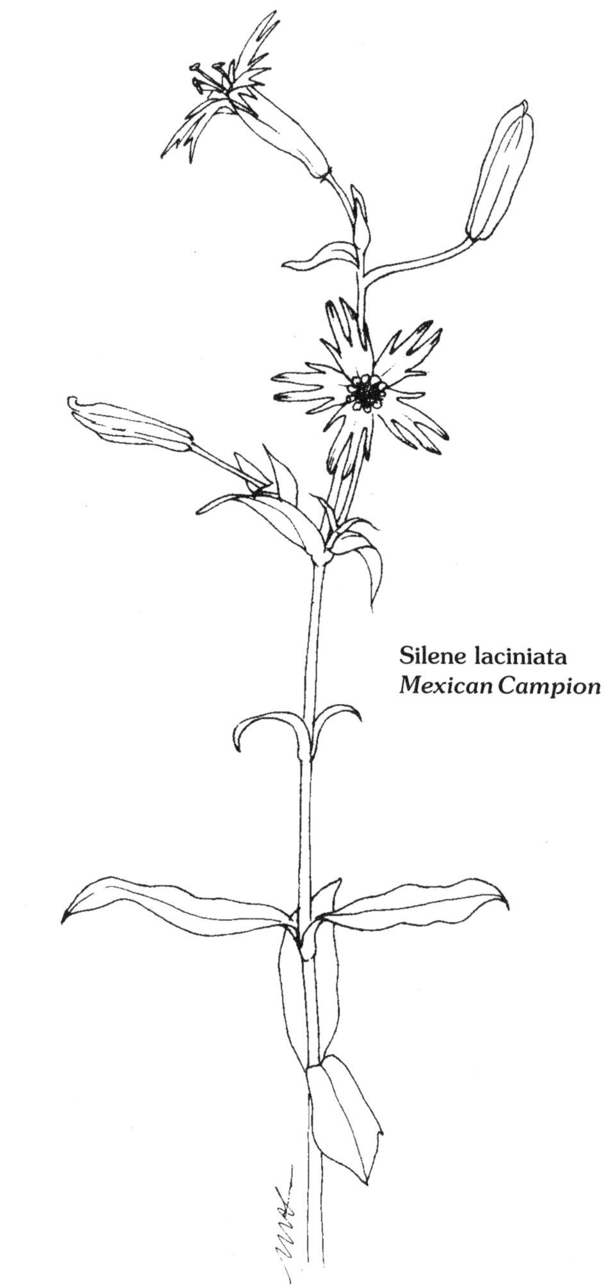

Silene laciniata
Mexican Campion

Remarks: Use Mexican campion with other moisture-loving and shade-tolerant native plants such as golden columbine and indigo bush. The bright red, star-shaped flowers are a favorite of hummingbirds.

Species Name: *Zinnia grandiflora*

Family: Asteraceae (Compositae) (Sunflower)

Common Name(s): DESERT ZINNIA, ROCKY MOUNTAIN ZINNIA, PRAIRIE ZINNIA

Description: *Zinnia grandiflora* is a low-growing perennial with branching stems which grows to about 8 inches (20 centimeters) in height. It spreads by means of deep, underground rhizomes.

Leaves: The small, three-ribbed leaves are light green. They grow up to 3/8 inch (1 centimeter) and are very abundant on this small plant.

Flowers: The cheery, bright yellow blossoms with orange centers dry to persistent, papery, straw-colored flower heads. The flowers are 3/4 inch (2 centimeters) across. Desert zinnia has a long flowering season from May through October. From late summer onward it attracts a lot of honeybees.

Fruit: The seeds are produced by the ray flowers. Seeds produced by the disk flowers are usually nonviable and empty.

Range and Habitat: Found in New Mexico, Colorado, Arizona, Texas, and northern Mexico from 4,000 to 6,500 feet (1,200 to 1,500 meters) on dry plains and slopes in the Chihuahuan Desert, the desert grassland, oak woodland, and other habitats.

Hardiness: Zone 4

Planting and Care: Seeds and plants are available at nurseries throughout the Southwest. Seeds are also available by mail order. While the seeds sprout without any special treatment, germination is erratic and can take several weeks.

Remarks: Desert zinnia is a very drought-tolerant perennial, surviving on less than 8 inches (20 centimeters) of precipitation a year. Its spreading habit makes it a good ground cover for hot, dry areas. Growing quickly, desert zinnia is a colorful addition to the desert garden and is an excellent plant for the dry-country rock garden.

Zinnia grandiflora, *Desert Zinnia*

Related Species: Desert zinnia (*Zinnia acerosa*) is a close relative of *Zinnia grandiflora* which blooms from June to October. Similar in habit, its main difference is its white flowers. Hardiness: Zone 7.

CACTI

Cacti are among the most unusual plants of the desert Southwest. As such, they are highly prized around the world for their unusual forms and brilliant-colored flowers.

The northern Chihuahuan Desert contains only a couple of large cactus species; however, it has a large number of intriguing smaller varieties, many of which are found nowhere else. Plants such as these are known by the term "endemic"; that is, they are found only in a particular habitat, specific place, or biological province.

To say that cactus nomenclature is a mess is an understatement. The botanical names given in the following descriptions are those which appear most frequently in the literature, and/or are in common usage by those interested in cacti. There are also several common names for most of these spiny denizens, and I have chosen the one most frequently used when discussing these plants. All cacti are members of the Cactaceae, or cactus, family.

The fruit of many cacti are edible. This has given us some of our common names for these plants, such as prickly pear and strawberry hedgehog. With most cacti in order to get the fruit you must have two or more plants to achieve cross-pollination since most cacti are not self-fertile.

Seeds and plants for all of the cacti listed in this section are available from nurseries specializing in cacti and succulents. Except for the opuntias, all are easily grown from seed without any pretreatments.

Most cacti have similar cultural requirements. These include basic soils, careful watering, full sun to partial shade, and good drainage. "Good drainage" is used here for lack of a better term. In reality, a cactus couldn't care less if the soil drains well; it just wants air around the roots and can't stand being waterlogged. In fact, during the spring and summer growing season, cacti can take quite a lot of water.

Cacti do not need large amounts of fertilizers. In fact, they can be easily burned if the fertilizer used is too strong. Since you're basically dealing with a stem and not leaves, any damage that occurs is difficult, if not impossible, to reverse. Liquid kelp is a mild fertilizer that is excellent for cacti. Use it occasionally for optimum growth and health of your plants in both the garden and containers.

Cacti should be planted after danger of frost is past. Plant them outside in late spring or early summer if possible so the cacti have time to establish themselves before winter. When planting cacti, remember to knock all the dirt off the roots of the plants or even wash the roots and trim any that are dead. This will help the roots grow out into the surrounding soil.

A garden in the Southwest is incomplete without a representative of the cactus clan. With such a wide variety of sizes, shapes, and spination (including spineless forms), the old myth of their being difficult to keep tidy is laid to rest. From small to large gardens, there is a cactus suitable for everyone's plot.

Species Name: *Coryphantha macromeris*

Common Name(s): DOÑA ANA CACTUS, LONG MAMMA, BIG NIPPLE CORYCACTUS, NIPPLE BEEHIVE

Description: *Coryphantha macromeris* is an endemic plant of the Chihuahuan Desert, often forming large clumps up to fifty stems over a foot (30 centimeters) in diameter. Along with the mammillarias, escobarias, and other coryphanthas, it is a member of the group of cacti commonly called pincushion cacti.

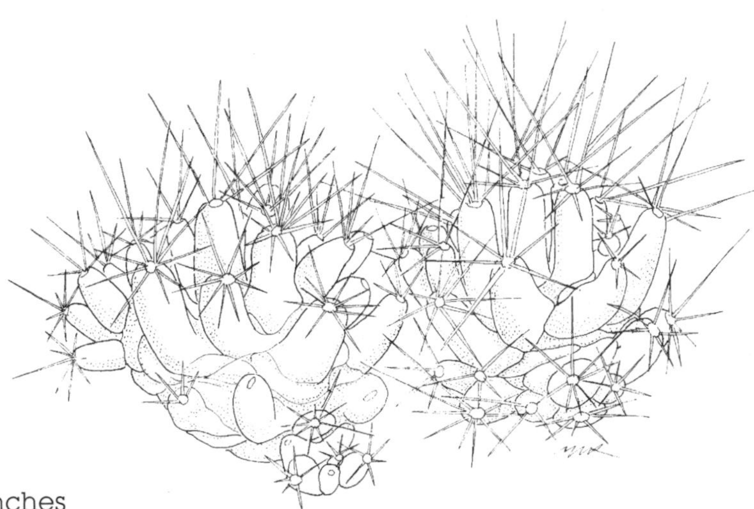

Coryphantha macromeris
Doña Ana Cactus

Stems: Short columns grow up to 4 inches (10 centimeters) tall, sometimes up to 8 inches (20 centimeters) tall, and 3 inches (8 centimeters) wide. It is easy to identify due to its tubercles 1 to 1½ inches (2.5 to 4 centimeters) in length. Typical of the genus, *Coryphantha macromeris* has a deep groove halfway down the tubercle.

Spines: *Coryphantha macromeris* is covered with 9 to 15 gray radial spines, ¾ to 1 inch (2 to 2.5 centimeters) long, per areole. The central spines, approximately 2 inches (5 centimeters) long, may be brown, purple, or black.

Flowers: The light purple or pinkish flowers, which are 2 inches (5 centimeters) tall and wide, bloom anytime from March to August.

Fruit: The green fruits are round to oval in shape and 1 inch (2.5 centimeters) long.

Range and Habitat: Found in southern New Mexico, Trans-Pecos Texas, and northern Mexico at 4,000 to 6,500 feet (1,200 to 1,950 meters) on gravelly soils and on rocky slopes in the Chihuahuan Desert.

Hardiness: Zone 7

Planting and Care: Doña Ana cactus is among the easiest cacti to grow in the desert garden. All it needs is a site with well-drained soil so that it has room to develop its long taproot.

Remarks: In nature Doña Ana cactus tends to grow under shrubs, where it is partially shaded. In the garden this can be used to advantage by placing Doña Ana cactus under a shrub where it can be discovered as if by chance, particularly when its spectacular flowers bloom. Another landscape advantage of Doña Ana cactus is the fact that it blooms later than most other cacti, and thus its flowering can provide the delight of the unexpected. I remember the first time I saw this cactus in full bloom in the desert near Las Cruces, New Mexico. Its bright pink blossoms were a real standout in the late summer, an unusual time for cactus flowers.

Species Name: *Coryphantha scheeri* var. *scheeri*

Common Name(s): SCHEER'S PINCUSHION CACTUS, MULEE, NEEDLE MULEE, LONG-TUBERCLED CORYPHANTHA

Description: *Coryphantha scheeri* var. *scheeri* has large, somewhat soft tubercles. The plant itself is quite large for a pincushion cactus.

Stems: The yellow-green stems grow up to 9 inches (23 centimeters) tall and up to 5½ inches (14 centimeters) in diameter. The long tubercles characteristic of the species grow up to 1½ inches (4 centimeters) long. It is usually single-stemmed.

Spines: The six to twelve radial spines per areole are yellowish white, occasionally with red or pink tips. The solitary central spine is a characteristic of var. *scheeri*. The nonwoolly areoles are another varietal characteristic.

Flowers: Var. *scheeri* has large, 2-inch (5-centimeter-) wide, bright yellow flowers with red streaks. Scheer's pincushion cactus flowers from August to November.

Fruit: The long, green fruit is elliptical shaped and 1 to 1½ inches (2.5 to 4 centimeters) long.

Range and Habitat: Found in southeastern New Mexico, Trans-Pecos Texas, and northern Mexico at 3,000 to 4,000 feet (900 to 1,200 meters) on sandy plains and alluvial flats in the Chihuahuan Desert.

Hardiness: Zone 7

Planting and Care: Scheer's pincushion cactus is easy to grow in cultivation. This cactus prefers sandy soil, full sun, or light shade. Place it under the branches of an airy shrub, such as bird-of-paradise or mesquite.

Remarks: Scheer's pincushion cactus is becoming rare due to overcollection. As with all our native plants, be sure to buy only nursery-propagated specimens. Var. *scheeri* can be seen growing in Carlsbad Caverns National Park, New Mexico.

Species Name: *Coryphantha scheeri* var. *valida*

Common Name(s): SCHEER'S PINCUSHION CACTUS, LONG NIPPLE CACTUS, MULEE, NEEDLE MULEE, LONG-TUBERCLED CORYPHANTHA

Coryphantha scheeri var. valida
Scheer's Pincushion Cactus

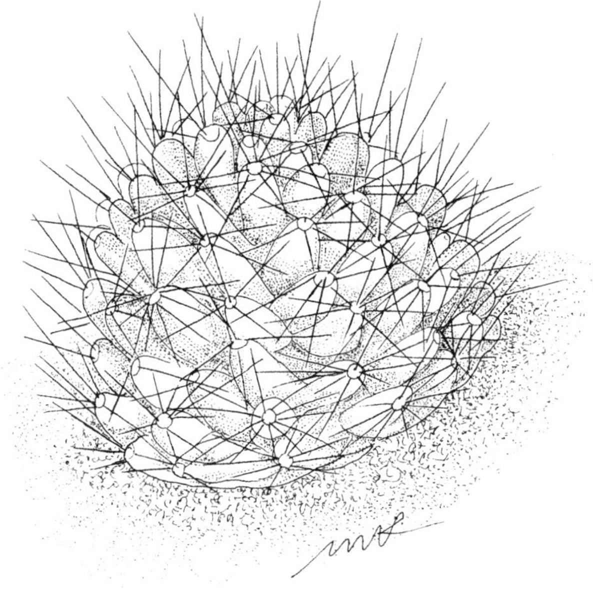

Description: *Coryphantha scheeri* var. *valida* is very similar to var. *scheeri* with a few exceptions, noted in the descriptions.

Stems: Same as var. *scheeri*.

Spines: Var. *valida* differs from var. *scheeri* in the higher number of spines. Var. *valida* has one to four central spines and nine to sixteen radial spines per areole. The young areoles of var. *valida* are very woolly as opposed to those of var. *scheeri*.

Flowers: Var. *valida* has large flowers 2 inches (5 centimeters) wide, similar to var. *scheeri*; however, they are not streaked with red. It also flowers earlier, sometimes as early as April or May, but usually from June to September.

Fruit: Same as var. *scheeri*.

Range and Habitat: Found in southern New Mexico, Trans-Pecos Texas, southeastern Arizona, and northern Mexico at 4,000 to 5,000 feet (1,200 to 1,500 meters) on sandy soils of desert plains, alluvial flats, hills, and valleys. Var. *valida* is also found in the desert grassland.

Hardiness: Zone 6

Planting and Care: Var. *valida* prefers the same conditions as var. *scheeri.*

Remarks: Var. *valida* is becoming rare due to overcollection. Always purchase plants or seeds of this or any other rare plant. Scheer's pincushion cactus, var. *valida*, can be seen growing in White Sands National Monument, New Mexico.

Species Name: *Echinocactus horizonthalonius* var. *horizonthalonius*

Common Name(s): BLUE BARREL, TURK'S HEAD, EAGLE'S CLAW, DEVIL'S HEAD, BISNAGRE

Description: *Echinocactus horizonthalonius* var. *horizonthalonius* is a widespread, endemic cactus of the Chihuahuan Desert. This small barrel cactus is hardier than its larger ferocactus cousins, making it more useful in high desert gardens.

Stems: Blue barrel is a round, small, globe-shaped plant. While it can have seven to thirteen blue-green ribs, it almost always has eight ribs. It grows 5 to 8 inches (13 to 20 centimeters) in diameter and up to 8 to 12 inches (20 to 30 centimeters) tall.

Spines: The six to nine curved radial spines and solitary central spine per areole are pale to dark gray and $^3/_4$ to $1^1/_2$ inches (2 to 4 centimeters) long. Sometimes they are pinkish or reddish tinged. The heavy spines tend to lie flat against the body of the plant.

Flowers: Blue barrel has beautiful, large, brilliant pink flowers 2 to 3 inches (5 to 8 centimeters) wide, with fringed petals. It flowers several times during the summer from March to September.

Fruit: While the fruit is $1^1/_4$ inches (3 centimeters) long and red in color, it is difficult to see, as it is covered with dense, white wool in the center of the plant.

Range and Habitat: Found in southern New Mexico, Trans-Pecos Texas, and northern Mexico at 3,000 to 5,000 feet (900 to 1,500 meters) on limestone soils of rocky slopes and hills.

Hardiness: Zone 7, warmer parts of Zone 6

Planting and Care: Blue barrel is easily grown from seeds without any pretreatments. It is a difficult plant to grow in the garden, as it is very temperamental as far as watering is concerned. It must be kept very dry or it will rot. When establishing blue barrel in the landscape, water it sparingly. Full sun and a warm microclimate are absolute musts. Blue barrels have survived temperatures of -2°F (-19°C) without damage in our gardens.

Remarks: Blue barrel is an attractive little plant found among the desert scrub vegetation of the Chihuahuan Desert. It is hardier than many of its larger barrel cousins. Use it as an accent plant in an area where both its showy pink flowers and its blue-green body can be seen.

Species Name: *Echinocactus texensis* (*Homalocephalus texensis*)

Common Name(s): HORSE CRIPPLER, DEVIL'S CLAW, EAGLE'S CLAW, VIZNAGA

Description: *Echinocactus texensis* is a large, flat cactus that is often hidden by grass. One of its common names, horse crippler, is derived from the fact that horses which have stepped on the stout, sharp spines have been injured.

Stems: The stem is usually solitary, very broad, and dome shaped or flattened. While the plant may only be 2 to 8 inches (5 to 20 centimeters) high, it can be over

Echinocactus texensis • *page 116* ▶

12 inches (30 centimeters) wide. The dark green body has thirteen to twenty-seven ribs.

Spines: The very rigid, large spines are brownish to reddish gray, becoming whitish with age. There are usually six radial spines per areole; however, that can vary from five to seven, up to 2 inches (5 centimeters) long. There is one stout central spine that grows up to 3 inches (8 centimeters) long and may be curved.

Flowers: The bell-shaped flowers, 2 to 3 inches (5 to 8 centimeters) wide, vary in color from red to pink to purple. They have fringed petals and a slight fragrance. Horse crippler blooms from April to December, depending on the temperatures and rains.

Fruit: The bright red fruit is large, $1^1/_2$ inches (4 centimeters) long, and round. It is fleshy and edible.

Echinocactus texensis, *Horse Crippler*

Range and Habitat: Found in southeastern New Mexico, central and Trans-Pecos Texas, and northeastern Mexico at 3,000 to 4,000 feet (900 to 1,200 meters) on a variety of soils, including limestone, sandy soil, clay, silty soils, and so forth. Horse crippler is a cactus of the high plains, but it is also found on the edges of the Chihuahuan Desert and desert grassland.

Hardiness: Zone 7

Planting and Care: Horse crippler is easily grown from seeds as long as close attention is paid to watering once they have germinated; otherwise seedlings are prone to rot. It is one of the easier barrel cacti to grow in cultivation, as it can take more cold, -2° to 0°F (-19° to -18°C), and moisture than its western cousins. Large specimens do not transplant well because of a large taproot. It requires a basic soil and full sun to partial shade. Grow it with low-growing natives much as it would in the wild for a natural effect, or use it in a desert-style garden in the colder parts of the high deserts where other barrel cacti aren't hardy. During establishment in the garden, water should also be given sparingly. After the initial adjustment, horse crippler will prove to be one of the more interesting acquisitions to your garden.

Remarks: Horse crippler is an unusual-looking cactus due to its large, round but flattened body. It is becoming increasingly rare, as much of its habitat has been plowed under for cultivation or the plants have been destroyed by ranchers who view its stout spines as hazardous to livestock. Horse crippler is such a sculptural plant that it would be a shame if we were to lose it in the wild.

Species Name: *Echinocereus chloranthus* var. *chloranthus*

Common Name(s): NEW MEXICO RAINBOW CACTUS, BROWN-FLOWERED CACTUS, GREEN-FLOWERED HEDGEHOG, BROWN SPINE HEDGEHOG

Description: *Echinocereus chloranthus* var. *chloranthus* is a member of the genus *Echinocereus*, the hedgehog cacti, that are very popular in desert-style gardens due to their ease of cultivation, showy flowers, and colorful spination. It is endemic to the Chihuahuan Desert region.

Stems: The stems are cylindrical and grow to 10 inches (25 centimeters) tall and 3 inches (8 centimeters) wide. They are usually solitary but sometimes have two to three stems. There are twelve to eighteen ribs.

Spines: New Mexico rainbow cactus varies greatly in the number of radial spines, from twelve to thirty-eight per areole. The radials vary from white to yellow or red and grow up to 3/4 inch (2 centimeters) long. There are three to six brown, red, or red and white central spines that grow from 1/4 to 1 1/4 inches (.6 to 3 centimeters) long.

Flowers: The flowers, which are 1 inch (2.5 centimeters) wide, appear on the side of the plant. They vary in color from dark green to reddish brown. New Mexico rainbow cactus blooms in May and June. It is very closely related to *Echinocereus viridiflorus*, from which it differs in its funnel-shaped flowers. *E. viridiflorus* has flowers which open widely.

Fruit: The fruits, 1/2 inch (1+ centimeters) long, turn from green to purplish red when they are ripe.

Range and Habitat: Found in southern New Mexico, Trans-Pecos Texas, and northern Mexico at 3,000 to 4,500 feet (900 to 1,350 meters) on rocky limestone hills and slopes in the Chihuahuan Desert and adjacent desert grassland and oak woodland.

Echinocereus chloranthus var. chloranthus
New Mexico Rainbow Cactus

Hardiness: Zone 6

Planting and Care: New Mexico rainbow cactus is easily grown from seeds and will reach flowering size in about five years. As with most of our desert cacti, it requires full sun and little water. It is hardy to 0°F (-18°C) and perhaps a few degrees colder.

Remarks: With its beautifully colored spines and unusual-colored flowers, New Mexico rainbow cactus should be planted in more Southwest landscapes. It is a good accent plant for small gardens.

Species Name: *Echinocereus chloranthus* var. *cylindricus*

Common Name(s): GREEN-FLOWERED TORCH CACTUS, GREEN-FLOWERED PITAYA, GREEN-FLOWERED HEDGEHOG, BROWN SPINE HEDGEHOG

Description: *Echinocereus chloranthus* var. *cylindricus* is an attractive, robust form of the species. Due to its great hardiness, it can be used in colder areas of the desert, desert grassland, and even higher elevations.

Stems: The solitary, cylindrical stem tends to be somewhat barrel shaped. It grows up to 8 inches (20 centimeters) tall and 3 inches (8 centimeters) wide. There are ten to fourteen ribs.

Spines: Green-flowered torch cactus has twelve to twenty-four radial spines per areole, varying in color from red to brown to white. While there can be up to three central spines, they are usually absent altogether. The lack of a central spine is a distinguishing feature of var. *cylindricus*.

Flowers: The same as var. *chloranthus*, although it may bloom earlier in April.

Fruit: The same as var. *chloranthus*.

Range and Habitat: Found in southern New Mexico, Trans-Pecos Texas, and northern Mexico at 3,500 to 6,000 feet (1,050 to 1,800 meters) on rocky, limestone hills and slopes in the Great Plains grassland, Chihuahuan Desert, and desert grassland.

Hardiness: Zone 5

Planting and Care: The seeds germinate readily without any special treatment. Green-flowered hedgehog is very hardy, to -20°F (-29°C) and can be planted almost anywhere in the Southwest, except at very high elevations.

Remarks: Green-flowered hedgehog is more commonly found than New Mexico rainbow cactus. The body is tightly covered with its colorful spines. This and var. *chloranthus* look especially nice when planted in groups.

Species Name: *Echinocereus coccineus* var. *gurneyi*

Common Name(s): RED-FLOWERED HEDGEHOG CACTUS, CLARET-CUP CACTUS

Description: *Echinocereus coccineus* var. *gurneyi* and its relatives are very popular in Southwest gardens because of their waxy-looking, bright red flowers.

Stems: The individual stems grow up to 14 inches (36 centimeters) tall and 4 inches (10 centimeters) wide. There are ten to twelve ribs on the very thick stems. Red-flowered hedgehog cactus tends to form clusters of two to ten stems. Apparently, those from higher elevations form clumps of many smaller stems than those from lower elevations, which tend to have fewer but larger stems.

Spines: There are normally seven to nine radial spines per areole that can be 1 1/8 inches (3 centimeters) long, although they are usually shorter. The one to two central spines are about the same length as the radials. All spines are yellowish to tan to dark brown in color.

Flowers: The waxy flowers are 1 to 2 inches (2.5 to 5 centimeters) wide. They are typically scarlet, red, or orange in color; however, due to hybridization with other *Echinocereus* species, especially *Echinocereus pectinatus* var. *dasyacanthus*, they vary considerably from pink to white or from yellow to orange. The flowers remain open day and night for several days, unlike many other *Echinocereus* and cacti. They usually bloom in April and May.

Fruit: The spherical fruits, which grow up to 1 1/4 inches (3 centimeters) long, are red and edible when ripe.

Range and Habitat: Found in southeastern and south-central New Mexico, Trans-Pecos Texas, and northern Mexico at 4,500 to 6,000 feet (1,350 to 1,800 meters) on rocky limestone slopes and in canyons of the Chihuahuan Desert and desert grassland.

Hardiness: Zone 5

Planting and Care: The seeds germinate readily without any special treatment. While red-flowered hedgehog cactus is readily propagated by seeds, it takes several years to flower. Stem

Echinocereus coccineus var. gurneyi
Red-flowered Hedgehog Cactus

cuttings are not difficult to take, root readily, and will flower sooner than seed-grown plants. It takes full sun to partial shade and very little watering. Red-flowered hedgehog cactus is very hardy, to -10°F (-23°C).

Remarks: Red-flowered hedgehog cactus is not only beautifully flowered, but it is easy to grow. The bright, usually orange-red flowers are pollinated by hummingbirds, among others. Red-flowered hedgehog cactus and its relatives are very useful as accent plants. Forming clumps of large stems, they should be placed in a conspicuous spot in the landscape where they can be easily seen.

Related Species: The red-flowered hedgehog cactus *Echinocereus coccineus* var. *coccineus* is quite similar to var. *gurneyi* except it has seven to twelve (sometimes as few as five) radial spines and one to six (usually four) central spines. This variety of red-flowered hedgehog cactus blooms in May and June. It tends to occur north of the Chihuahuan Desert at higher elevations but sometimes enters the desert at these northern locations. Hardiness: Zone 4.

Claret-cup hedgehog cactus (*Echinocereus triglochidiatus*) is a close relative of the *coccineus* group. It is normally found in the mountains of the Southwest. It differs from *E. coccineus* in having fewer ribs and fewer, heavier spines. A form that is sometimes distinguished as var. *gonacanthus* occurs in the Tularosa Basin of southern New Mexico. This is one of the few areas where this species enters the Chihuahuan Desert. This particular population of plants is very robust with very large stems and flowers. The red flowers appear from May into July. Claret-cup cactus is particularly attractive as a garden specimen. Hardiness: Zone 5.

Species Name: *Echinocereus enneacanthus* var. *brevispinus*

Common Name(s): STRAWBERRY HEDGEHOG CACTUS, STRAWBERRY CACTUS, PITAYA

Description: *Echinocereus enneacanthus* var. *brevispinus* is a large, clump-forming cactus endemic to the Chihuahuan Desert.

Stems: On desert flats, the strawberry hedgehog cactus can form low-growing clumps from thirty to two hundred stems, 5 to 6 feet (150 to 180 centimeters) wide. The individual stems are cylindrical, green, and not obscured by spines (as in the similar species *Echinocereus stramineus*). They have seven to ten ribs and grow up to 12 inches (30 centimeters) tall and up to 4 inches (10 centimeters) thick.

Spines: The six to thirteen mostly radial spines per areole are straight, gray to straw colored, often with darker tops, and grow to 1 inch (2.5 centimeters) long. The one to five (usually one) central spines are straight or curved, brownish to straw colored, and grow to 2 inches (5 centimeters) long.

Flowers: The showy, large flowers, 2 to 3 inches (5 to 8 centimeters) wide, are a beautiful magenta to purple. Strawberry hedgehog cactus blooms in May or June.

Fruit: The greenish to purplish fruits are 1 inch (2.5 centimeters) long and have an edible, strawberry-flavored, pink flesh that gives the cactus its common name strawberry hedgehog. The fruit is covered with small, bristlelike spines.

Range and Habitat: Found in south-central New Mexico, southern and Trans-Pecos Texas, and northern Mexico from near sea level up to 5,000 feet (1,500 meters) on rocky, limestone soils on hills and in canyons in the Chihuahuan Desert, surrounding grasslands, and other habitats.

Hardiness: Zone 8

Planting and Care: Strawberry hedgehog cactus requires a very sandy soil in cultivation, as it cannot take excessive watering. As with most of our desert cacti, it requires full sun. During establishment in the garden, it should have some shade initially to prevent the stems from sunburning. It is hardy to 10°F (-12°C) and perhaps as low as 0°F (-18°C).

Remarks: Strawberry hedgehog cactus is a spectacular specimen when it is covered with its large flowers in spring. There are several other species also known as strawberry hedgehog cactus (*Echinocereus fendleri, Echinocereus stramineus*) in our area.

Species Name: *Echinocereus fendleri* var. *rectispinus*

Common Name(s): FENDLER'S HEDGEHOG CACTUS, STRAWBERRY HEDGEHOG CACTUS, TORCH CACTUS

Description: *Echinocereus fendleri* var. *rectispinus* is a desert form of *Echinocereus fendleri*, which is a hardy plant from higher elevations in New Mexico and elsewhere in the Southwest.

Stems: Var. *rectispinus* is a robust form of *E. fendleri* that forms small clumps of up to six to eight stems, 8 inches (20 centimeters) tall and 2 to 4 inches (5 to 10 centimeters) thick, with eight to twelve ribs.

Spines: There are seven to twelve radial spines per areole, which are variegated with light brown and white or black and white to gray or whitish, and grow up to $1^1/_4$ inches (3 centimeters) long. The solitary central spine is light gray tipped with brown or black. The central spines, which are 1 inch (2.5 centimeters) long, stand at right angles to the stem, as opposed to typical *fendleri*'s upward-curving central spines. This is var. *rectispinus*'s distinguishing feature.

Flowers: Fendler's hedgehog cactus has very large, reddish purple flowers that are approximately 3 inches (8 centimeters) wide. It can bloom from March to August but usually flowers in April or May.

Fruit: The fruit, 1 to $1^1/_2$ inches (2.5 to 4 centimeters) long, is green, becoming reddish to purplish with ripening; and it is covered with spines.

Range and Habitat: Found in southwestern New Mexico, southeastern Arizona, Trans-Pecos Texas, and northern Mexico at 3,000 to 6,800 feet (900 to 2,040 meters) on sandy or gravelly slopes or plains of the desert grassland and on the edges of the Sonoran and Chihuahuan deserts.

Hardiness: Zone 6

Planting and Care: Fendler's hedgehog cactus is very hardy to 0°F (-18°C) and perhaps lower. With moderate watering, a well-drained soil, and full sun, Fendler's hedgehog cactus is easy to grow. It will reach flowering size in about five years when grown from seed.

Remarks: Both the form and flower of Fendler's hedgehog cactus make it an attractive cactus.

Related Species: *Echinocereus fendleri* var. *fendleri*, Fendler's hedgehog cactus, is sometimes found in the Chihuahuan Desert but is more at home in the desert grassland and Southwest woodlands. It is hardier than var. *rectispinus*. More widespread, var. *fendleri* is found in Colorado as well as New Mexico, Arizona, Texas, and Mexico. Its reddish purple flowers usually appear in May or June; however, Fendler's hedgehog cactus can bloom from March into fall, depending on location. Hardiness: Zone 5.

Species Name: *Echinocereus pectinatus* var. *dasyacanthus* (*E. pectinatus*, var. *neomexicanus*)

Common Name(s): TEXAS RAINBOW CACTUS, NEW MEXICO RAINBOW CACTUS, RAINBOW HEDGEHOG, YELLOW-FLOWERED PITAYA, GOLDEN RAINBOW CACTUS

Description: *Echinocereus pectinatus* var. *dasyacanthus* is a very common cactus in its range. In the spring its yellow flowers brighten the desert's hills and flats.

Stems: The cylindrical stems grow up to 14 inches (36 centimeters) tall and 4 inches

Echinocereus pectinatus • *page 122* ▶

Echinocereus pectinatus var. dasyacanthus
Texas Rainbow Cactus

(10 centimeters) thick. With age, the plants will form clumps of two to ten stems. Each stem has twelve to twenty-one ribs.

Spines: Texas rainbow cactus is densely spined with twelve to twenty-five tan to pink radials, 1/2 inch (1+ centimeter) long, per areole, covering the surface of the stem. The two to five or more central spines are also tan to pink and grow up to 1 inch (2.5 centimeters) long.

Flowers: Texas rainbow cactus has huge, very showy flowers up to 3 to 5 inches (8 to 13 centimeters) wide. They are usually yellow, but they can be orangish or pink, and bloom in April or May.

Fruit: The large fruits, 1 to 2 inches (2.5 to 5 centimeters) in diameter, are covered with spines and are reddish brown to purplish when ripe.

Range and Habitat: Found in southern New Mexico, Trans-Pecos Texas, southeastern Arizona, and northern Mexico at 4,000 to 5,000 feet (1,200 to 1,500 meters) on limestone soils on slopes and flats in the Chihuahuan Desert and desert grassland.

Hardiness: Zone 6

Planting and Care: Texas rainbow cactus has the usual requirements of a well-drained, preferably sandy, soil, full sun, and little watering. It has survived -6°F (-21°C) in our garden.

Remarks: Texas rainbow cactus is named for the colored bands of pink and tan spines surrounding the body of the plant. The large body and flowers make this an outstanding cactus to use as a small accent in the garden.

Species Name: *Echinocereus russanthus* (*E. chloranthus* var. *russanthus*)

Common Name(s): RUSTY HEDGEHOG CACTUS

Description: *Echinocereus russanthus* is an uncommon, endemic Chihuahuan Desert cactus known for its unusual-colored flowers.

Stems: The stems, which are 10 inches (25 centimeters) tall and 2 to 3 inches (5 to 8 centimeters) in diameter, occur in clumps of up to a dozen. The medium-green stems have thirteen to eighteen ribs.

Spines: Rusty hedgehog cactus is very heavily spined. There are thirty to forty-five radial spines and seven to twelve central spines, 3/4 to 1 1/4 inches (2 to 3 centimeters) long. The central spines vary from being reddish or purplish tipped to the whole spine being red or purple.

Flowers: The flowers, which are 1 inch (2.5 centimeters) long and 1/2 to 1 inch (1 to 2.5 centimeters) wide, are bright red to rust-red in color. They bloom in May and June.

Fruit: The oval fruit, which is 1/2 inch (1+ centimeters) long, is covered with white spines.

Range and Habitat: Found in south-central New Mexico, Trans-Pecos Texas, and Chihuahua, Mexico, at 3,000 to 4,500 feet (900 to 1,350 meters) in the Chihuahuan Desert.

Hardiness: Zone 5

Planting and Care: Like its cousin *Echinocereus chloranthus*, rusty hedgehog cactus requires full sun and little water. It is very hardy and can take temperatures well below 0°F (-18°C). As such, rusty hedgehog cactus can be used in gardens outside the region, for example in the colder, arid areas of the western United States.

Remarks: Rusty hedgehog cactus is a very colorful addition to the desert garden, especially those specimens with bright red spines. While not particularly showy, the unusual rust-colored flowers are an interesting addition to the range of colors of cactus flowers.

Species Name: *Echinocereus stramineus*

Common Name(s): STRAWBERRY CACTUS, PITAYA

Description: *Echinocereus stramineus* is a very large, distinctive cactus endemic to the Chihuahuan Desert. All parts of the strawberry cactus are big: the flowers, the spines, and the stems.

Stems: The individual green stems grow up to 3 inches (8 centimeters) wide and up to 10 inches (25 centimeters) tall with ten to seventeen ribs, usually around twelve, however. They form tremendous mounds up to 4 feet (120 centimeters) across and 2 to 3 feet (60 to 90 centimeters) high of three hundred fifty to five hundred stems.

Spines: Strawberry cactus is covered with seven to fourteen radial spines, 1½ inches (4 centimeters) long, per areole. They are pink to straw colored and obscure the stems. The two to five central spines are very long and sharp, up to 3½ inches (9 centimeters) long; they are also pink to straw colored.

Flowers: The very large and beautiful flowers of strawberry cactus are showy magenta to purple. They are 3 to 5 inches (8 to 13 centimeters) wide and 4 to 5 inches (10 to 13 centimeters) long. Strawberry cactus blooms from March to June.

Fruit: The red fruit, which is 1½ to 2 inches (4 to 5 centimeters) long, is edible and tastes like strawberries, hence the cactus's name. They are covered with long, bristly spines which must be removed first. The seeds are edible and can be eaten along with the fleshy fruit.

Range and Habitat: Found in southeastern New Mexico, Trans-Pecos Texas, and north-central Mexico at 4,000 to 5,300 feet (1,200 to 1,590 meters) on rocky, limestone slopes in the Chihuahuan Desert.

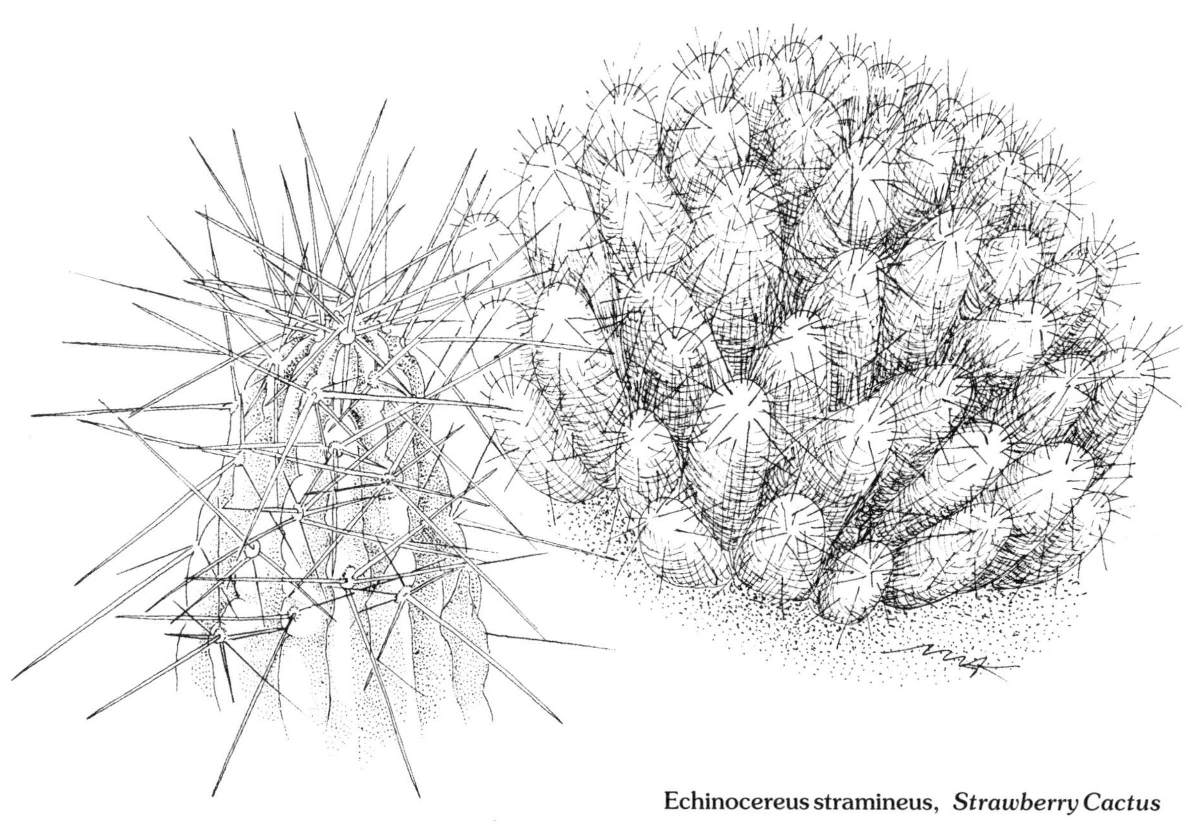

Echinocereus stramineus, ***Strawberry Cactus***

Hardiness: Zone 8

Planting and Care: Strawberry cactus is difficult to transplant from the wild, which should not be attempted unless the plants are being rescued from destruction by a highway or housing development. If so, they should be planted in sandy soil, given very little water, and provided with temporary shade. Strawberry cactus is easy to grow from seeds; however, it takes a long time for clumps to form.

Remarks: Strawberry cactus is a large plant In the landscape, it should be given a place of its own, where its form can be admired. When it's in flower, strawberry cactus is a real showstopper.

Species Name: *Echinomastus intertextus* var. *intertextus*

Common Name(s): EARLY BLOOMER, WOVEN SPINE PINEAPPLE CACTUS, WHITE-FLOWERED VISNAGITA

Description: *Echinomastus intertextus* var. *intertextus* is a diminutive, hard-to-find barrel cactus. It grows among the grasses where it is well hidden until it blooms. Then it is easy to spot, as it is among the earliest flowers of spring.

Stems: The solitary stems are cylindrical to egg shaped and have thirteen broad ribs with protruding tubercles. Early bloomer grows up to 6 inches (15 centimeters) tall and 4 inches (10 centimeters) wide.

Spines: Early bloomer is covered with many (sixteen to twenty-seven) stout radial spines up to 3/4 inch (2 centimeters) long that are pressed against the stem. They are gray or yellow in color, often with reddish brown tips. It has about four pinkish or gray central spines, usually less than 1/4 inch (6 millimeters) in length.

Flowers: The flowers, 1 inch (2.5 centimeters) wide, of early bloomer are white to cream colored. Blooming as early as February and as late as August, it is the earliest cactus to flower in our area. Most flowering is in the early spring.

Fruit: The fruits, which are 1/2 inch (1+ centimeters) long, are green when young, turning brown as they dry.

Range and Habitat: Found in southern and central New Mexico, Trans-Pecos Texas, southeastern Arizona, and northern Mexico at 4,000 to 5,000 feet (1,200 to 1,500 meters) on grassy slopes on limestone soils in the desert grassland and less often on the edges of the Chihuahuan Desert.

Hardiness: Zone 6

Planting and Care: Unfortunately, early bloomer is among the more difficult of our native cacti to grow. However, it is worth the challenge of growing it successfully. It must be given full sun, a very well-drained soil, and very little water; otherwise, it tends to die out in a few years. It is very prone to rot. It is easy to grow from seeds, however, and it should be kept pot-bound or planted outside to avoid any problems. It is hardy to at least -2°F to -3°F (-19°C to -19.4°C).

Remarks: Early bloomer is a delightful plant for the desert garden, with its white flowers, a rare color among cacti of the Chihuahuan Desert. Being a plant of grassland areas, in the landscape it combines well with native grasses.

Species Name: *Echinomastus intertextus* var. *dasyacanthus*

Common Name(s): EARLY BLOOMER, WOVEN SPINE PINEAPPLE CACTUS, WHITE-FLOWERED VISNAGITA

Description: *Echinomastus intertextus* var. *dasyacanthus* is very similar to var. *intertextus* and is most easily distinguished from it by the attractive, stout spines of this variety.

Echinomastus intertextus • *page 126* ▶

Stems: The stems are similar to var. *intertextus*; however, in var. *dasyacanthus* the ribs are narrower, and the plants tend to be a little larger.

Spines: Var. *dasyacanthus* has longer central spines, over 1/2 inch (1+ centimeters) long, and more upright spines; that is, they are not strongly appressed against the stem.

Flowers: The same as var. *intertextus*.

Fruit: The same as var. *intertextus*.

Range and Habitat: Found in southern and central New Mexico, Trans-Pecos Texas, and northern Mexico at 4,000 to 5,000 feet (1,200 to 1,500 meters) on dry, limestone slopes in the Chihuahuan Desert and less often in the desert grassland.

Hardiness: Zone 6

Planting and Care: Var. *dasyacanthus* has the same cultural requirements and the same attributes as var. *intertextus*. It is the more common form of early bloomer in the central Rio Grande Valley of New Mexico. Keep in mind that both varieties of early bloomer are somewhat rare. Be sure to purchase seeds and nursery-propagated plants only.

Remarks: The upright spines of this variety of early bloomer are an attractive feature.

Echinomastus intertextus var. dasyacanthus
Early Bloomer

Species Name: *Epithelantha micromeris*

Common Name(s): BUTTON CACTUS, MULATO

Description: *Epithelantha micromeris* is a tiny plant highly prized by cactus collectors. It is an endemic plant of the Chihuahuan Desert.

Stems: The small stems grow up to 2 inches (5 centimeters) wide and 3/4 to 4 inches (2 to 10 centimeters) tall. They are often solitary; however, they also form small clumps. Button cactus has the smallest tubercles of any American cactus.

Spines: The tiny, white spines are very numerous, twenty to sixty per areole, and lie flat against the stem. The body of the cactus is practically obscured by the spines.

Flowers: Button cactus has tiny, pale pink flowers, up to 3/16 inch (5 millimeters) wide. It blooms anytime from March to May.

Fruit: The small red fruits, 3/4 inch (2 centimeters) long, are club shaped. They are called *chilitos* (little chiles) by the Spanish-speaking people of the region.

Range and Habitat: Found in southern New Mexico, Trans-Pecos Texas, and northern Mexico at 3,400 to 5,000 feet (1,020 to 1,500 centimeters) on rocky, limestone ledges and slopes in the Chihuahuan Desert.

Hardiness: Zone 7

Planting and Care: Button cactus is easy to grow if it is given a well-drained soil, a little shade, and very little water. It is becoming rare due to overcollection. As with many of our cacti, it is easily propagated from seeds, and only nursery-propagated plants should ever be purchased.

Remarks: Button cactus is a cute little plant. It is one of our best native plants for growing in containers. While its flowers are pretty, the contrast of the bright red fruit against its white-spined body is very attractive.

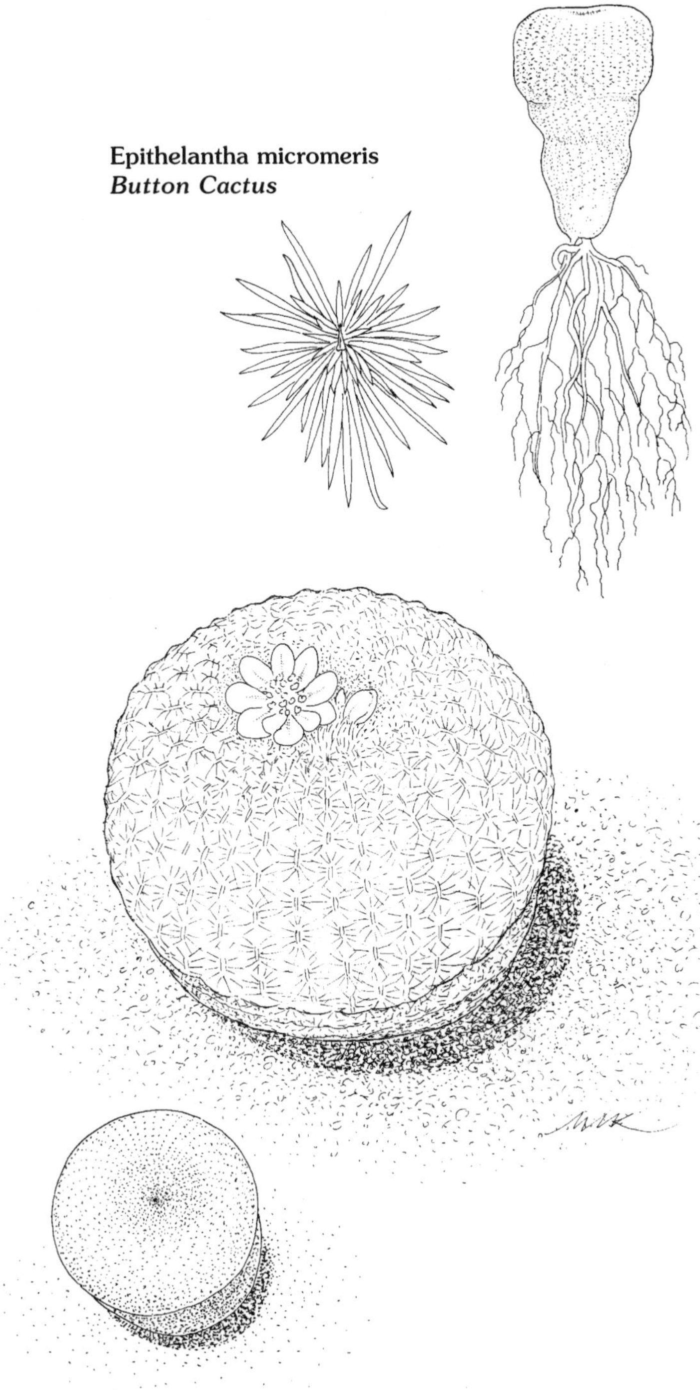

Epithelantha micromeris
Button Cactus

Species Name: *Escobaria dasyacantha*

Common Name(s): MOUNTAIN COB CACTUS, COB CACTUS

Description: *Escobaria dasyacantha* is a rare little cactus. It is a Chihuahuan Desert endemic that is highly prized by collectors.

> ***Stems:*** The thick stems of the mountain cob cactus, which are 3 inches (8 centimeters) wide and 8 to 14 inches (20 to 36 centimeters) tall, occur as white, solitary cylinders or in small clusters.
>
> ***Spines:*** The sixteen to thirty-five or more radial spines are white or straw colored and grow 1/2 to 1 inch (1 to 2.5 centimeters) long. The one to seventeen spines are black or reddish brown at the tip, pink or gray at the base. They grow 3/8 to 1 inch (1 to 2.5 centimeters) long.
>
> ***Flowers:*** The whitish to pale pink flowers of the mountain cob cactus do not open widely, are 1/2 to 3/4 inch (1 to 2 centimeters) wide, and bloom in April and May. The stigma is bright green.
>
> ***Fruit:*** The red, egg-shaped fruit are 1/2 to 3/4 inch (1 to 2 centimeters) long.

Range and Habitat: Found in southern New Mexico, Trans-Pecos Texas, and Chihuahua, Mexico, at 2,700 to 5,800 feet (810 to 1,740 meters) on rocky slopes in the Chihuahuan Desert and surrounding desert grassland.

Hardiness: Zone 7

Planting and Care: Mountain cob cactus is easily grown from seeds and requires full sun and little water in the desert garden. Since it is a relatively small plant and not dangerously spined, it can be planted near walkways and other areas where larger, more sharply-spined plants can't be used.

Remarks: Mountain cob cactus is similar to *Escobaria tuberculosa* only larger. Also the tubercles around the base of the stem are not bare as in *E. tuberculosa*. Due to overcollection, mountain cob cactus is becoming rare.

Species Name: *Escobaria duncanii*

Common Name(s): DUNCAN'S PINCUSHION CACTUS, DUNCAN'S CACTUS

Description: *Escobaria duncanii* is a tiny plant endemic to the Chihuahuan Desert. It is very rare, and overcollecting is a threat to its existence. Duncan's pincushion cactus has a fleshy taproot that is an identifying feature.

Stems: The small stems, which are 1¼ inches (3 centimeters) wide and 2 inches (5 centimeters) tall, are usually solitary; however, clusters of two to three stems are sometimes found.

Spines: There are thirty to seventy-five spines per areole that are difficult to separate into radial and central spines, although there are approximately twenty-four to forty radials and three to sixteen centrals. These are all white or white with dark brown tips, and they completely hide the stem.

Flowers: Duncan's pincushion cactus has pale pink or whitish flowers, ½ inch (1 centimeter) wide, that bloom from May to July. The flowers are comparatively large for a cactus this small.

Fruit: The red, club-shaped fruit is ½ to ¾ inch (1 to 2 centimeters) long.

Range and Habitat: Found in south-central New Mexico and Trans-Pecos Texas at 3,000 to 5,400 feet (900 to 1,620 meters) on limestone soils and on hills in the Chihuahuan Desert and desert grassland.

Hardiness: Zone 7

Planting and Care: Duncan's pincushion cactus requires well-drained, basic soils and full sun in the desert garden. Place it carefully since it could easily be overwhelmed by larger species of cacti and other plants.

Remarks: The inconspicuous Duncan's pincushion cactus is a rare little cactus in nature and deserves protection. As such, it is imperative that seeds and plants be purchased from reputable nurseries only. Blooming when less than 1 inch (2.5 centimeters) wide, Duncan's pincushion cactus is an excellent small cactus for growing in containers.

Species Name: *Escobaria leei* (*Escobaria sneedii* var. *leei*)

Common Name(s): LEE'S PINCUSHION CACTUS

Description: *Escobaria leei* is a very rare, small, endemic cactus of the Chihuahuan Desert. Only one thousand to two thousand plants are known to exist over its entire range.

Stems: The short, cylindrical stems grow to ⅛ inch (3 millimeters) thick and up to 3 inches (8 centimeters) tall. They can occur in clumps of one hundred or more very closely packed stems.

Spines: There are usually twenty to twenty-five white or yellowish white spines per areole, but there can be as many as ninety or more. The six to seven more stout centrals are not always easily differentiated from the radials. The central spines are sometimes tipped with light brown. The large number of spines is a distinguishing factor between *E. leei* and *E. sneedii*, a close relative.

Flowers: The pink or brownish pink flowers, which are ½ inch (1+ centimeters) wide, bloom in April or May and again sometimes in the fall after the summer rains.

Fruit: The thick fruit is greenish or pinkish when ripe and is ½ inch (1+ centimeters) long.

Range and Habitat: Found in southeastern New Mexico at 4,100 to 5,900 feet (1,230 to 1,770 meters) on dry, rocky limestone slopes and ledges in the Chihuahuan Desert.

Hardiness: Zone 7

Planting and Care: This interesting little cactus will grow in the garden with well-drained soil, full to partial sun, and little watering. As with other plants, Lee's pincushion cactus should always be purchased from a reputable nursery that sells only legally obtained seeds or plants. This cactus does well in containers. Its small size allows it to flourish for some time before it needs to be transplanted.

Remarks: Lee's pincushion cactus is threatened due to illegal overcollection of the plants. It is protected by law as a federally-listed threatened plant. Much of its habitat is within Carlsbad Caverns National Park, and therefore it is not as endangered perhaps as *E. sneedii*, which also occurs there and elsewhere. Many botanists consider *E. leei* to be a variety of *E. sneedii*; however, they both live within the same range, and there is apparently no hybridization or integration between the two. For this reason they are listed as separate species in this book.

Lee's pincushion cactus has clumps of many stems—some larger than others and the majority small and short. The shorter stems carry on photosynthesis and act as food producers only, while the larger stems flower and act as the reproductive parts of the plants. If one or more of the larger stems is destroyed, a smaller one will change character and grow larger to take its place.

Escobaria orcuttii var. orcuttii
Orcutt's Pincushion Cactus

Species Name: *Escobaria orcuttii* var. *orcuttii*

Common Name(s): ORCUTT'S PINCUSHION CACTUS

Description: *Escobaria orcuttii* var. *orcuttii* is a densely spined, fuzzy-looking cactus of the desert grasslands.

Stems: The cylindrical stems are often clustered but sometimes solitary, and they appear pointed at the top. They grow up to 2½ inches (6 centimeters) wide and up to 6 inches (15 centimeters) tall.

Spines: The bright white spines number thirty to forty-one radial spines and fifteen to eighteen central spines, up to ½ inch (1 centimeter) long. Orcutt's pincushion cactus differs from the closely related *Escobaria tuberculosa* by not having spine-covered tubercles at the base.

Flowers: The pink flowers grow up to ¾ inch (2 centimeters) wide. They bloom in May and June.

Fruit: The fruit is yellowish green and is ⅜ to ¾ inch (1 to 2 centimeters) long.

Range and Habitat: Found in southern New Mexico, southeastern Arizona, and northern Chihuahua, Mexico, up to 4,000 feet (1,200 meters) in grassy areas on limestone slopes primarily in desert grassland.

Hardiness: Zone 6

Planting and Care: Orcutt's pincushion cactus is easily grown from seeds and easy to grow in the desert garden. It has the usual requirements of full sun, little water, and a well-drained, basic soil.

Remarks: Orcutt's pincushion cactus is a very attractive little cactus that is not very well known. It looks like a clump of prickly snowballs, with its white spines and round stems. Orcutt's pincushion cactus needs careful placement in a garden because it is so small it could get lost. Place it in the foreground with other small plants.

Species Name: *Escobaria orcuttii* var. *koenigii*

Common Name(s): KOENIG'S PINCUSHION CACTUS

Description: *Escobaria orcuttii* var. *koenigii* is a very rare variety of *E. orcuttii* and an endemic cactus of the Chihuahuan Desert region.

Stems: Koenig's pincushion cactus has solitary stems or clusters of up to twelve heads. The stems, which grow up to 6 inches (15 centimeters) tall, differ from the species by being rounded at the top.

Spines: The usually white or occasionally straw-colored spines are very dense and hide the gray-green body of the cactus. The thirty to thirty-six radial and up to twenty-one central spines are sometimes tipped with reddish brown and grow to 3/8 inch (1 centimeter) long.

Flowers: The funnel-shaped flowers range from deep pink to brownish pink and differ from the species by being darker colored. The flowers grow up to 1 inch (2.5 centimeters) long and 2/5 to 4/5 inch (1 to 2 centimeters) wide.

Fruit: The fruit is smaller than var. *orcuttii*, about 3/8 inch (1 centimeter) long.

Range and Habitat: Found in southern New Mexico at 5,000 feet (1,500 meters) on rocky, limestone hillsides of the Florida Mountains.

Hardiness: Zone 5

Planting and Care: Koenig's pincushion cactus is one of our rarest cacti and is threatened by overcollection. This is unfortunate, as it is easily grown from seeds. Koenig's pincushion cactus requires the same growing conditions as var. *orcuttii*. Be sure to buy plants or seeds from a reputable nursery that doesn't collect from wild populations.

Remarks: Koenig's pincushion cactus is an interesting and unusual cactus for your desert garden. As its spines are not particularly stout, it can be placed close to walkways and other areas where more heavily spined cacti species would be too dangerous.

Species Name: *Escobaria sandbergii*

Common Name(s): SANDBERG'S PINCUSHION CACTUS

Description: *Escobaria sandbergii* is a very rare endemic cactus of the Chihuahuan Desert region.

Stems: The cylindrical stems grow up to 2 3/4 inches (7 centimeters) wide and 6 inches (15 centimeters) tall and occur in clusters of up to twenty or more.

Spines: Sandberg's pincushion cactus has twenty-three to fifty-five white radial spines up to 3/8 inch (1 centimeter) long, one to five white with brown or reddish brown tipped central spines, and five to fifteen all white or white with reddish brown tipped peripheral centrals. The dense spines give this cactus a very bristlelike appearance.

Flowers: The light to medium pink flowers are tinged with violet or purple. They grow up to 1 inch (2.5 centimeters) wide and bloom from April to June.

Fruit: The fruit is pale green to greenish yellow.

Range and Habitat: Found in south-central New Mexico at 5,000 to 7,400 feet (1,500 to 2,220 meters) on limestone outcrops in the desert grassland and surrounding woodlands. Known only from the San Andres Mountains on Department of Defense property.

Hardiness: Zone 7, warmer parts of zone 6

Planting and Care: Sandberg's pincushion cactus is very rare. Fortunately, it is fairly protected due to its inaccessible location; also, seeds are available, and it is easily propagated. It is one of the more hardy cacti if given the usual growing conditions of full sun, basic soil, careful watering, and good drainage, and can take several degrees below 0°F (-18°C).

Remarks: Sandberg's pincushion cactus is one of a group of cacti, including Sneed's pincushion cactus, Lee's pincushion cactus, Orcutt's pincushion cactus, and Villard's pincushion cactus, that are very closely related. In fact, there are some taxonomists who consider them all variants of the same species. Whatever the case may be, it is a curious example of genetic mutation resulting from isolation. All of these plants are native to their own particular mountain ranges, or "islands," which are surrounded by a desert "sea." The fun is in collecting each of them in a garden, if you have the collecting bug.

Species Name: *Escobaria sneedii*

Common Name(s): SNEED'S PINCUSHION CACTUS

Description: *Escobaria sneedii* is a rare endemic cactus native to the Chihuahuan Desert region. As with many of the escobarias, it is restricted in range, making it very desirable to collectors of cacti.

Stems: The stems, which are 1 inch (2.5 centimeters) wide and 2 to 5 inches (5 to 13 centimeters) tall, form dense clusters up to 2 feet (60 centimeters) in diameter, although the clusters are usually much smaller, from a few inches (5+ centimeters) to 6 or 8 inches (15 to 20 centimeters) wide. A few larger stems protrude above several smaller ones. These are the flowering stems, while the smaller ones produce food for the overall cluster.

Spines: Sneed's pincushion cactus is a densely spined cactus. The tubercles are almost hidden by the twenty-five to thirty-five white radials, which are 1/8 inch (3 millimeters) long, and the six to nine centrals, which are 1/8 to 5/16 inch (3 to 8 millimeters) long and either white, pink, or purple tipped.

Flowers: The pink or pinkish brown flowers, which are 1/2 inch (about 1 centimeter) wide, bloom from May to June and sometimes again in July, August, or September following the summer rains.

Fruit: The green to greenish brown fruit is approximately 1/4 inch (6 millimeters) long.

Range and Habitat: Found in Doña Ana and Eddy counties of New Mexico, and adjacent Texas at 4,000 to 7,000 feet (1,200 to 2,100 meters) on rocky, limestone slopes in the Chihuahuan Desert and adjacent desert grassland.

Hardiness: Zone 7, warmer parts of zone 6

Planting and Care: In the desert garden Sneed's pincushion cactus is very hardy and easily grown in well-drained soil. It can tolerate partial shade and extra watering. Sneed's pincushion cactus will grow to flower size in three years from seeds and will form clusters in five years. Due to its rarity, compactness, beauty, and ease of cultivation, Sneed's pincushion cactus is a very desirable plant for Southwest gardens.

Remarks: Sneed's pincushion cactus is very

threatened due to poaching by cactus thieves. As such, it is on the Federal Endangered Species List, and legal seed and plants are available only through nurseries with special permits. Be very careful as to the source of plants, as you could be fined for purchasing illegal cacti.

Species Name: *Escobaria tuberculosa*

Common Name(s): COB CACTUS

Description: *Escobaria tuberculosa* is an uncommon but widespread member of the flora of the Chihuahuan Desert. The delicate, pinkish flowers make cob cactus a very desirable plant for the desert garden.

> ***Stems:*** The cylindrical stems grow 1 to 2 inches (2.5 to 5 centimeters) thick and up to 7 inches (18 centimeters) tall, although they are usually shorter. They are prominently tubercled, with the lower tubercles on the stems becoming spineless with age, and are commonly found in clumps of two to fifteen stems.
>
> ***Spines:*** The twenty to thirty radial spines are white or off-white. They grow up to 3/8 inch (1 centimeter) long. The four to nine central spines are grayish white to straw colored with pink, purple, or red tips. They grow up to 5/8 inch (1.6 centimeters) long.
>
> ***Flowers:*** The petite pretty pink flowers, which are up to 1 3/8 inches (3.5 centimeters) long, open widely in late afternoon. Cob cactus may bloom in May and June or in August and September, depending on rainfall.
>
> **Fruit:** The small fruits, 3/4 inch (2 centimeters) long, are red when ripe, and they are edible.

Range and Habitat: Found in southern New Mexico, Trans-Pecos Texas, southeastern Arizona, and northern Mexico at 2,500 to 5,000 feet (750 to 1,500 meters) on limestone slopes in the Chihuahuan Desert and surrounding desert grassland.

Hardiness: Zone 7

Planting and Care: Cob cactus is an interesting plant that is easy to grow and flowers profusely under cultivation. It will form clusters of stems in a short time (two years or so) and does well with the usual cactus requirements of full to partial sun, well-drained soil, and little water.

Remarks: Cob cactus is named for its resemblance to a corncob due to the loss of the spines on the knobby lower tubercles of the plant. These distinctive lower tubercles and larger flowers are features that distinguish it from mountain cob cactus (*Escobaria dasyacantha*), which is similar in form. Cob cactus is an unusual cactus that does well in containers as well as in the desert garden.

Species Name: *Escobaria villardii*

Common Name(s): VILLARD'S PINCUSHION CACTUS

Description: *Escobaria villardii* is a very rare endemic cactus of the Chihuahuan Desert. It is a good plant for those who want something unusual in their gardens.

> ***Stems:*** The rounded to club-shaped stems grow up to 6 inches (15 centimeters) tall and form clusters of ten or more.
>
> ***Spines:*** The twenty to forty slender radial spines and six to seventeen central spines grow up to 3/4 inch (2 centimeters) long. They are usually white to straw colored. The rigid centrals have reddish brown tips which are a distinguishing feature of Villard's pincushion cactus.
>
> ***Flowers:*** The pale pink to magenta flowers are 3/4 to 1 inch (2 to 2.5 centimeters) wide, which is larger than most others of the genus. They bloom in May and June.

Fruit: The cylindrical-shaped fruits grow up to 3/4 inch (2 centimeters) long and are greenish colored.

Range and Habitat: Found in south-central New Mexico at 4,500 to 6,000 feet (1,350 to 1,800 meters) on limestone outcrops in the Chihuahuan Desert region. *Escobaria villardii* is known only from the Sacramento Mountains of Otero County, New Mexico.

Hardiness: Zone 7

Planting and Care: Villard's pincushion cactus is a very rare little cactus and is threatened by overcollection. Seeds and plants are available from legal sources, and there is no need for wild plants being sold, as this plant is easily propagated. It requires full sun, little water, and well-drained soil.

Remarks: The size of Villard's pincushion cactus makes it an ideal plant for use in containers and small gardens. Growing naturally in rocky areas, it is a good choice for the dry-country rock garden.

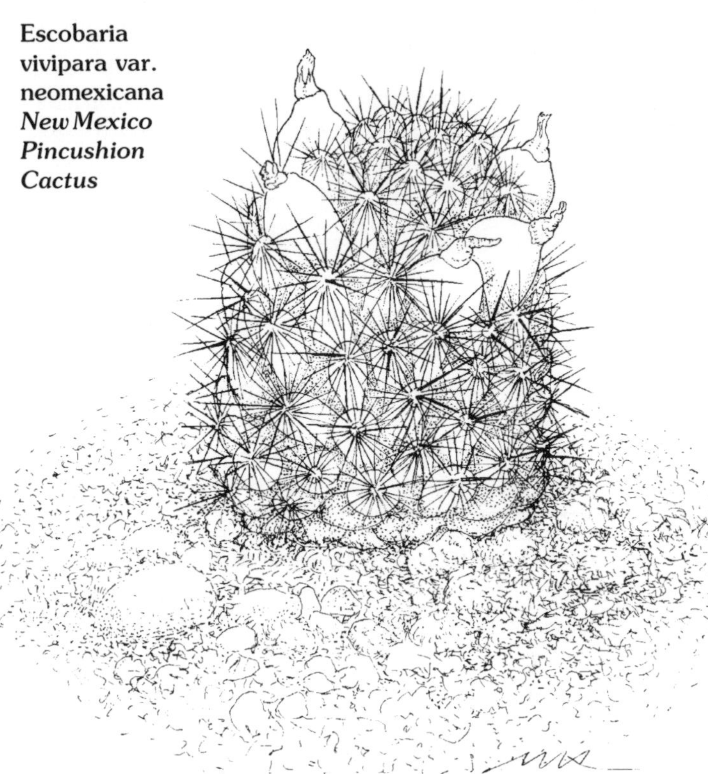

Escobaria vivipara var. neomexicana ***New Mexico Pincushion Cactus***

Species Name: *Escobaria vivipara* var. *neomexicana* (*Coryphantha vivipara* var. *neomexicana*)

Common Name(s): NEW MEXICO PINCUSHION CACTUS, NEW MEXICO CORYPHANTHA, ESTRIA DEL TARDE

Description: *Escobaria vivipara* var. *neomexicana* is found in a wide range of habitats, and it is very adaptable and desirable in cultivation.

Stems: The medium-green, ovoid to cylindrical stems grow up to 2 1/2 inches (6 centimeters) wide and 4 inches (10 centimeters) tall and often form small clusters. They consist of tubercles 1/2 inch (approximately 1 centimeter) in length.

Spines: The twenty to forty round, slender, white to pink radials are 3/4 inch (2 centimeters) long. At the ends of the tubercles are four to fifteen centrals, which are 3/8 inch (1 centimeter) long and white or pink, sometimes tipped with red or purple to light brown.

Flowers: The five to six large, pink to violet flowers are found at the top of the cactus and are 1 inch (2.5 centimeters) wide. New Mexico pincushion cactus blooms from March to August, with May being the usual time of flowering.

Fruit: The edible green fruit grows up to 1 5/8 inches (4 centimeters) long.

Range and Habitat: Found in New Mexico, southern Colorado, West Texas, eastern Arizona, and Chihuahua, Mexico, at 5,000 to 9,000 feet (1,500 to 2,700 meters) in the Chihuahuan Desert, desert grassland, and pinyon-juniper woodland.

Hardiness: Zone 4

Planting and Care: New Mexico pincushion cactus is one of our most cold-hardy desert plants, and as such, it has been collected for some time for the nursery trade. As always, be sure to purchase only nursery-propagated plants or seeds. New Mexico pincushion cactus is very easy to grow from seeds, and it grows quickly into flowering-sized plants in three to four years. It can form small clusters in four to five years. This cactus requires well-drained soil, little water, and full sun or partial shade.

Remarks: New Mexico pincushion cactus has beautiful, large flowers that make it a very desirable little cactus. It stands out when in bloom, but it is unobtrusive during the rest of the year, blending into the landscape. While this would be undesirable with many other ornamentals, in this case it adds to the charm of this plant. One of my favorite spring pastimes is walking in the garden, waiting for the New Mexico pincushion cactus's satiny pink flowers to appear. It does well in containers as well as in gardens in a variety of climates. New Mexico pincushion cactus is one of our most desirable and widely available cacti.

Species Name: *Ferocactus hamatacanthus*

Common Name(s): GIANT FISHHOOK CACTUS, TEXAS BARREL CACTUS, TURK'S HEAD, VISNAGA

Description: *Ferocactus hamatacanthus* is an endemic plant of the Chihuahuan Desert. This large cactus and its other barrel cactus cousins are among our most distinctive native plants.

Stems: The large, rounded stems become cylindrical with age. They grow up to 1 foot (30 centimeters) in diameter and 2 feet (60 centimeters) tall. The thirteen to seventeen ribs have large, round tubercles.

Spines: There are eight to fourteen reddish or gray radial spines, which are $^3/_4$ to $3^1/_4$ inches (2 to 8 centimeters) long; one very large, hooked, reddish or gray central spine, which is 2 to 6 inches (5 to 15 centimeters) long; and up to six additional, smaller central spines, which are 1 to $3^1/_2$ inches (2.5 to 9 centimeters) long.

Flowers: The yellowish flowers with or without red centers grow up to 3 inches (8 centimeters) wide and bloom anytime from March to July.

Fruit: The large, brownish red, ovoid fruits grow up to 2 inches (5 centimeters) long and are covered with small scales.

Range and Habitat: Found in south-central New Mexico, Trans-Pecos Texas, and northern Mexico up to 5,000 feet (1,500 meters) on gravelly soils in the Chihuahuan Desert and desert grassland.

Hardiness: Zone 8, warmer parts of zone 7

Planting and Care: Giant fishhook cactus is not as winter hardy as many other cacti of the northern Chihuahuan Desert. It should only be planted in areas where temperatures don't fall below 10° F (-11°C). In the desert garden, giant fishhook cactus will rot if given too much water.

Remarks: Giant fishhook cactus is rarely found in large groups in the wild. In the desert garden it deserves a place where its sculptural form can be displayed. Place a few large rocks around giant fishhook cactus in areas where it may need additional protection from winter's cold. Not only will this help it survive, but the rocks are a natural way to show off this plant.

Species Name: *Ferocactus wislizenii*

Common Name(s): FISHHOOK BARREL CACTUS, BARREL CACTUS, CANDY BARREL, BISNAGA

Description: *Ferocactus wislizenii* is one of the largest cacti in the American Southwest. As such, they are widely used as specimen or accent plants in many desert landscapes.

Stems: The huge, cylindrical stems are usually solitary. They grow 2 to 4 feet (60 to 120 centimeters) in diameter and up to 10 feet (300 centimeters) or more in height, although they're usually much shorter. There are up to twenty-five vertical ribs.

Spines: There are twelve to twenty ashy gray radial spines, which are 1 to 2 inches (2.5 to 5 centimeters) long; and four reddish central spines, which are 1½ to 3 inches (4 to 8 centimeters) long.

Flowers: The yellow to orange-yellow flowers grow up to 3 inches (8 centimeters) wide and occur in a ring around the top of the cactus. Fishhook barrel cactus normally blooms in the summer months from June to August; but it can bloom as early as March and as late as September.

Fruit: The large, yellow, ovoid fruits grow up to 2¼ inches (6 centimeters) long and are covered by rounded scales.

Range and Habitat: Found in southwestern New Mexico, Trans-Pecos Texas, southeastern Arizona, and northern Mexico at 3,000 to 5,000 feet (900 to 1,500 meters) on rocky, gravelly, or sandy slopes.

Hardiness: Zone 8

Planting and Care: Fishhook barrel cacti grow surprisingly fast from seeds, forming large specimens in five to eight years. In the desert garden, they should be planted in full sun, sandy soil, and be given little water. They are winter hardy to about 0°F (-18°C), and consequently they should be planted in the warmer parts of the region at their natural elevation. Fishhook barrel cactus is a striking accent plant and should be situated where it is the center of attention.

Remarks: Fishhook barrel cactus is the largest barrel cactus in the United States, and it is also the largest cactus found in New Mexico and Texas. At one time it was harvested in large quantities for making cactus candy, and many large specimens were destroyed. Thank goodness this practice has been stopped, but unfortunately fishhook barrel cacti are still being overcollected for landscaping.

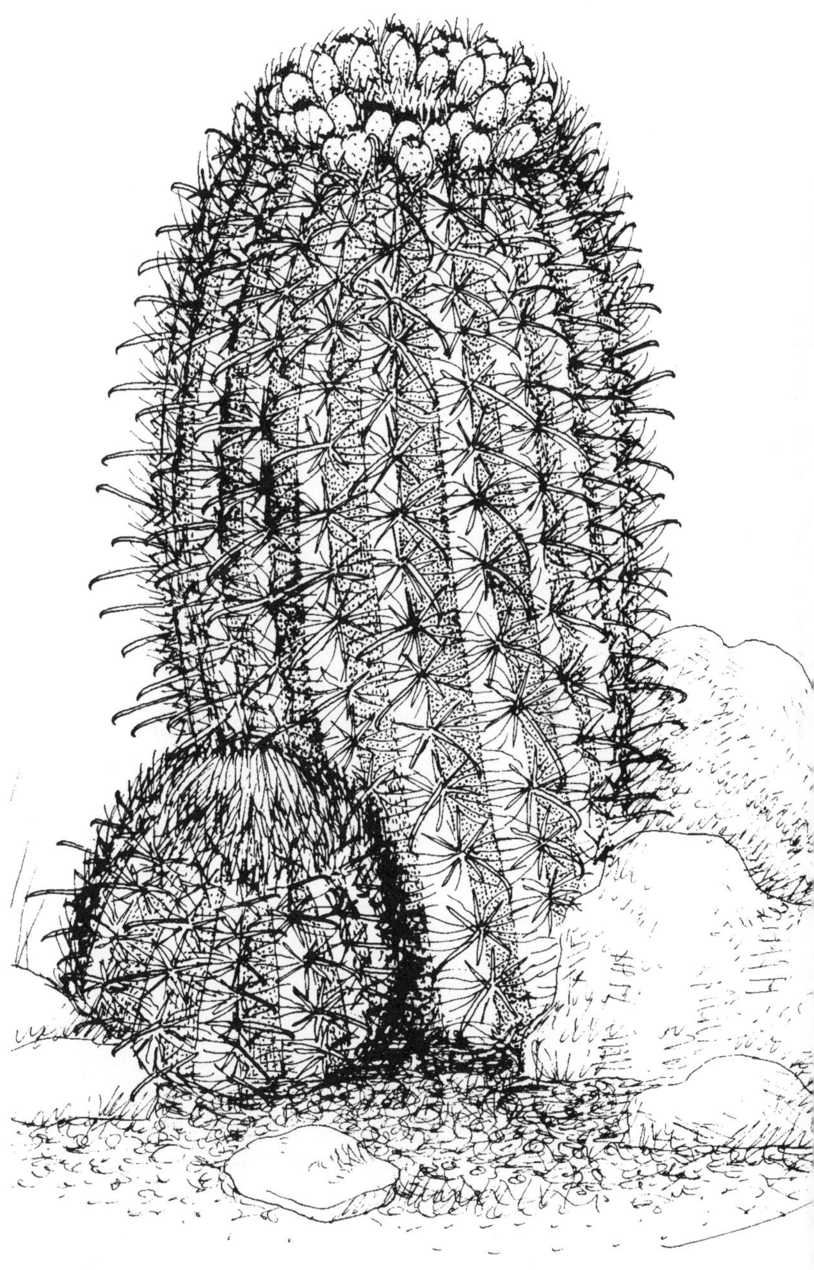

Ferocactus wislizenii, ***Fishhook Barrel Cactus***

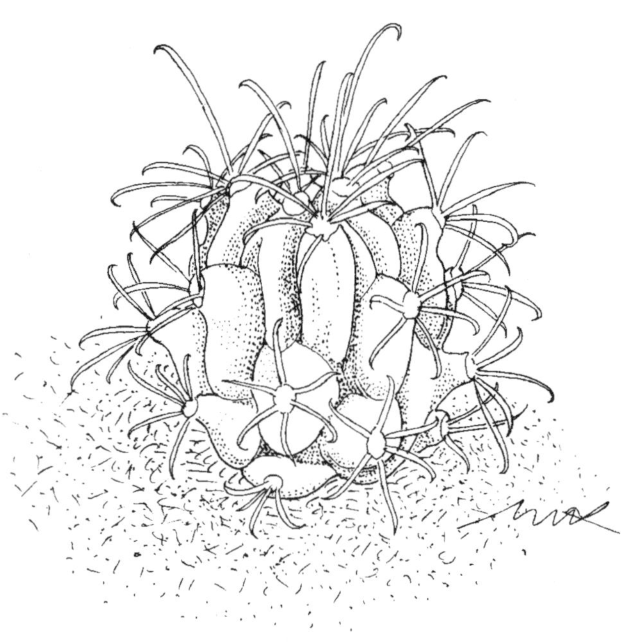

Glandulicactus wrightii, *Catclaw Cactus*

Species Name: *Glandulicactus wrightii* (*Ancistrocactus uncinatus* var. *wrightii*)

Common Name(s): CATCLAW CACTUS, BROWN-FLOWERED HEDGEHOG

Description: *Glandulicactus wrightii* is an unusual cactus of the Chihuahuan Desert. Its very long, sharp-hooked spines and unusual-colored flowers make catclaw cactus a curious addition to the desert garden.

Stems: The bluish green stems are 4 to 6 inches (10 to 15 centimeters) in diameter and up to 6 to 12 inches (15 to 30 centimeters) tall, although most specimens are under 6 inches (15 centimeters) in height. The nearly cylindrical, ribbed stems are constricted between the tubercles.

Spines: The seven to ten radial spines per areole are 3/4 to 2 inches (2 to 5 centimeters) long. The long, hooked, central spines are 2 to 4 inches (5 to 10 centimeters) long. The spines vary in color from reddish brown to straw colored.

Flowers: The 1-inch (2.5-centimeter), funnel-shaped flowers are of such an unusual coloration that many people have had a difficult time describing them. Their color has been described as being anywhere from chocolate-orange to chocolate brown to brownish purple to brownish red to brick-red. Catclaw cactus blooms from March to June and sometimes at later intervals throughout the summer.

Fruit: The red fruits are scaly and fleshy at maturity. They are oblong and grow to about 1 inch (2.5 centimeters) long.

Range and Habitat: Found in southern New Mexico, Trans-Pecos Texas, and northern Mexico at 3,000 to 4,500 feet (900 to 1,350 meters) on limestone soils of rocky ridges and on gravelly hills in the Chihuahuan Desert.

Hardiness: Zone 8

Planting and Care: Catclaw cactus seeds germinate readily. The young plants will reach flowering size in five years. This small barrel cactus is sensitive to overwatering and will rot quickly if given too much moisture. It requires very little attention other than full sun and a well-drained site. Catclaw cactus is hardy to about 0°F (-18°C).

Remarks: Although it is not a very big plant, catclaw cactus should be included in a desert landscape whenever possible. It looks very interesting when planted among large rocks, much as it occurs in nature. This also gives it some extra protection from frosts, as the rocks store heat during cold, sunny winter days.

Species Name: *Mammillaria grahamii* (*Mammillaria microcarpa* var. *grahamii*)

Common Name(s): LIZARD-CATCHER, FISHHOOK CACTUS, PINCUSHION CACTUS, SUNSET CACTUS

Description: *Mammillaria grahamii* is a very attractive cactus and a true desert dweller. Its sharp-hooked spines snag things quite easily. Reportedly, small lizards have been found caught by these, giving this cactus the common name lizard-catcher.

Stems: Although the ovoid stems can grow up to 6 inches (15 centimeters) tall, they are usually only 3 to 4 inches (8 to 10 centimeters) in height. They grow up to $3^1/_2$ inches (9 centimeters) in diameter. There can be up to six or more stems in small clusters, even though there is often only one.

Spines: There are twenty to thirty-five white or pale tan, spreading radial spines that grow up to $^1/_2$ inch (1 centimeter) long. The red to dark reddish brown or black central spines are noticeably hooked. There are one to three spines per areole, and they grow up to $^3/_4$ inch (2 centimeters) long.

Flowers: The rose-purple, pink, or white flowers form a ring around the top of the plant. They grow up to $1^1/_8$ inches (3 centimeters) wide. Lizard-catcher blooms from March to May.

Fruit: The barrel-shaped fruit is red when ripe and $^3/_4$ to 1 inch (2 to 2.5 centimeters) long.

Range and Habitat: Found in southern New Mexico, Trans-Pecos Texas, southern Arizona, and northern Mexico at 3,000 to 5,000 feet (900 to 1,500 meters) on rocky or gravelly soils in the Chihuahuan Desert, desert grassland, and the Sonoran Desert.

Hardiness: Zone 8

Planting and Care: Lizard-catcher should be watered carefully, as it needs perfect drainage. It is not one of the more winter-hardy cacti and shouldn't be planted outside its natural range without being placed in a warm microclimate. Lizard-catcher makes a fine plant for containers anywhere, as long as it has a well-drained soil and adequate sunlight.

Remarks: Lizard-catcher is usually found growing under bushes or grasses and, as such, prefers partial shade in the desert garden. Its brightly colored blooms in spring are an eye-catching sight. Be sure to plant far enough away from walks and paths, as the hooked spines will "grab hold" of those who get too close.

Species Name: *Mammillaria heyderi* var. *heyderi*

Common Name(s): NIPPLE CACTUS, LITTLE CHILES, BIZNAGA DE CHILITOS, PINCUSHION CACTUS

Description: *Mammillaria heyderi* var. *heyderi* is an interesting-looking, flat-bodied cactus that is one of the hardier mammillarias.

Stems: The usually solitary stems grow up to 5 inches (13 centimeters) wide and 2 inches (5 centimeters) tall. They are flattened or concave in the center. The body is made up of numerous tubercles or nipples that contain a milky sap.

Spines: The ten to twenty-six white to brownish radial spines grow up to $^1/_2$ inch (1 centimeter) long. The solitary central spine grows up to 3 $^8/_{10}$ inches (1+ centimeters) long and is brown to reddish brown in color.

Flowers: The tiny pink to white or cream flowers are $^3/_4$ to 1 inch (2 to 2.5 centimeters) wide and occur in rings around the top of the plant. Nipple cactus blooms from April to May.

Fruit: The small, oval-shaped red fruits look like tiny red chile peppers, which is the source of some of the common names for this cactus. They can be as long as $1^1/_2$ inches (4 centimeters).

Range and Habitat: Found in southern New Mexico, Trans-Pecos Texas, southeastern Arizona, and northern Mexico at 4,000 to 4,500 feet (1,200 to 1,350 meters) on gravelly, limestone soils in the Chihuahuan Desert and desert grassland.

Hardiness: Zone 7

Planting and Care: In the desert garden nipple cactus should be planted in semishade under bushes as it is found in nature. The seeds germinate readily, and the seedlings grow quickly. Although it can take more watering

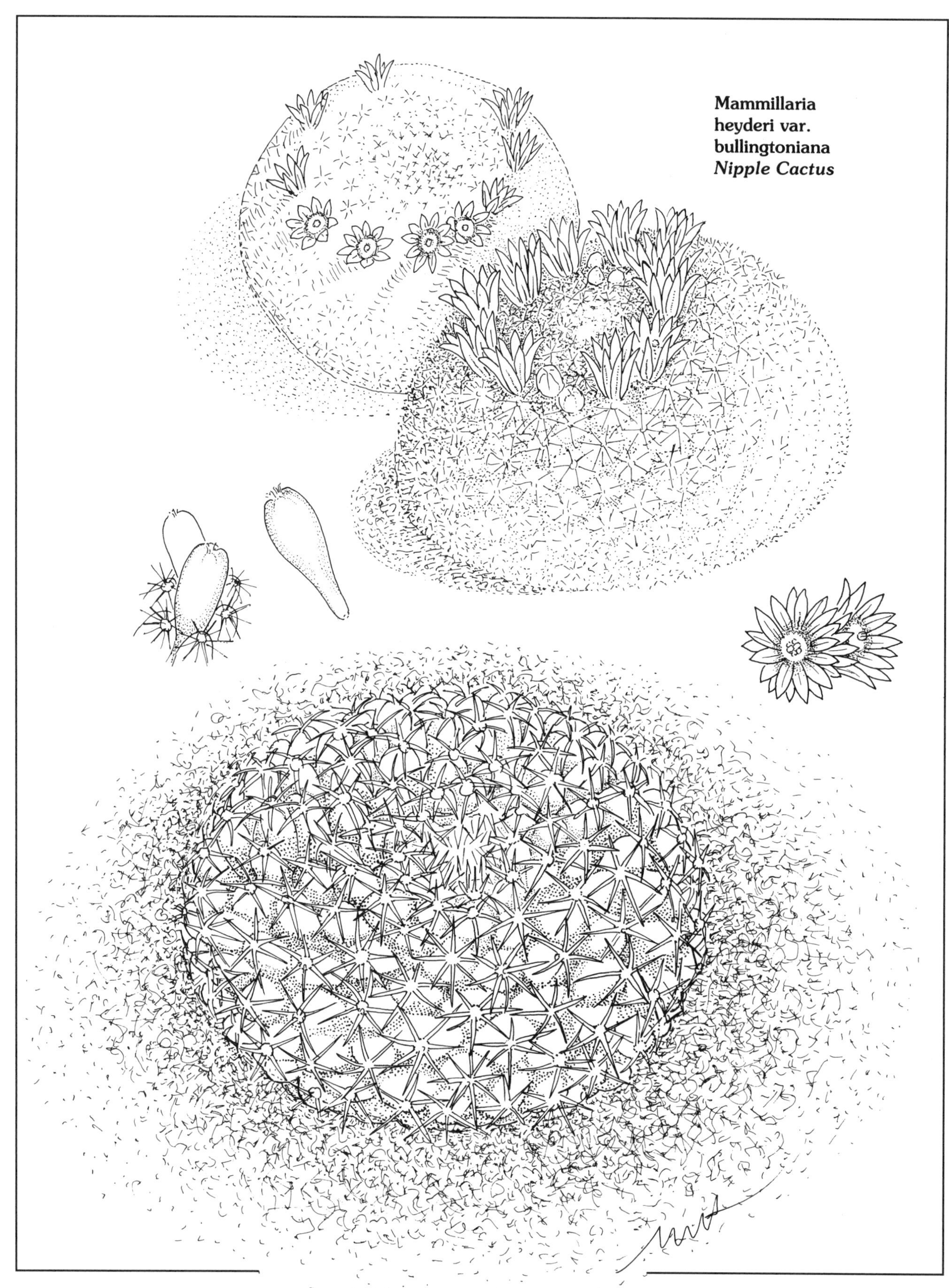
Mammillaria
heyderi var.
bullingtoniana
Nipple Cactus

than many other cacti, it prefers a well-drained soil typical of the family. Nipple cactus can be difficult to get established in the garden if the plant is not grown under the above conditions.

Remarks: Nipple cactus is an unusual-looking cactus, as it doesn't have the typical conical shape of so many other varieties. Its red fruits brighten up the garden long after its blossoms have faded.

Species Name: *Mammillaria heyderi* var. *bullingtoniana*

Common Name(s): NIPPLE CACTUS, LITTLE CHILES, BIZNAGA DE CHILITOS

Description: *Mammillaria heyderi* var. *bullingtoniana* is a form that is found at higher elevations than the species.

> ***Stems:*** Same as the species var. *heyderi*.
>
> ***Spines:*** Same as the species var. *heyderi* except var. *bullingtoniana* has ten to fourteen radials.
>
> ***Flowers:*** The white to cream to pink flowers have a brownish green midstripe and grow up to 5/8 inch (2 centimeters) wide. Nipple cactus blooms in May and June.
>
> ***Fruit:*** Same as the species var. *heyderi* except they can be red or green when ripe.

Range and Habitat: Found in southern New Mexico, Trans-Pecos Texas, southeastern Arizona, and northern Chihuahua and Sonora, Mexico, at 4,500 to 6,300 feet (1,350 to 1,890 meters) in desert grassland.

Hardiness: Zone 7

Planting and Care: This variety of nipple cactus is very similar to the species var. *heyderi*. It is even less tolerant of full sun in the Southwest, and it must be planted where it receives partial shade.

Remarks: Nipple cactus is a good choice for a rock garden, where its small size and unusual shape can be appreciated. To get the fruit, which gives us the common name little chiles, you must have two or more plants, as with most cacti, in order to achieve cross-pollination. As mentioned in the introductory remarks on cacti this is because most cacti are not self-fertile.

Species Name: *Mammillaria lasiacantha*

Common Name(s): GOLF BALL CACTUS, BUTTON MAMMILLARIA, CHILITOS

Description: *Mammillaria lasiacantha* is one of the miniature cacti endemic to the Chihuahuan Desert region. It has a smooth appearance due to the small, white spines covering its body.

> ***Stems:*** The small stems of this cactus are difficult to find, as they only rise slightly above the surface of the soil. They only grow up to 2 inches (5 centimeters) wide and 1 1/2 inches (4 centimeters) high. While usually solitary, they sometimes form small clusters of two or three stems.
>
> ***Spines:*** Golf ball cactus has no central spines. It has thirty to eighty white radial spines which grow up to 3/16 inch (5 millimeters) long.
>
> ***Flowers:*** For such a small cactus, golf ball cactus has fairly large flowers, 1/2 to 3/4 inch (1 to 2 centimeters) wide. The blossoms are white or pinkish white with a reddish center stripe and form a circle around the top of the cactus. They can bloom in the spring and again during the summer rainy season.
>
> ***Fruit:*** The cylindrical fruits are bright red and grow 3/8 to 5/8 inch (1 to 2 centimeters) long.

Range and Habitat: Found in southeastern New Mexico, Trans-Pecos Texas, adjacent Mexico, and possibly southeastern Arizona at 3,000 feet (900 meters) to just above 4,000 feet (1,200 meters) on limestone hills in the Chihuahuan Desert and desert grassland.

Hardiness: Zone 8, warmer parts of zone 7

Planting and Care: In nature golf ball cactus grows in rocky crevices and under partial shade. Give it a similar place in the garden, under a bush or somewhere else for shade. Be careful with watering, as these plants have a tendency to rot easily. Golf ball cactus is not as cold hardy as most of the other cacti of the northern Chihuahuan Desert. It shouldn't be planted above its natural elevation without some type of protection. Golf ball cactus does very well in containers. In containers as well as in the garden, to be successfully grown, golf ball cactus must have a well-drained soil and full sun.

Remarks: Golf ball cactus is named for its round, white, ball-like appearance. It looks very much like *Epithelantha micromeris* and grows in the same habitat, although the flowers of golf ball cactus have a different color and are much larger.

Species Name: *Mammillaria meiacantha*

Common Name(s): LITTLE CHILES, NIPPLE CACTUS, BIZNAGA DE CHILITOS

Description: *Mammillaria meiacantha* is a close relative and sometimes listed as a subspecies of *M. heyderi*. However, it gets much wider and has fewer radial spines.

Stems: Little chiles grows 6 to 12 inches (15 to 30 centimeters) wide. The plants are flat, rising only 1 to 2 inches (2.5 to 5 centimeters) above the ground with many firm green tubercles, which are filled with a milky sap.

Spines: There is one central spine or none at all. It is a little darker than the radials and grows up to 3/8 inch (1 centimeter) long. The five to nine stout radial spines grow up to 1/2 inch (1 centimeter) long. They are yellowish to gray and always have dark brown or blackish tips.

Flowers: The pink to white flowers have a purplish midstripe. Growing up to 1 3/4 inches (4.5 centimeters) wide, they form a ring around the top of the plant. Little chiles blooms in May and June.

Fruit: Little chiles is named for the red fruits, which are 7/8 to 1 1/4 inches (2.2 to 3.2 centimeters) long. They form a ring around the plant where the flowers were and take nearly a year to mature.

Range and Habitat: Found in southern and central New Mexico, Trans-Pecos Texas, southeastern Arizona, and northern Mexico at 4,000 to 5,300 feet (1,200 to 1,590 meters) on rocky or gravelly soils in the Chihuahuan Desert, desert grassland, Great Plains grassland, and pinyon-juniper woodland.

Hardiness: Zone 5

Planting and Care: Little chiles is probably the hardiest of the mammillarias, surviving temperatures well below 0°F (-18°C). While it can take more sun than *Mammillaria heyderi*, little chiles still likes a partially shaded location. It also takes less watering than its close relative and will rot more easily if watered too much.

Remarks: Little chiles is a very desirable plant for the desert garden. It is an interesting plant for those who want a display that represents as many genera of cacti of the Southwest as possible. With its wide elevational range, it can be grown throughout much of our region.

Mammillaria meiacantha, *Little Chiles*

Species Name: *Mammillaria wrightii* var. *wrightii*

Common Name(s): WRIGHT'S PINCUSHION CACTUS

Description: *Mammillaria wrightii* var. *wrightii* is a rare, soft-bodied cactus of the desert grassland and surrounding areas.

Stems: When moist and growing, the stems are 2 to 3 inches (5 to 8 centimeters) wide and up to 4 inches (10 centimeters) tall and are ball shaped or top shaped. During the cooler times of year, the cactus withdraws down into the surrounding soil and appears to be quite flat.

Spines: There are seven to twenty white, tan, or gray radial spines tipped with brown. They can grow up to 5/8 inch (2 centimeters) long. There can be one to five reddish brown or blackish central spines, although there are usually two to three centrals. They are hooked and grow 3/8 to 1/2 inch (approximately 1 centimeter) long.

Flowers: The large pink to purple flowers, which are 1 to 3 inches (2.5 to 8 centimeters) wide, bloom from May through October, depending upon the rainfall. Late summer is the usual time of bloom.

Fruit: The round or oval fruit is 3/4 to 1 inch (2 to 2.5 centimeters) long and reddish brown to dull purple.

Range and Habitat: Found in central and western New Mexico, eastern Arizona, and perhaps Trans-Pecos Texas at 3,000 to 7,000 feet (900 to 2,100 meters) on clay soils on low hills and foothills in a variety of habitats, including the desert grassland, pinyon-juniper woodland, Great Plains grassland, and Southwest oak woodland.

Hardiness: Zone 6

Planting and Care: Wright's pincushion cactus is easily propagated from seeds and grows rapidly. It is very sensitive to overwatering and needs a well-drained soil in the desert garden. Wright's pincushion cactus also prefers the light shade of bushes and grasses, especially when planted at the lower elevations of its range. This cactus is quite winter hardy for a mammillaria. Growing at higher elevations, it is able to take temperatures of 0°F (-18°C) and lower.

Remarks: Wright's pincushion cactus has a wide range; however, it is never common. Habitat destruction and overcollection are the primary threats to this unique little mammillaria. Urbanization, particularly in the Northeast Heights area of Albuquerque, New Mexico, destroyed some of the few large populations of this cactus. Wright's pincushion cactus is another of the jewels of the cactus family that is an interesting addition to the small and large garden alike. Although it is difficult to grow, its beautiful, satiny flowers and interesting spination make this plant a worthwhile challenge.

Species Name: *Mammillaria wrightii* var. *wilcoxii*

Common Name(s): WILCOX'S PINCUSHION CACTUS

Mammillaria wrightii var. wrightii
Wright's Pincushion Cactus

Description: *Mammillaria wrightii* var. *wilcoxii* is a more western form of the species. It is another cactus prized by collectors.

Stems: Although it is usually much smaller, it can grow up to 6 inches (15 centimeters) in diameter.

Spines: Wilcox's pincushion cactus has more spines than Wright's pincushion cactus. There are twelve to thirty radial spines, the average number being twenty. The central spines also tend to be longer, up to 1 1/4 inches (3 centimeters) long.

Flowers: The pink to pale purple flowers are 1 to 2 inches (2.5 to 5 centimeters) wide, smaller on the average than the species. Wilcox's pincushion cactus blooms in May and June.

Fruit: As with the flowers, the fruit, which is 5/8 to 1 inch (2 to 2.5 centimeters) long, tends to be smaller than the species. It is pink to greenish purple in color.

Range and Habitat: Found in southwestern New Mexico, southeastern Arizona, and northern Mexico at 3,000 to 6,500 feet (900 to 1,950 meters) in canyons and on rocky or gravelly hills in the desert grassland and bordering areas.

Hardiness: Zone 7

Planting and Care: Wilcox's pincushion cactus requires the same growing conditions as Wright's pincushion cactus, except it is not as winter hardy and should be planted in lower elevations of the region. Wilcox's pincushion cactus is a plant of the Sierra Madrean region that borders the Chihuahuan Desert.

Remarks: Wilcox's pincushion cactus is a rare cactus threatened by overcollection. This is a cactus for the more experienced gardener, but well worth the effort to grow for its appealing form and pretty, dainty flowers.

Opuntias

Opuntias are different from other cactus genera in that they grow in the form of jointed stems. There are two basic types: the chollas, with cylindrical stems, and the prickly pears, with flat pads. Prickly pears are so named because the edible "pears" are covered with spines. Once the spines are removed by brushing them off with a vegetable brush under running water, the fruit can be eaten raw or made into juice, jams, wine, and so forth. The pads are also called *nopalitos* by the Spanish-speaking people of the area, who slice the young pads and eat them as a vegetable in omelets, salsas, and other dishes.

Prickly pears are the widest ranging of the cacti, being native in every state except Alaska, Hawaii, and Maine. Their hardiness and adaptability to a wide range of growing conditions have made them popular plants for both desert and non-desert gardens. They also do very well in containers and can add a touch of the Southwest to a sunny windowsill.

Opuntias are easily propagated by taking cuttings of the stems or joints, allowing them to dry out, and planting them in containers or directly into the ground. They are difficult to grow from seed, which requires scarification followed by a period of cold stratification.

Opuntias range in size from miniatures to large, treelike plants. They can be spineless or armored with many sharp, long spines. The heavily spined and those with many glochids have given not only opuntias but all other cacti a bad name. This is unfortunate because, as previously discussed, both opuntias and other cacti have their place in the desert garden along with other native plants.

Species Name: *Opuntia clavata*

Common Name(s): CLUB CHOLLA, DAGGER CHOLLA

Description: *Opuntia clavata* is very common in its range, which is restricted to the Rio Grande Valley and Tularosa Basin of New Mexico. Its extensive mats help to control soil erosion in those areas.

Stems: Club cholla forms extensive mats up to 6 feet (180 centimeters) across of joints that are 3 to 6 inches (8 to 15 centimeters) high. The individual club-shaped joints are 1 inch (2.5 centimeters) thick.

Spines: There are ten to twenty white spines up to 1¼ inches (3 centimeters) long. When young and growing, the spines are bright pink. The lower three to four and main central spine are thick and flat. The white or straw-colored glochids vary in number from a few to many.

Flowers: The yellow to yellow-green flowers are 2 inches (5 centimeters) wide and bloom from April to July.

Fruit: The elongated, club-shaped fruits grow up to 2 inches (5 centimeters) long and 1 inch (2.5 centimeters) thick. They are yellowish when ripe and are covered with very tiny white, yellow, or straw-colored spines.

Range and Habitat: Found in central New Mexico from 4,600 to 8,000 feet (1,380 to 2,400 meters) on sandy soils of valleys and dry plains of the Chihuahuan Desert, desert grassland, and Great Plains grassland.

Hardiness: Zone 5

Planting and Care: In the desert garden club cholla needs to be planted well away from areas where someone could trip and fall on it. Club cholla, broom dalea (*Dalea scoparia*), and Indian rice grass (*Oryzopsis hymenoides*) grow in a unique, specialized habitat in sandy soils in the Rio Grande Valley region. Sandy soils are the best areas in the desert garden for growing this plant. Club cholla requires full sun and little water.

Remarks: Club cholla is found growing in huge mats that belie their grasslike appearance when stepped on. The common name dagger cholla comes from the largest daggerlike spines, which can cause harm to people and animals alike.

Species Name: *Opuntia davisii* (*Opuntia tunicata* var. *davisii*)

Common Name(s): GOLD CHOLLA

Description: *Opuntia davisii* is a rare cholla that forms small golden bushes, 12 to 30 inches (30 to 76 centimeters) tall. Its common name, gold cholla, comes from the golden appearance of its spines.

Stems: There are numerous, branching stems. These cylindrical joints are 3 to 6 inches (8 to 15 centimeters) long and 1/4 to 3/4 inch (6 millimeters to 2 centimeters) wide. The tubercles on the joints are very conspicuous. The overall color of the stems is a light green.

Spines: There are six to thirteen reddish brown or bright brown spines per areole. The four to seven main spines, up to 2 inches (5 centimeters) long, are covered with straw-colored or golden tan, papery sheaths. The remaining two to five smaller radials, up to 1/2 inch (1 centimeter) long are brownish without sheaths. The yellow or brownish glochids occur in a small cluster in the areole.

Flowers: Unlike many other opuntias, *Opuntia davisii* has firm, waxy flowers that are 1 1/2 inches (4 centimeters) wide and similar to those of *Echinocereus triglochidiatus*. They are dark to pale green in color with yellowish centers, and sometimes there is a reddish or brownish tinged border around the outside of the flowers. Gold cholla blooms in June.

Fruit: The fleshy, greenish yellow fruit grows up to 3/4 inch (2 centimeters) thick and 1/2 inch (1 centimeter) long. The seeds are light tan and possibly sterile. Asexual reproduction by dropping joints, which then root, is very common among opuntias and is the case with gold cholla.

Range and Habitat: Found in eastern New Mexico, West Texas, including the Trans-Pecos region, and southwestern Oklahoma at 2,000 to 5,000 feet (600 to 1,500 meters) on sandy soils mostly in the Great Plains grassland but also in the Chihuahuan Desert and desert grassland.

Hardiness: Zone 7

Planting and Care: Although gold cholla is somewhat rare, it is easily propagated from cuttings. It is hardy to at least 0°F (-18°C) and probably can take even lower temperatures.

Remarks: Gold cholla's attractively colored spines are also quite sharp. Therefore, be sure to plant gold cholla away from paths. Its unusual-looking flowers and shrubby form make gold cholla a good choice for the desert garden.

Species Name: *Opuntia grahamii* (*Opuntia schottii* var. *grahamii*)

Common Name(s): MOUNDED DWARF CHOLLA, GRAHAM DOG CACTUS, DWARF CHOLLA, GRAHAM'S CACTUS, DOG CHOLLA

Description: *Opuntia grahamii* is a miniature cholla that spreads out for a foot or more across the ground. It is an endemic cactus of the Chihuahuan Desert.

Stems: The elongated, club-shaped joints grow up to 1 inch (2.5 centimeters) wide and 1 1/2 to 2 1/2 inches (4 to 6 centimeters) long. They are covered with oblong-shaped tubercles 1/2 inch (1 centimeter) or more long. These stems form small mounds that grow 3 to 6 inches (8 to 15 centimeters) high.

Spines: The plant has eight to fourteen brownish or gray spines tinged with pink or red that grow up to 2 1/2 inches (6 centimeters) long. There are lots of tiny, brown glochids, which are 1/4 inch (6 millimeters) long, in each areole.

Flowers: The yellow flowers, which are 2 to 2 1/2 inches (5 to 6 centimeters) wide, bloom from March to August but usually in late May or early June.

Fruit: The oblong, egg-shaped yellow fruit grows up to 1 3/4 inches (4.5 centimeters) long. The fleshy fruit is covered with white glochids and several slender white spines.

Range and Habitat: Found in southern New Mexico, Trans-Pecos Texas, and Chihuahua, Mexico, at 2,300 to 5,000 feet (690 to 1,500 meters) on sandy flats and dunes in the Chihuahuan Desert.

Hardiness: Zone 7

Planting and Care: Mounded dwarf cholla requires full sun, a sandy soil, and little water when grown in cultivation. This little novelty is reportedly hardy to at least 0°F (-18°C).

Remarks: Mounded dwarf cholla is a good choice for the collector or gardener who has a small garden and wants a representative cholla. This is one of the few chollas small enough for growing in containers, in which it flourishes.

Species Name: *Opuntia imbricata*

Common Name(s): TREE CHOLLA, CANE CHOLLA

Description: *Opuntia imbricata* is the tallest cactus found in the Chihuahuan Desert in the United States. In some areas it occurs in such densities as to form pygmy "forests," or thickets, 3 to 10 feet (90 to 300 centimeters) in height.

Stems: The cylindrical joints grow up to 1 1/2 inches (4 centimeters) wide and 8 inches (20 centimeters) long on round trunks of 3 to 4 inches (8 to 10 centimeters) in diameter. Individual, older branches grow 3 to 4 feet (90 to 120 centimeters) long.

Spines: The barbed spines are often covered with loose, papery sheaths. There are two to ten spines on new growth. With age, these number twenty to thirty, and one to eight of these will develop central spines that spread in all directions. The central spines grow up to 1 1/4 inches (3 centimeters) long. Glochids are few or nonexistent on tree chollas.

Flowers: The large, magenta flowers are very showy and abundant on a single plant. The flowers, which are 3 inches (8 centimeters) in diameter, open for about two days and close at night. They bloom in May or June.

Fruit: The fruits, which are 1 inch (2.5 centimeters) wide and long, are yellow when ripe and remain on the plants for many months before falling off. People often mistake ripe fruits for flowers as they drive by a group of tree chollas.

Range and Habitat: Found across New Mexico, West Texas, eastern Arizona, parts of Colorado, extreme southwestern Kansas, the extreme western end of the panhandle of Oklahoma, and northern Mexico at 4,000 to 6,000 feet (1,200 to 2,250 meters) on gravelly or rocky slopes of the Chihuahuan Desert, desert grassland, Great Plains grassland, southwestern oak woodland, and chaparral.

Hardiness: Zone 5

Planting and Care: Tree cholla is very hardy to well below zero, and I have seen full-sized tree chollas growing outside in a central Pennsylvania garden! The main form of propagation is from stem cuttings, which root easily in warm weather. Once new growth has started, tree cholla can be watered fairly frequently. It requires full sun and prefers a sandy soil.

Remarks: Tree cholla is a large, dramatic plant that makes a very fine specimen plant. In spring its vibrant flowers are as beautiful as any rose bush. The dried, woody stems are used for a variety of items from lamps to walking sticks, hence the common name cane cholla. Wildlife is attracted to it for both food and shelter. For those who have the space, tree cholla is a must in the desert garden.

Opuntia kleiniae, *Klein Cholla*

Species Name: *Opuntia kleiniae*

Common Name(s): KLEIN CHOLLA, CANDLE CHOLLA

Description: *Opuntia kleiniae* is a bushy, medium-sized cholla found in a wide variety of habitats. One of its common names, candle cholla, is derived from the branched joints that look like a candelabra.

Stems: This many-branched cactus grows 3 to 6 feet (90 to 120 centimeters) tall. It is composed of cylindrical joints, $^1/_2$ inch (1 centimeter) wide, that grow 4 to 12 inches (10 to 30 centimeters) long. These stems branch off of woody trunks, which are 1 to $1^1/_2$ inches (2.5 to 4 centimeters) wide and covered with brown bark. The tubercled stems are a pretty mint green color.

Spines: Klein cholla has one to four grayish or reddish spines per areole. There is always one main spine, $^1/_2$ to $1^1/_2$ inches (1 to 4 centimeters) long, and two to three shorter ones are possible.

Flowers: The flowers, which are 1 to $1^1/_4$ inches (2.5 to 3 centimeters) in diameter, are pale greenish purple, lavender, or pinkish, edged with red or brown. Klein cholla blooms in May and June.

Fruit: The fruits, which are $^3/_4$ to $1^1/_2$ inches (2 to 4 centimeters) long, are fleshy, red or greenish red, and spineless. The seeds are light brown.

Range and Habitat: Found in southern and eastern New Mexico, Trans-Pecos Texas, central Oklahoma, and northern Mexico from 2,400 to 4,000 feet (720 to 1,200 meters) on rocky soils of hillsides and canyons in the Chihuahuan Desert, desert grassland, Great Plains grassland, and other grassland habitats.

Hardiness: Zone 6

Planting and Care: Klein cholla is easily propagated from stem cuttings, which will root directly in the ground without any special treatment other than letting the cut end of the joint callous over by drying it for three or four days before planting. Klein cholla is very hardy, to 0°F (-18°C) and lower, and consequently has a wide range of planting possibilities.

Remarks: Klein cholla is a nice compact shrub for use as a background plant. In spring it bursts forth with apple-blossom-pink flowers. Because of the sharp spines, this accent plant should be sited away from walkways.

Species Name: *Opuntia leptocaulis*

Common Name(s): DESERT CHRISTMAS CACTUS, TASAJILLO, PENCIL CHOLLA, SLENDER STEM CACTUS

Description: *Opuntia leptocaulis* is a small bush that grows 2 to 5 feet (60 to 150 centimeters) tall. The name desert Christmas cactus is derived from the bright red fruits that stay on the plant long after ripening and into the winter season.

Stems: The cylindrical joints are 1 to 12 inches (2.5 to 30 centimeters) long and $^1/_8$ to $1^1/_4$ inches (3 millimeters to 3 centimeters) thick. These deep green stems are the size of a pencil and form a compact shrub with a main trunk that grows up to $1^1/_4$ inches (3 centimeters) in diameter.

Spines: Most often there is one spine per areole, although there can be zero to three. The spines are gray and usually covered with yellow sheaths. There are long- and short-spined forms with spines from 1/8 to 2 inches (3 millimeters to 5 centimeters) long, respectively. The tiny glochids are few in number.

Flowers: The unusual-colored, greenish yellow flowers are 1/2 to 1 inch (1 to 2.5 centimeters) wide. They bloom anytime from April to July.

Fruit: The bright red, small fruit persist through the winter, giving desert Christmas cactus one of its common names. These fruits are pear shaped and grow up to 1 inch long. They are smooth-skinned, often with tiny brown glochids. In Texas some plants have yellowish fruits when ripe.

Range and Habitat: Found in eastern, central, and southern New Mexico, and from eastern Texas westward through West Texas, Oklahoma, Arizona, California, and northern Mexico, including Baja California, at 3,000 to 5,000 feet (900 to 1,500 meters) on a variety of soils. Desert Christmas cactus is found in the Chihuahuan, Sonoran, and Mojave deserts.

Hardiness: Zone 6

Planting and Care: Desert Christmas cactus is easily propagated from stem cuttings, which only need to be placed in the ground after having been left to callous over for three or four days. This cactus is very hardy and can take temperatures well below 0°F (- 18°C).

Remarks: Desert Christmas cactus is highly ornamental and provides winter color for the native desert garden. The fruits are excellent food for quail in wintertime. Because of its shrubby quality, this plant lends itself well to planting in the middleground of the garden.

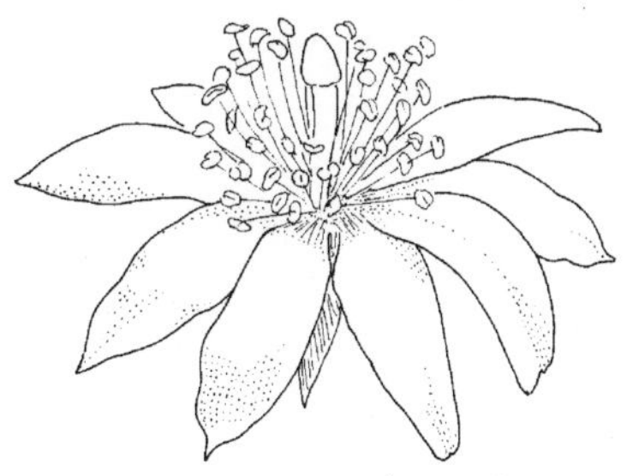

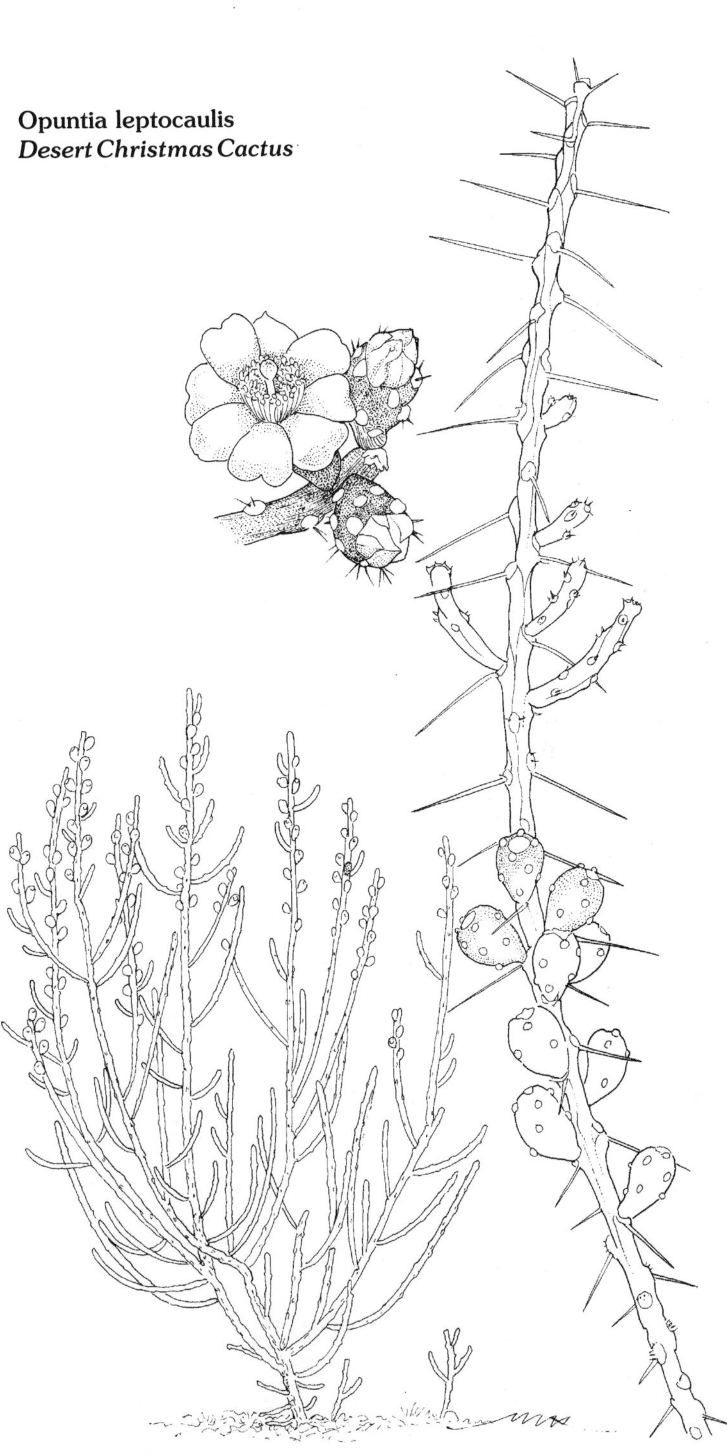

Opuntia leptocaulis
Desert Christmas Cactus

Species Name: *Opuntia arenaria*

Common Name(s): SAND PRICKLY PEAR

Description: *Opuntia arenaria* is a very rare endemic prickly pear cactus of the Chihuahuan Desert. It is threatened due to urban development throughout its known range.

Stems: The small, pale pads are $1^1/_4$ to 4 inches (3 to 10 centimeters) long and $^3/_4$ to 2 inches (2 to 5 centimeters) wide. The plants are composed of these pads, which form clumps up to 12 inches (30 centimeters) high. They spread by rhizomelike roots, which grow into clumps or strings of pads as big as 4 to 6 feet (120 to 180 centimeters) broad or long. Young pads are shiny green.

Spines: There are three to ten spines that are white or sometimes brownish or grayish with red or brown. They grow up to $1^1/_5$ inches (3 centimeters) long. The one rigid central spine grows $^3/_4$ to 2 inches (2 to 5 centimeters) long. There are also many clustered glochids, which grow up to $^1/_4$ inch (6 millimeters) long.

Flowers: The very delicate-looking, lemon yellow flowers grow from $1^1/_2$ to $2^3/_4$ inches (4 to 5 centimeters) wide. They bloom in April and May then off and on again through fall, depending upon moisture. There is also reportedly a rose-colored form.

Fruit: The green, club-shaped fruits have white spines and grow up to $1^1/_2$ inches (4 centimeters) long and $^3/_8$ inch (1 centimeter) thick.

Range and Habitat: Found in Doña Ana County, New Mexico, and adjacent Texas and Mexico from 3,500 to 4,500 feet (1,050 to 1,350 meters) on sandy soils of dunes and floodplains in the Chihuahuan Desert.

Hardiness: Zone 5

Planting and Care: While it is rare due to its restricted range and overcollection, sand prickly pear is easily propagated from stem cuttings. As long as it is grown in sandy soil and full sun, it will be happy in cultivation. Despite being from a fairly warm climate, sand prickly pear is very hardy and has reportedly survived several winters outdoors in Denver, Colorado. As with all our rare species, be sure to buy only nursery-propagated plants, and avoid buying from anyone who sells plants collected from the wild.

Remarks: Sand prickly pear is an interesting opuntia, spreading as it does from rhizomelike roots. This is apparently an adaptation to growing in shifting sands. It can "move" through the dunes by this means, ensuring its survival. Otherwise, it would be buried alive. Its small size, satiny flowers, and rarity make this little cactus a good plant for desert or rock gardens.

Species Name: *Opuntia engelmanii* (*Opuntia phaeacantha* var. *discata*)

Common Name(s): ENGELMANN PRICKLY PEAR, NOPAL

Description: *Opuntia engelmanii* is the largest native prickly pear in the Southwest. Its big, edible fruits, called *tunas* in Spanish, are made into jelly, preserves, wine, and so forth.

Stems: Engelmann prickly pear forms bushes of large, green dinner-plate-sized pads, which are 3 to 6 feet (90 to 180 centimeters) tall. The thick pads are 8 to 14 inches (20 to 35 centimeters) long when mature.

Spines: The whitish to grayish spines grow up to $2^1/_2$ inches (6 centimeters) long. There can be as few as one spine per areole on young pads and up to twelve or more on older ones. There are many glochids on the edges of older pads but few on the sides.

Flowers: As with everything else about this plant, the brightly colored flowers are large, up to 4 inches (10 centimeters) in diameter. Ranging in color from yellow to orange or reddish, they bloom from March to July, depending on different factors such as weather and location.

Fruit: The dark red to purple fruits are somewhat pear shaped and grow up to 3 inches (8 centimeters) long.

Range and Habitat: Found in southern and central New Mexico, West Texas, southern Arizona, southern California, extreme south-central Oklahoma, and northern Mexico from 2,000 to 5,000 feet (600 to 1,500 meters) on a variety of soils, including sandy, gravelly, and rocky, on slopes and plains in the Chihuahuan, Sonoran, and Mojave deserts, the desert grassland, and other habitats.

Hardiness: Zone 7

Planting and Care: Engelmann prickly pear is easily propagated from cuttings of the big, rounded pads. It requires a well-drained soil and full sun and is hardy to 0°F (-18°C), perhaps a few degrees lower.

Remarks: Engelmann prickly pear is a must for all but the smallest desert garden. Its size, flowers, and fruit make it an effective accent plant. Keep it away from walkways, as the spines are quite formidable. Engelmann prickly pear makes a good living fence due to its large size and spines. As with all things, there are exceptions. In the case of Engelmann prickly pear, there are spineless forms! One in particular from southern New Mexico, sometimes referred to as var. *dillei,* has very large pads and is very attractive.

Species Name: *Opuntia macrocentra* (*Opuntia violacea* var. *macrocentra*)

Common Name(s): PURPLE PRICKLY PEAR, BLACK-SPINED PRICKLY PEAR

Description: *Opuntia macrocentra* is one of the most beautiful of the opuntias, as its pads turn a vivid violet in the winter. The extremely long, blackish spines are in sharp contrast to the purple pads.

Stems: The pads, which are 4 to 8 inches (10 to 20 centimeters) long, are somewhat wider than long, or broadly oval shaped. They are thin for an opuntia, 1/2 to 5/8 inch (1 to 2 centimeters) thick. When in partial shade and well watered, the pads are a medium to yellowish green, turning purplish in the winter and in the heat of summer.

Spines: The few long spines are found on the upper areoles and on the edges of the pads. There are one to four per areole, reaching 2 to 5, sometimes 6 inches (15 centimeters) or more long. These black spines are among the longest of the genus. The brown or reddish brown glochids grow up to 1/2 inch (1 centimeter) long on the edges of the pads.

Flowers: Purple prickly pear has very pretty yellow flowers with red centers. They are 3 inches (8 centimeters) in diameter and open for two days, closing at night. Purple prickly pear blooms anytime from April to July.

Fruit: The spherical, red to orange-red fruit grows up to 1 1/2 inches (4 centimeters) long.

Range and Habitat: Found in central and southern New Mexico, Trans-Pecos Texas, southern Arizona, and northern Mexico from 3,500 to 5,500 feet (1,050 to 1,650 meters) on sandy, gravelly, and other soils of plains, washes, and slopes in the Chihuahuan Desert, desert grassland, and rarely in the Sonoran Desert.

Hardiness: Zone 6

Planting and Care: Purple prickly pear requires good drainage, and it is prone to rot if kept continually moist. Cuttings of pads must be placed in dry soil at first in order to prevent rotting and promote rooting. Once rooted, they may then be given a little water to help the roots spread in the soil.

Remarks: Purple prickly pear is a desirable cactus for almost every landscape, as it requires very little space for an opuntia. Its beautiful, violet pads; long, black spines; and attractive two-tone flowers make purple prickly pear one of the best cacti for desert gardens.

Opuntia macrocentra • *page 150* ▶

Opuntia macrocentra, *Purple Prickly Pear*

Species Name: *Opuntia phaeacantha*

Common Name(s): BROWN-SPINED PRICKLY PEAR, NEW MEXICO PRICKLY PEAR

Description: *Opuntia phaeacantha* has been subdivided into many varieties which intergrade throughout its range. It also hybridizes with many other species of opuntias, making it difficult to determine the species. *Opuntia phaeacantha* is the most abundant prickly pear in the southwestern deserts.

Stems: The pads are 4 to 9 inches (10 to 23 centimeters) long and 3 to 7 inches (8 to 18 centimeters) wide. They are dull to grayish green or yellow-green. Brown-spined prickly pear forms 3-foot- (90-centimeter-) high clumps that spread 6 to 8 feet (15 to 20 centimeters) wide.

Spines: There are one to eight usually dark brown spines on the upper areoles of the pad. They grow up to 3 inches (8 centimeters) long. With the various subspecies, the spine color can vary from whitish to yellow, brown, or reddish. The edges of old pads have numerous brown to reddish brown glochids, which are 1/2 to 5/8 inch (1 to 2 centimeters) long.

Flowers: The showy flowers are 2 to 3 inches (5 to 8 centimeters) in diameter with golden yellow to orange petals that are yellow or red in the center. Brown-spined prickly pear blooms anytime from May to July.

Fruit: The oval- or goblet-shaped fruit is 1 to 2 1/2 inches (2 1/2 to 6 centimeters) long. It is various shades of red when ripe.

Range and Habitat: Found in all of New Mexico, the western halves of Texas and Oklahoma, north through Nebraska, Colorado, and Montana, and westward practically to the Pacific from 3,000 to 8,000 feet (900 to 2,400 meters) on sandy, gravelly, or rocky slopes.

Hardiness: Zone 5

Planting and Care: Brown-spined prickly pear is easily propagated from cuttings of the pads. Allow them to dry out for three to four days and plant the pads in the garden to a depth of 1/3 of the pad from the bottom. They can also be started the same way in pots of well-drained soil.

Remarks: Brown-spined prickly pear is a very hardy opuntia. It can be used to advantage in a garden that is too cold for some of the other large-padded opuntias.

Species Name: *Opuntia polyacantha*

Common Name(s): PLAINS PRICKLY PEAR

Description: *Opuntia polyacantha* is a low-growing, spreading plant found across a large area of North America.

Stems: The circular to oval-shaped pads grow up to 5 inches (13 centimeters) long and 4 inches (10 centimeters) wide. They range in color from pale green and yellow-green to gray-green. Never more than a few pads high, they creep along the ground, rooting as they go.

Spines: The spines of plains prickly pear vary as can be expected with such a wide-ranging plant. There can be anywhere from one to fifteen spines on almost all the areoles and up to five main spines that grow up to 3 inches (8 centimeters) long. They are whitish to reddish brown in color.

Flowers: The large flowers are 2 to 3 1/2 inches (5 to 9 centimeters) wide. While they are usually bright yellow, they can be beautiful shades of rose or pink. Plains prickly pear blooms in May and as late as July in some locations.

Fruit: The fruit varies in shape, from almost spherical to egg shaped. It is 3/4 to 2 inches (2 to 5 centimeters) long and 1/2 to 2 inches (1 to 5 centimeters) thick. Unlike the more juicy fruits of other prickly pears, plains prickly pear has dry, brownish fruit at maturity. They are covered with spines.

Range and Habitat: Found over much of New Mexico, parts of Colorado, Oklahoma, and Trans-Pecos Texas, almost as far north as the Arctic Circle in Canada, west into Arizona, California, and the northwestern states on sandy soils in a variety of habitats, including the Chihuahuan Desert, desert grassland, Great Plains grassland, and pinyon-juniper woodland.

Hardiness: Zone 4

Planting and Care: Plains prickly pear requires sandy soil and very little water in order to look its best. It is easily propagated from cuttings of the pads, which root readily.

Remarks: Plains prickly pear is an extremely hardy cactus and, as a result, can be used in gardens across the country. It is a low-growing plant that can be easily lost if planted among larger plants. Because of its sharp spines, you should not plant it too close to walkways. Put it behind some lower-growing plants, such as some of the wildflowers. Plains prickly pear's large, bright flowers justify its careful placement. The pink-flowered varieties are particularly attractive with their satiny-looking blossoms.

Species Name: *Opuntia pottsii* (*Opuntia macrorhiza* var. *pottsii*)

Common Name(s): GRASSLANDS PRICKLY PEAR, PLAINS PRICKLY PEAR

Description: *Opuntia pottsii*, a small cactus that forms clumps of bluish stems, is often hidden by the taller grasses that it grows among.

Stems: The round pads, which are 1½ to 5 inches (4 to 13 centimeters) long, taper at the base. These blue-green pads do not form mats. Instead, the plants tend to grow as small, upright clumps up to 1 foot (30 centimeters) tall.

Spines: Grasslands prickly pear has one to three gray, tan, or brownish spines that grow ½ to 2½ inches (1 to 6 centimeters) long. The yellowish or tannish glochids grow up to ¼ inch (6 millimeters) long.

Flowers: The showy, purplish or reddish flowers are 2 to 3 inches (5 to 8 centimeters) wide. They bloom in May and June.

Fruit: The club-shaped, light red fruit grows up to 2 inches (5 centimeters) long.

Range and Habitat: Found in southern New Mexico, Trans-Pecos Texas, southeastern Arizona, and adjacent Mexico from 3,500 to 6,000 feet (1,050 to 1,800 meters) on alluvial flats and plains in the Chihuahuan Desert, desert grassland, and Great Plains grassland.

Hardiness: Zone 4

Planting and Care: While it prefers dry conditions, grasslands prickly pear is not as prone to rot if given too much water as some other cacti. A friend showed me a small plant growing in Alamogordo, New Mexico, in a vacant field. I took a couple of cuttings (in this case, pads), rooted them in pots, and now have several plants of my own. By doing this you can acquire new plants without removing them from their habitat. It does very well in containers if given a sunny location.

Remarks: Grasslands prickly pear is a small prickly pear that is easy to grow in the desert garden. The unusual flower color for a prickly pear makes this little plant a worthy choice for cultivation.

Species Name: *Peniocereus greggii* (*Cereus greggii*)

Common Name(s): NIGHT-BLOOMING CEREUS, QUEEN-OF-THE-NIGHT, REINA-DE-LA-NOCHE

Description: *Peniocereus greggii* is an unusual plant of the southwestern deserts, being quite different in appearance from other cacti in our area.

Stems: The stems are quite long, up to 6½

Peniocereus greggii
Night-blooming Cereus

feet (198 centimeters) but are usually about 3 feet (91 centimeters) in length. They are very slender, $^1/_2$ to 1 inch (1 to 2.5 centimeters) wide, and have three to six very strong ribs. The individual stems can have one or more branches that grow among the branches of brushy plants for support. The stems grow out of a large, underground tuber.

Spines: There are six to nine spreading radials and one to two central spines. The spines are blackish fading to gray or whitish and about $^1/_8$ inch (3 millimeters) long.

Flowers: The large, creamy white flowers are 5 to 8 inches (13 to 20 centimeters) long and 2 to 3 inches (5 to 8 centimeters) wide. They open in the evening and close soon after sunrise. The extremely fragrant flowers are sweet smelling and last only one night. Night-blooming cereus blooms in May and June.

Fruit: The red, oval fruits are 1 to 2 inches (2.5 to 5 centimeters) long and have short spines.

Range and Habitat: Found in southwestern New Mexico, southern Arizona, Trans-Pecos Texas, and in northern Mexico from 3,000 to 5,000 feet (900 to 1,500 meters) on gravelly soils of washes and flats in the Chihuahuan and Sonoran deserts.

Hardiness: Zone 8, warmer parts of zone 7

Planting and Care: Night-blooming cereus is relatively rare, and cactus poachers have been a problem, as they quickly collect most populations when they're discovered. This is truly unfortunate, as night-blooming cereus is easily grown from seeds and will grow up to 1 foot (30 centimeters) in height by the second year. The large, tuberous root also makes it difficult to successfully transplant this cactus from the wild. In a container it requires enough soil and space for the root to develop, or the plant may rot. The root can weigh as much as 125 pounds (56 kilograms) and be 2 feet (60 centimeters) in diameter; it was used as a food source at one time by Native Americans of the area.

In the garden night-blooming cereus should be planted under the branches of an open bush, such as mesquite or creosote bush, for support and the light shade it desires. It can take partial shade to full sun. Night-blooming cereus is reportedly hardy to 0°F (-18°C); however, it is not particularly adapted to climates outside its natural range.

Remarks: Night-blooming cereus is a choice specimen for the desert garden or for growing in containers in cooler climates. Where it can be grown, night-blooming cereus adds an exotic touch to the landscape. It is particularly effective when planted near patios and other areas where its sweet fragrance can perfume the night air. Avoid buying collected plants and purchase night-blooming cereus from reputable sources only.

SUCCULENTS

While all cacti are succulents, not all succulents are cacti. Many plant families have succulent members; that is, plants which have evolved fleshy parts, usually leaves and/or stems, to store moisture. The plants in this section range from those with succulent leaves such as agaves and broad-leaved yuccas to those that are sometimes referred to as stem-succulents or semisucculents, such as the narrow-leaved yuccas and ocotillo. Many of these plants are found in the family Agavaceae, a large number of whose species are desert dwellers.

These plants are among the truly unique and spectacular-looking garden specimens of the world. They can't be beaten for giving our area its character. Those of us who live here are lucky to be able to use them outside in our landscapes. Those who live elsewhere, however, can easily grow these plants in large containers. They can bring a piece of the desert into anyone's home.

Some of these plants require careful thought and placement. The bigger century plants and yuccas not only need a large space to grow and look good but also need to be placed where they are out of harm's way if someone were to fall down.

Give these plants extra water during the spring and summer growing season and they will grow surprisingly fast. Be careful not to overwater, particularly during the cool, winter months when the plants are dormant. With a minimum amount of care, succulent plants will provide the dramatic masterpieces only a Southwest desert garden can have.

Species Name: *Agave lechuguilla*

Family: Agavaceae (Agave)

Common Name(s): LECHUGUILLA

Description: *Agave lechuguilla* is a relatively small member of the family. But what it lacks in size, it makes up for in numbers. Lechuguilla is the most abundant wild agave and has one of the largest ranges. It is one of the indicator plants of the Chihuahuan Desert.

Leaves: The ten to thirty dark green leaves grow up to 2 feet (60 centimeters) long and 1¼ inches (3 centimeters) wide, forming a rosette. They are tipped with sharp points and have numerous prickles running down the leaf margins.

Flowers: The small, tubular flowers are borne on a tall flower stalk up to 13 feet (390 centimeters) tall. They range in color from pinkish white to yellow to green, and grow in clusters of two to three or more. After flowering, the parent plant dies, having produced several offsets to ensure its replacement. Lechuguilla blooms from May to July.

Fruit: The seed capsules, which are 1 inch (2.5 centimeters) long, are brown to black in color. They contain many black, flat, shiny seeds.

Range and Habitat: Found in southern New Mexico, Trans-Pecos Texas, and northern Mexico south to the states of Mexico and Hidalgo up to 5,000 feet (1,500 meters) on limestone cliffs, hills, and mesas in the Chihuahuan Desert.

Hardiness: Zone 7, warmer parts of zone 6

Planting and Care: Seeds and plants are available from nurseries specializing in cacti and succulents. The young offsets produced around the base of the parent can be cut off and potted up to produce new plants. Lechuguilla is also easily propagated from seeds, which need no special treatment. It is hardy to about 6,500 feet (1,950 meters) in the Southwest.

Agave lechuguilla • *page 156* ▶

Agave lechuguilla
Lechuguilla

Remarks: Lechuguilla is a highly desirable ornamental for desert and rock gardens It suckers quite freely and should be planted where it can spread. It is also very adaptable to growing in containers. The leaf fibers have been used to make rope.

Related Species: Shindagger (*Agave schottii*) is another narrow-leaved agave from southwestern New Mexico, southeastern Arizona, and northern Mexico with sweetly scented, yellow flowers. It blooms from June to September. As with lechuguilla, it needs room in the desert garden where it can spread. Hardiness: Zone 8, warmer parts of zone 7.

Species Name: *Agave neomexicana*

Family: Agavaceae (Agave)

Common Name(s): NEW MEXICO AGAVE, MESCAL, CENTURY PLANT

Description: *Agave neomexicana* is a medium-sized agave forming rosettes 1½ to 2 feet (45 to 60 centimeters) in diameter. This Chihuahuan Desert region endemic produces many offsets.

Leaves: New Mexico agave consists of numerous bluish green leaves up to 1 foot (30 centimeters) long. They are tipped with very sharp, black to gray-colored spines.

Flowers: The flowers, which are approximately 2 to 2½ inches (5 to 6 centimeters) long, are borne on stalks 8 to 15 feet (240 to 450 centimeters) high. They are reddish on the outside and deep yellow to orange inside. New Mexico agave blooms from June to August.

Fruit: The fruit is oblong and 1 to 1½ inches (2.5 to 4 centimeters) long. Its light brown capsule contains numerous black, flat seeds.

Range and Habitat: Found in south-central and southeastern New Mexico and Trans-Pecos Texas from 5,000 to 6,000 feet (1,500 to 1,800 meters) on dry, rocky slopes and hills in the Chihuahuan Desert and desert grassland.

Hardiness: Zone 5

Planting and Care: Seeds and plants of New Mexico agave are available from nurseries specializing in cacti and succulents. New Mexico agave is easily propagated from offsets or seeds. The seeds germinate readily without pretreatment. New Mexico agave prefers full sun to partial shade in the garden. It is tolerant of a wide variety of soils but prefers a well-drained location. Plant it at least 3 feet (90 centimeters) away from walkways, as its sharp points could injure anyone who fell on it.

Remarks: New Mexico Agave is well suited for native gardens from the desert to the transition zone. It is an excellent accent plant, a real attention-getter. New Mexico agave is one of those plants that evokes the image of the Southwest.

The Mescalero Apaches were given this name by the Spanish, who observed their use of mescal as an important food source, roasting wild mescal heads in a pit filled with hot stones.

Related Species: Parry agave (*Agave parryi*) is a larger close relative of New Mexico agave. Although it is found at higher elevations, it is adaptable to desert gardens. Parry agave is one of the hardiest agaves. Its yellow flowers bloom from June to August. It is native to southwestern New Mexico, southeastern and central Arizona, and northern Mexico. Hardiness: Zone 5.

Desert agave (*Agave deserti*) is a Sonoran Desert species native to southwestern Arizona, southern California, and northern Mexico. It is not as hardy as the previous species and should be grown in the deserts only. Desert agave is one of the most drought-tolerant century plants. Its yellow flowers bloom in May and June. Hardiness: Zone 8.

Agave neomexicana • *page 158* ▶

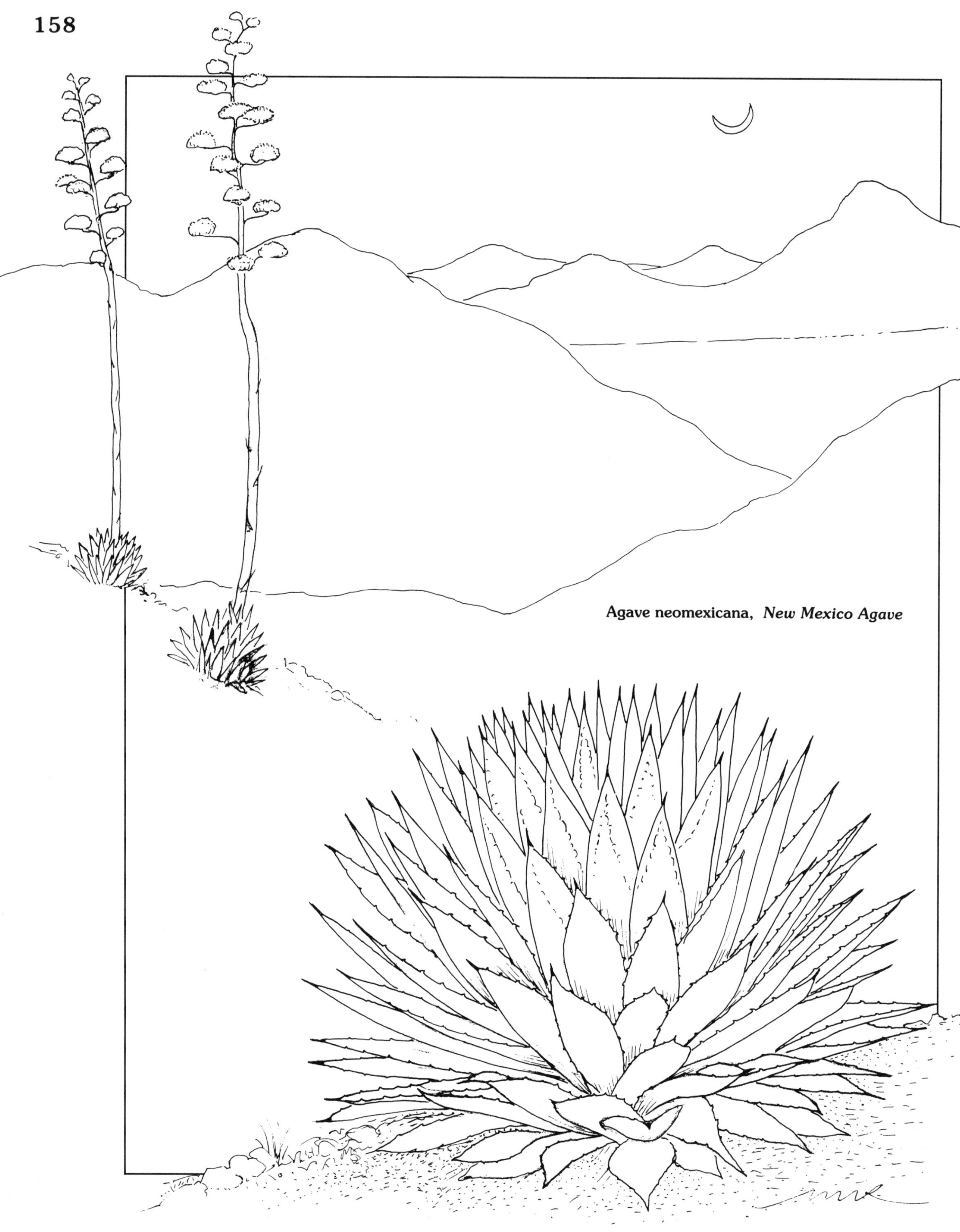

Agave neomexicana, *New Mexico Agave*

Species Name: *Agave palmeri*

Family: Agavaceae (Agave)

Common Name(s): PALMER AGAVE, CENTURY PLANT, MESCAL

Description: *Agave palmeri* is the largest agave native to the United States. It is a plant of the desert grasslands.

Leaves: Palmer agave has long, lanceolate leaves which were used for fiber by the Native Americans of the area. The leaves grow up to 3 feet (90 centimeters) long and 4 inches (10 centimeters) wide. They are coated with waxes that help conserve water. The brown to green terminal spine grows up to 2¼ inches (6 centimeters) in length and is very sharp.

Flowers: Its flower stalk, which is approximately 18 feet (540 centimeters) tall, shoots up in June and July. While hummingbirds and other birds are attracted to the flowers, night-flying bats of the genus *Leptonycteris* are its primary pollinators. The flowers range from pale greenish yellow to golden yellow and have purple-tinged parts.

Fruit: The fruit is a brown, cylindrical capsule, which is 1½ to 2½ inches (4 to 6 centimeters) wide. The entire plant dies once the fruit has set; however, there are usually several offsets to replace it.

Range and Habitat: Found in southwestern New Mexico, southeastern Arizona, and Sonora and Chihuahua, Mexico, from 3,000 to 7,800 feet (900 to 2,340 meters) on rocky hillsides in the desert grassland and adjacent woodlands.

Hardiness: Zone 7

Planting and Care: Palmer agave is available as plants and seeds from nurseries specializing in cacti and succulents and is sometimes available in native plant nurseries in the Southwest. As with most agaves, Palmer agave is easily grown from offsets and seeds. Due to its large size, it should not be planted close to walkways or where small children or pets could be injured by its sharp, spined leaves.

Remarks: In the desert garden Palmer agave makes a striking accent plant. It combines well with other desert plants, such as ocotillo, prickly pear, and acacias. There is some danger of Palmer agave being overcollected for the bootleg mescal industry in northern Mexico.

Related Species: Other agaves are very useful in the desert gardening style landscape, ranging from the small, heavily spined Utah agave (*Agave utahensis*) to the giant American agave (*Agave americana*) of old Mexico. Hardiness: Zone 6 and zone 8, respectively.

Species Name: *Dasylirion wheeleri*

Family: Agavaceae (Agave)

Common Name(s): SOTOL, DESERT SPOON, DESERT SOTOL, DESERT CANDLE

Description: *Dasylirion wheeleri* is a large plant with long, slender leaves that occur in basal clusters on subterranean stems or short trunks up to 3 feet (90 centimeters) tall. Sotol is often mistaken for a yucca, which it resembles.

Leaves: The flat, linear, blue-green leaves grow up to 3 feet (90 centimeters) long and 1 inch (2.5 centimeters) wide. They have prickles on the margins that are pointed towards the tip of the leaf. The leaves, having a spoon-shaped base, were once used as spoons, hence the common name desert spoon.

Flowers: The tiny, creamy white flowers are borne on a dense terminal spike on a flower stalk that grows 9 to 15 feet (270 to 450 centimeters) high. Sotol blooms from May to June.

Fruit: The three-winged fruit consists of a capsule containing a solitary seed inside the center.

Range and Habitat: Found in southern New Mexico, southern Arizona, Trans-Pecos Texas, and Sonora and Chihuahua, Mexico, at 3,000

to 5,000 feet (900 to 1,500 meters) on gravelly or rocky slopes and hills in the Chihuahuan and Sonoran deserts and the surrounding desert grassland and southwestern oak woodland.

Hardiness: Zone 7

Planting and Care: Sotol is widely available as plants throughout nurseries in the desert Southwest. It is also available as seed and plants through mail-order nurseries specializing in native southwestern plants or in cacti and succulents. Sotol is easily grown from seeds, which germinate in three to four weeks without pretreatment. It grows quickly in cultivation and is a very hardy plant that probably can be grown in elevations up to about 6,500 feet (1,950 meters) in the Southwest.

Remarks: Sotol has been used by the Native Americans and Mexican people for many things. An alcoholic beverage also known as "sotol" is made by roasting the head in a pit for twenty-four hours and then distilling the juice. The fibers of the leaves have been used for various products such as mats and baskets.

Related Species: *Dasylirion leiophyllum* is very similar to *D. wheeleri* except the prickles on the leaf margins are pointed down towards the base of the leaf. The creamy white flowers bloom from May into August. This sotol is native to rocky hillsides in the Chihuahuan Desert and desert grassland from southern New Mexico to West Texas and Chihuahua, Mexico. Hardiness: Zone 7.

Species Name: *Fouquieria splendens*

Family: Fouquieriaceae (Candlewood)

Common Name(s): OCOTILLO, COACHWHIP

Description: *Fouquieria splendens* is a spiny-branched shrub of the warm deserts of the Southwest. Ocotillo is often mistaken for a cactus due to its whiplike stems covered with thorns. The stems can grow 8 to 20 feet (240 to 600 centimeters) tall and 3 inches (8 centimeters) in diameter.

Leaves: The green leaves grow 1/2 to 2 inches (1 to 5 centimeters) long. During dry spells it sheds its leaves to conserve moisture. After spring or summer rains it grows new leaves.

Flowers: Ocotillo has clusters of bright red flowers on the ends of its many stems. The tubular flowers, which are 1 inch (2.5 centimeters) long, bloom in April or May and occasionally again after the summer rains.

Fruit: The fruit is an oval capsule filled with many flat seeds.

Range and Habitat: Found in southern New Mexico, Trans-Pecos Texas, southern Arizona, southern California, and northern Mexico from sea level to 5,000 feet (1,500 meters) on rocky, gravelly slopes, hills, and plains in the Mojave, Sonoran, and Chihuahuan deserts and surrounding desert grasslands.

Hardiness: Zone 7

Planting and Care: Ocotillo is widely available at nurseries in the desert Southwest. Seeds and plants are available through mail-order sources specializing in southwestern native plants or cacti and succulents. Ocotillo is easy to grow from seeds, which require no special treatment other than warm temperatures and moisture. Ocotillo can be grown successfully in marginal areas where it might freeze by planting it in a warm microclimate, such as up against a south wall. It is not reliably hardy above 5,000 feet (1,500 meters).

Remarks: Ocotillo's bright red flowers are a favorite of hummingbirds. Living fences are often made from the cut branches, which root when placed in the ground. A unique desert plant, it is a must for desert landscaping.

Species Name: *Nolina texana*

Family: Agavaceae (Agave)

Common Name(s): BEARGRASS, SACAHUISTA

Description: *Nolina texana* looks like a large clump of grass. The long leaves fan out from the plants, which are 1½ to 2½ feet (45 to 75 centimeters) tall.

Leaves: The yellowish green to olive green leaves grow up to 3½ feet (105 centimeters) long and ⅛ to ⅕ inch (3 to 5 millimeters) wide. The sharp-edged leaves are smooth or slightly serrated.

Flowers: The tiny creamy white flowers, which are ⅛ to ⅙ inch (3 to 4 millimeters) wide, are borne in large clusters contained within the foliage of the plant. Beargrass blooms in May and June.

Fruit: The tan seeds are about ⅛ inch (3 millimeters) wide.

Range and Habitat: Found in central and southeastern New Mexico, Trans-Pecos Texas, southeastern Arizona, northeastern Sonora and Chihuahua, Mexico, from 3,500 to 5,500 feet (1,050 to 1,650 meters) on gravelly hills of several different soil types in the desert grassland and foothills of the mountains.

Hardiness: Zone 6

Planting and Care: Beargrass is occasionally offered as plants and seeds at nurseries specializing in native southwestern plants or in cacti and succulents. It is easy to grow from seeds, which don't require any special treatments. The young plants look like tiny grass plants and will grow quickly into plants suitable for your garden.

Remarks: Beargrass is a wonderful plant for the desert garden. Being very drought tolerant, it is an excellent substitute for water-thirsty

Nolina texana, *Beargrass*

ornamental grasses. It is a winter-hardy evergreen, a very desirable attribute as far as landscapes are concerned.

Beargrass is also known as basket grass, as it has been used for making baskets. Whether used for baskets or for its striking appearance, beargrass is a choice addition to your desert garden.

Species Name: *Yucca elata*

Family: Agavaceae (Agave)

Common Name(s): SOAPTREE YUCCA, PALMILLA, AMOLE

Description: *Yucca elata* is a large, treelike, narrow-leaved plant. It is characteristic of the Chihuahuan Desert and desert grasslands. The trunk can grow from 6 to 20 feet (180 to 600 centimeters) tall, is covered with a thatch of old leaves from previous years, and is often branched two or three times.

> ***Leaves:*** The bluish or grayish green leaves grow 2 to 4 feet (60 to 120 centimeters) long and 1/4 to 1 3/4 inches (6 millimeters to 4.5 centimeters) wide. They are sharply pointed and have fine fibers between the leaf margins.
>
> ***Flowers:*** Soaptree yucca sends up the tallest flower stalks of the yuccas, with a large head of creamy white flowers. The petals are 1/4 to 1 3/4 inches (6 millimeters to 4.5 centimeters) long. The edible flowers, which bloom from May into July, are rich in vitamin C.
>
> ***Fruit:*** The pale brown fruit is 2 to 3 1/8 inches (5 to 8 centimeters) long. It is a dry capsule and contains black, flat seeds.

Range and Habitat: Found in central and southern New Mexico, Trans-Pecos Texas, southern Arizona, and northern Mexico from 3,500 to 5,500 feet (1,050 to 1,650 meters) on dry hills and plains in the Chihuahuan and Sonoran deserts and the desert grasslands surrounding them.

Hardiness: Zone 6

Planting and Care: Soaptree yucca is widely available at nurseries throughout the Southwest. Seeds and plants are also available from mail-order nurseries. Collected plants often die back when transplanted, but usually they will eventually recover. Unlike the broad-leaved yuccas that transplant easily, this is a common problem with the narrow-leaved species. By using container-grown plants, this problem is avoided, as there is no root loss resulting in transplant shock. Soaptree yucca is easily grown from seeds, which will germinate in seven to ten days. For the first year or two, it will put much of its growth into its root system. Be sure to move it into larger containers as it grows, since the strong, growing roots can break a pot when they've outgrown it. Seed-grown plants will reach flowering size in about five years.

Remarks: Soaptree yucca is the state flower of New Mexico, where it occurs in "forests" covering large areas in the south-central and southwestern parts of the state. Forming large clumps at times, this beautiful yucca is particularly suited for desert gardens.

Soaptree yuccas and other yucca species are popularly used as specimen plants in both residential and commercial landscapes. The name soaptree derives from the fact that the roots and stems are beaten in water to make a soapy lather, which has been used by various inhabitants of the Southwest for washing their clothes and hair.

At night soaptree yucca is pollinated by a small, white pronuba moth that lays its eggs in the flower. While laying its eggs, the moth fertilizes the yucca with pollen from another plant. When the larvae hatch, they feed on some of the seeds. Enough seeds are left, however, to perpetuate the species.

Related Species: There are several other narrow-leaved yuccas which make good specimens for the garden. Soapweed yucca (*Yucca angustissima*) is a stemless, or nearly so, narrow-leaved yucca of the desert of the Colorado Plateau. The greenish white flowers bloom in May or June. Hardiness: Zone 5.

Plains yucca (*Yucca glauca*) is the hardiest of the yuccas and can be used to give a "desert look" to gardens in fairly cold climates, especially in conjunction with hardy cacti. The greenish white flowers bloom in May or June. Hardiness: Zone 4.

Species Name: *Yucca torreyi*

Family: Agavaceae (Agave)

Common Name(s): TORREY YUCCA, PALMA, SPANISH DAGGER, SPANISH BAYONET, PALM YUCCA

Description: *Yucca torreyi* is an endemic plant of the Chihuahuan Desert and is quite plentiful throughout a large area of the desert. The trunk can grow from 3 to 24 feet (90 to 720 centimeters) tall and is usually single and unbranched, although two or three branches are not uncommon.

Leaves: The trunk is covered with a thatch of dead leaves. The olive green to blue-green leaves grow up to 4½ feet (135 centimeters) long and 2 inches (5 centimeters) wide. They have a sharp spine at the tip, which is ¼ to ½ inch (6 millimeters to 1 centimeter) long, and curly to straight fibers along the leaf margins.

Flowers: The creamy white flowers are borne in dense, heavy-looking clusters on upright flower stalks 3 to 4 feet (90 to 120 centimeters) tall. The individual waxy, bell-shaped flowers are 3 to 4 inches (8 to 10 centimeters) long. Torrey yucca blooms from April to June.

Fruit: The fruit is a dark brown to black capsule 4 to 5½ inches (10 to 14 centimeters) long and 1¼ to 2 inches (3 to 5 centimeters) wide, bananalike in shape. The flat, black seeds are numerous.

Range and Habitat: Found in southeastern New Mexico, Trans-Pecos Texas, and northern Mexico at 3,500 to 5,000 feet (1,050 to 1,500 meters) on mesas, slopes, and foothills in the Chihuahuan Desert and surrounding desert grassland.

Hardiness: Zone 7, warmer parts of zone 6

Planting and Care: Torrey yucca is sometimes for sale in nurseries in the Southwest. It is occasionally offered as seeds or plants by mail-order nurseries specializing in cacti and succulents. Torrey yucca requires careful placement in the desert garden away from walkways and children's play areas. It is easily started from seeds, and growth is rapid in full sun and with extra water.

Remarks: Torrey yucca is an excellent ornamental plant. Its large size makes it very useful as an accent plant. It is one of the "palm yuccas," so called due to their resemblance to a palm tree.

Related Species: Datil yucca (*Yucca baccata*) is a closely related, trunkless species. It has dense clusters of white flowers tinged reddish brown on the outside. It blooms from April to July. Datil yucca is the hardiest of the broad-leaved yuccas, being found the furthest north and at relatively high altitudes in the mountains. Hardiness: Zone 5.

Other useful broad-leaved yuccas include the treelike Schott's mountain yucca (*Yucca schottii*) from the desert grassland, which blooms from April to August, and the giant palm yucca (*Yucca faxoniana*), also from the Chihuahuan Desert, which blooms from April to June. Both have white flowers and are hardy in zone 7 and above.

DESERT SHRUBS

Among the most plentiful of desert plants, shrubs such as creosote bush and the acacias cover thousands of acres in the Chihuahuan Desert. Since many of the trees in the desert are small and few in number, shrubs are the dominant and, therefore, most visible plants. As in the desert, they should form the foundation of your landscaping scheme.

Just like their non-desert relatives, these arid-region shrubs can be used for a wide variety of purposes. As accent plants Chihuahuan whitethorn, bird-of-paradise, and shrubby senna all have colorful flowers and bloom for long periods of time. All of the desert shrubs can be used as informal hedges. The larger ones such as Apache plume and little-leaf sumac can screen out unsightly views. Large shrubs can also be used for windbreaks, either by themselves or in combination with desert trees.

Desert shrubs can be used in all watering zones in a Xeriscape. They are a good choice for covering large expanses in a low-water-use zone. Apache plume, for example, is an excellent plant for this zone and is often used for revegetation of disturbed areas. This and other desert shrubs help stabilize the soil while also providing beauty.

Adapted to the heat, aridity, and intense sunlight of the desert, these shrubs are also able to adapt to other climates as well. Legumes in particular seem to be able to survive in wetter climates as long as winter temperatures are similar to those in the Chihuahuan Desert. In order to give them the dry conditions they require, plant them in sand beds in non-desert regions, as described in Chapter 5.

Species Name: *Acacia neovernicosa* (*Acacia constricta* var. *vernicosa*)

Family: Fabaceae (Leguminosae) (Pea); Subfamily: Mimosoideae (Mimosa)

Common Name(s): CHIHUAHUAN WHITETHORN, VISCID ACACIA

Description: *Acacia neovernicosa* is a thorny shrub that grows up to 10 feet (300 centimeters) or more tall. The entire plant, including the leaves, seedpods, and small branches, are slightly sticky.

> ***Leaves:*** The tiny leaves are only 1/2 to 1 inch (1 to 2.5 centimeters) long. There are usually one to two primary leaflets, sometimes three or four, and six to ten secondary leaflets, up to 1/8 inch (3 millimeters) long.
>
> ***Flowers:*** The fragrant flowers, which are 1/2 inch (1 centimeter) wide, are shaped like yellow globes. They flower in May and June and again following summer rains.
>
> ***Fruit:*** The fruit is a slender pod that grows up to 2 3/4 inches (7 centimeters) long and 1/5 inch (5 millimeters) wide. It tends to be curved with slight constrictions between the seeds. The gray or black spotted seeds grow up to 1/4 inch (6 millimeters) long and are oval shaped.

Range and Habitat: Found in southern New Mexico, Trans-Pecos Texas, southern Arizona, and in the Mexican states of Zacatecas, Sonora, Chihuahua, and Puebla from 2,000 to 5,000 feet (600 to 1,500 meters) on gravelly hillsides, rocky hills, mesas, and caliche soils in the Chihuahuan Desert, desert grassland, and Sonoran Desert.

Hardiness: Zone 7

Planting and Care: Seeds and plants are sometimes available from mail-order nurseries located in the Southwest. Chihuahuan whitethorn is easily propagated from seeds, which should be collected from late summer through early fall before the pods split and the seeds disperse. Germination is delayed due to an impermeable seed coat, and scarification is necessary. A hot water bath is very effective.

Growth is rapid, and a good 1 gallon (3.8 liter)-sized plant can be grown in one or two seasons. Chihuahuan whitethorn and other legumes are very sensitive to having their roots disturbed and may defoliate when transplanted. If this happens, keep them well watered, and they should releaf in a short time.

Remarks: Chihuahuan whitethorn is very closely related to mescat acacia (*Acacia constricta*). Some authorities consider it to be a variety of the latter.

In the desert garden Chihuahuan whitethorn's pretty, sweet-scented yellow flowers are very attractive. Plant it where the thorns won't be a problem. The light shade of Chihuahuan whitethorn is a good place for growing those small cacti that prefer some extra shade, such as some of the mammillarias.

Related Species: Whitethorn acacia, largoncillo (*Acacia constricta*) is a close relative. The sweet-scented, bright yellow, powder puff flowers are a very attractive feature of this small

Acacia neovernicosa, *Chihuahuan Whitethorn*

desert tree. Whitethorn acacia blooms from May into September. The foliage is light and airy. It can reach 18 feet (540 centimeters) in height under good conditions. Hardiness: Zone 8.

Species Name: *Amorpha fruticosa*

Family: Fabaceae (Leguminosae) (Pea); Subfamily: Papilionoideae (Bean)

Common Name(s): INDIGO BUSH

Description: *Amorpha fruticosa* is a shrubby legume with dark purple, oddly-shaped flower spikes found along riparian areas and irrigation ditches in the Southwest. Indigo bush grows from 4 to 10 feet (120 to 300 centimeters) tall.

Amorpha fruticosa
Indigo Bush

> ***Leaves:*** The dark green leaves are 3 to 8 inches (7 to 20 centimeters) long. The nine to twenty-five leaflets are $^3/_5$ to 2 inches (1.5 to 5 centimeters) long.
>
> ***Flowers:*** The purplish flower spikes are 6 to 8 inches (15 to 20 centimeters) long. They have bright golden stamens which provide a stunning contrast with the single purple flower petal. Indigo bush blooms in May and June.
>
> ***Fruit:*** The tiny pod, which is $^1/_{10}$ to $^3/_{10}$ inch (3 to 7 centimeters) long, contains one to two seeds.

Range and Habitat: Found in New Mexico, Texas, Arizona to California, north to Wyoming, the eastern United States, and Chihuahua and Sonora, Mexico, from 4,500 to 8,000 feet (1,350 to 2,400 meters) in canyons and along stream banks and washes in the Chihuahuan, Sonoran, and Mojave deserts, the desert grassland, and a wide variety of other habitats.

Hardiness: Zone 4

Planting and Care: Indigo bush is easy to grow from seeds. It must be scarified with a hot water bath before planting. Some sources indicated better germination with a one-month period of cold stratification, although I haven't found this necessary. Indigo bush requires extra watering in arid regions. Seeds and plants are widely available through mail-order sources and at nurseries.

Remarks: Indigo bush is an attractive plant with a wide natural range. It can be grown in the desert areas with other desert trees and shrubs if it receives extra irrigation. One of its main assets in the desert garden is its hardiness, making it a good substitute in areas too cold to grow mesquites and acacias. The flowers are quite striking and will attract butterflies when in bloom.

Indigo bush can be pruned into a small tree by pruning off the lower branches for the first couple years. Being an adaptable plant, it is at home in sandy or clay soils. I have a favorite indigo bush that grows in the Rio Grande

Valley at the edge of an irrigated field from which I collect seed. One year it was mowed down, and I thought that was the end of it. But it came back more vigorous than ever. Since that time I have noticed numerous plants growing along local irrigation ditches that are often mowed as part of their maintenance. Each time the indigo bushes come back. While I think they respond well to selective pruning, I don't think such drastic pruning will be needed in the desert garden!

Species Name: *Atriplex canescens*

Family: Chenopodiaceae (Goosefoot)

Common Name(s): FOUR-WING SALTBUSH, CHAMISO

Description: *Atriplex canescens* is a large, evergreen shrub of the western deserts and grasslands. It is very drought tolerant and cold hardy. Four-wing saltbush grows up to 8 feet (240 centimeters) tall.

Leaves: The small, gray-green leaves are 3/8 to 2 inches (1 to 5 centimeters) long and 1/8 to 1/2 inch (3 millimeters to 1 centimeter) wide.

Flowers: The inconspicuous, yellow-green flowers bloom on male and female plants. Four-wing saltbush blooms from June to September.

Fruit: The fruits have two pairs of papery wings. They are 1/5 to 3/5 inch (6 to 14 millimeters) long. They appear on the plants, usually quite plentifully, in August and September.

Range and Habitat: Found in New Mexico, western and central Texas, Arizona, north to Alberta, Canada, west to the Pacific Coast, south to Baja California to Sonora, Chihuahua, Coahuila, and Zacatecas, Mexico, from sea level to 7,000 feet (2,100 meters) in the Chihuahuan, Sonoran, Mojave, and Great Basin deserts, the desert grassland, and other arid habitats.

Atriplex canescens
Four-wing Saltbush

Hardiness: Zone 4

Planting and Care: Plants and seeds are available throughout the West at nurseries and by mail order. The seeds require a period of dry after-ripening to break down germination inhibitors. Sow the seeds in early spring. As its name indicates, four-wing saltbush can tolerate alkaline, even salty soils. It is one of our most drought-tolerant shrubs and requires no supplemental water after it's established. Somewhat rangy in appearance, it looks better if it is lightly sheared periodically. In fact, it can be planted and pruned as a hedge.

Remarks: To be perfectly honest, it has taken me years to warm up to four-wing saltbush. It doesn't have pretty flowers, it has tiny, nondescript leaves, and it's weedy looking. But I've since come full circle and now consider it one of our most useful desert plants. Its durability under the harshest conditions makes it a good choice for areas with erosion problems and difficult soil conditions, such as excessive alkalinity. Four-wing saltbush is one of the best choices for nonirrigated areas, requiring only a minimal amount of watering to get established.

While it may not be the most beautiful plant in the world (but after all, beauty is in the eye of the beholder), it does have attractive qualities. The seeds on the female plants are very decorative in fall and early winter. They are also a good food for game birds. The light, gray-green foliage persists into winter. Four-wing saltbush is a tough plant that deserves a closer look and a place in the desert garden.

Species Name: *Caesalpinia gilliesii*

Family: Fabaceae (Leguminosae) (Pea); Subfamily: Caesalpinoideae (Bird-of- Paradise)

Common Name(s): BIRD-OF-PARADISE, PARADISE POINCIANA

Description: *Caesalpinia gilliesii* is a shrub or small tree that grows up to 15 feet (460 centimeters) tall, although 4 to 8 feet (120 to 240 centimeters) is the average. Unlike many other legumes, it is thornless. The branches are green, light brown, or reddish and carry on photosynthesis when the plant has shed its leaves.

Leaves: The bipinnate leaves are large, 3 to 5 inches (8 to 13 centimeters) long. The twelve to twenty-four primary leaves are $^3/_4$ to 1 inch (2 to 2.5 centimeters) long. The leaflets are $^1/_8$ to $^3/_{16}$ inch (3 to 5 millimeters) long and are medium green in color.

Flowers: Bird-of-paradise has beautiful long, red stamens up to 4 inches (10 centimeters) long and a light yellow corolla and calyx about $1^1/_4$ inches (3 centimeters) wide. It blooms for most of the summer.

Fruit: The fruit is a large, flat pod 4 inches (10 centimeters) long that splits open and ejects the seed with some force. The large seeds should be collected just before this happens, when the pods become brown and dry.

Range and Habitat: Native of Argentina and Chile, now found in southern New Mexico, Trans-Pecos Texas, and southeastern Arizona up to 6,000 feet (1,800 meters) in washes in the Chihuahuan Desert and desert grassland.

Hardiness: Zone 7

Planting and Care: Bird-of-paradise is widely available at nurseries throughout the Southwest. Seeds and plants are available from mail-order nurseries specializing in southwestern native plants. Since bird-of-paradise is a nitrogen-fixing plant, it requires little or no fertilizing in a garden situation. The plants are very fast growing from seeds, attaining several feet (meters) in height in just a couple of years. The seeds can be planted fresh; however, germination will be enhanced by a hot water bath. Bird-of-paradise may die back to the ground in the coldest winters but recovers quickly in the spring.

Remarks: Bird-of-paradise is a legume and is not to be confused with the tropical bird-of-

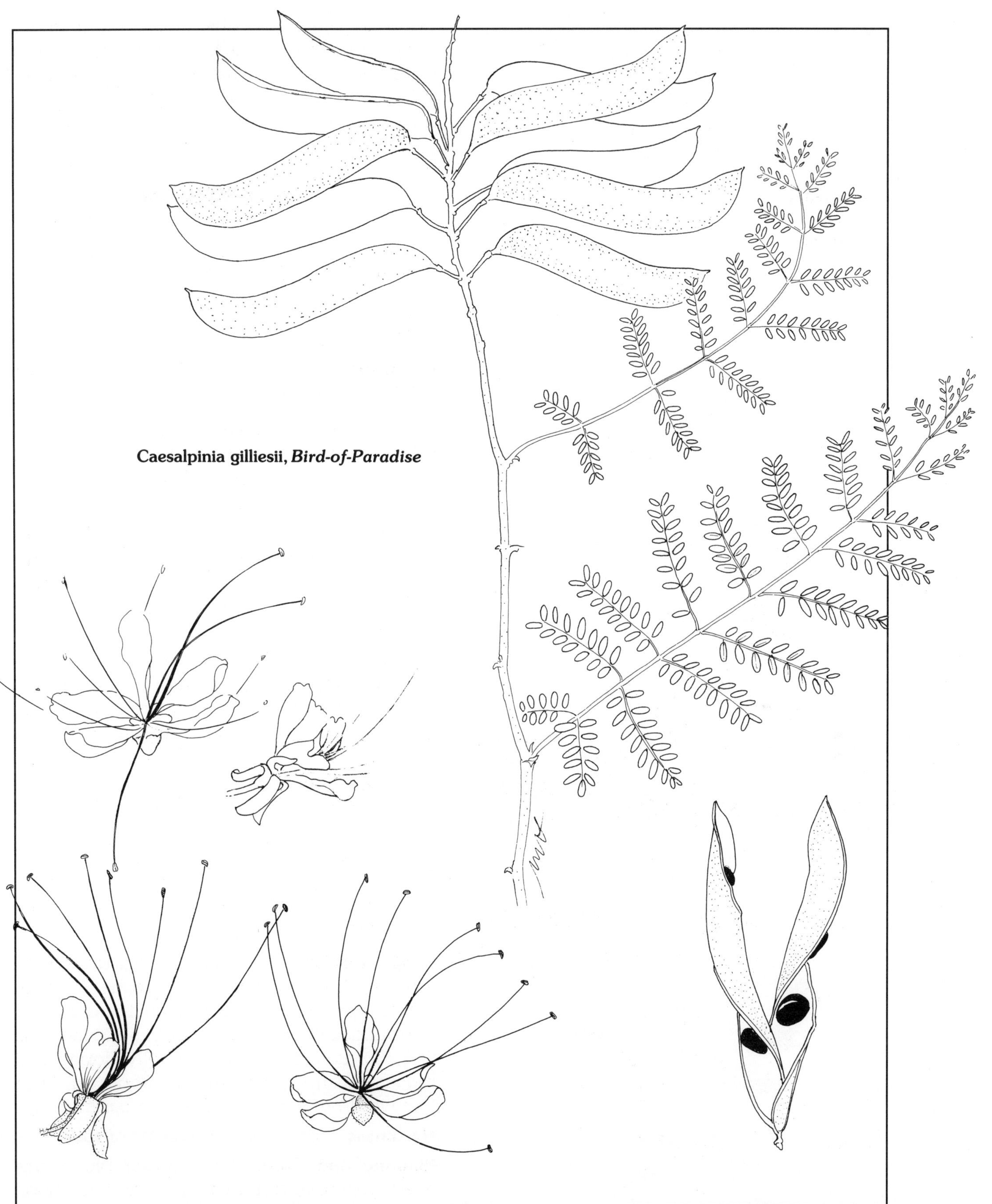

Caesalpinia gilliesii, *Bird-of-Paradise*

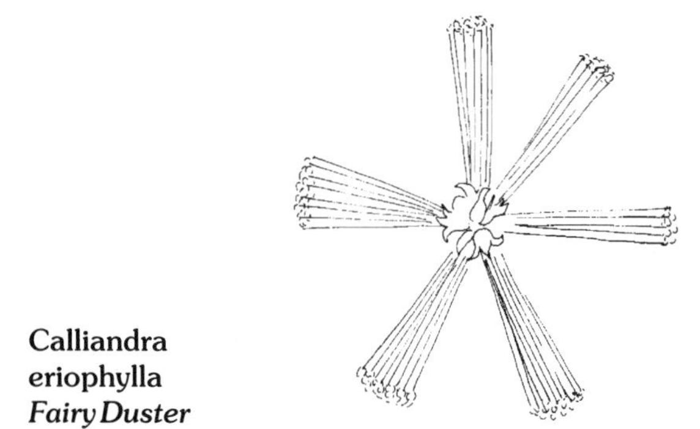

Calliandra eriophylla
Fairy Duster

paradise (*Strelitzia*). It is a good plant where the climate is too cold for acacias or where a desert-type legume without thorns is desired. The very showy flowers add an exotic, tropical-looking touch to the desert garden.

Species Name: *Calliandra eriophylla*

Family: Fabaceae (leguminosae) (Pea); Subfamily: Mimosoideae (Mimosa)

Common Name(s): FAIRY DUSTER, FALSE MESQUITE, HUAJILLO

Description: *Calliandra eriophylla* is a small, bushy shrub known for its pretty pink or purple powder puff flowers.

Leaves: The leaves are 1/4 to 1/2 inch (6 millimeters to 1 centimeter) long. There are usually six primary leaflets and fourteen to eighteen secondary leaflets up to 1/8 inch (3 millimeters) long.

Flowers: The flowers, which are 1 1/4 to 2 inches (3 to 5 centimeters) wide, consist of twenty or more filaments up to 1 inch (2.5 centimeters) long. They are pink or reddish purple and bloom from March to May.

Fruit: The fruit consists of large velvety pods, which are 1 1/2 to 3 inches (4 to 8 centimeters) long and 1/4 inch (6 millimeters) wide. The fruit matures from June to August, containing several gray to black, smooth seeds up to 1/4 inch (6 millimeters) long.

Range and Habitat: Found in central and southern New Mexico, Trans-Pecos Texas, Arizona, California, and Mexico from Sonora and Coahuila to Puebla from 2,000 to 5,000 feet (600 to 1,500 meters) on dry, gravelly slopes and mesas of the Chihuahuan, Sonoran, and Mojave deserts and the desert grassland.

Hardiness: Zone 8, warmer parts of zone 7

Planting and Care: Fairy duster plants are often available at nurseries in the Southwest.

Seeds are sometimes available from mail-order nurseries specializing in southwestern native plants. A hot water bath is the preferred treatment for getting the seeds to germinate. Amazingly enough, the seeds of fairy duster will actually be sprouted in the morning after soaking overnight! Plant them immediately into 1-gallon (3.8-liter) containers. They prefer a lot of room for their roots to grow.

Remarks: Fairy duster is a delightful, small plant for the desert garden. Its bright purple flowers make it among our most attractive desert shrubs. Unlike its relatives, the mimosas and most of the acacias, fairy duster has the added bonus of being thornless. Not only is fairy duster a beautiful ornamental; once established it will be one of the more drought-tolerant plants in a desert garden.

Species Name: *Fallugia paradoxa*

Family: Rosaceae (Rose); Subfamily: Rosoideae (Rose)

Common Name(s): APACHE PLUME, PONIL

Description: *Fallugia paradoxa* is a medium-sized, multibranched, semievergreen shrub that grows 3 to 8 feet (90 to 240 centimeters) tall. The word *paradox* in its botanical name is due to the unusual habit of this plant to produce both flowers and fruits at the same time.

> ***Leaves:*** The very small leaves are triangular shaped with three to seven deep lobes. They are dark green with a reddish, pubescent underside and grow 1/4 to 1/2 inch (5 to 10 millimeters) long.
>
> ***Flowers:*** The five-petaled, white flowers are something like an old-fashioned rose and are 1 to 1 1/3 inches (2.5 to 3 centimeters) wide. They bloom from May to October.
>
> ***Fruit:*** The fruit of Apache plume is perhaps even more attractive than its flowers. It is an achene, that is, a dry fruit that does not split open when ripe and contains a single seed. It is attached to a long, showy, delicate plume. The achenes are 1/8 inch (2.5 millimeters) long, and the plumes are 1 to 2 inches (2.5 to 5 centimeters) long. The common name Apache plume is derived from the clusters of these long-tailed, pinkish, feathery fruits which resemble an Apache Indian headdress.

Range and Habitat: Found in New Mexico, southern Colorado, West Texas, Arizona, southern California, southern Utah, southern Nevada, and northern Mexico from 3,000 to 8,000 feet (900 to 2,400 meters) on gravelly or rocky slopes and dry arroyos in the Chihuahuan, Sonoran, and Mojave deserts, the desert grassland, pinyon-juniper woodland, and other habitats.

Hardiness: Zone 4

Planting and Care: Seeds and plants of Apache plume are widely available at nurseries throughout the Southwest and by mail order from several sources. It is easily grown from seeds, which require no special treatment. The seedlings grow fast and will even flower the first year from seeds if started early in the year. Apache plume is very hardy and very drought tolerant. In fact, overwatering can ruin its appearance, causing it to become lanky and weedy.

Remarks: Apache plume is a favorite ornamental in the Southwest due to its white flowers and showy, feathery fruit. In the landscape, it has many uses, both as a background plant and as an accent plant. It also works well as a windbreak and in controlling erosion.

Fallugia paradoxa • *page 172* ▶

Fallugia paradoxa, *Apache Plume*

Species: *Fendlera rupicola*

Family: Saxifragaceae (Saxifrage)

Common Name(s): CLIFF FENDLERBUSH

Description: *Fendlera rupicola* is a small shrub found in the foothills and canyons of mountain ranges in the desert and elsewhere. It grows from 4 to 6 feet (120 to 180 centimeters) tall.

Leaves: The small, dark green leaves grow 3/8 to 5/8 inch (10 to 15 millimeters) long.

Flowers: The sweet-scented, white flowers are 1 to 2 inches (2.5 to 5 centimeters) wide. These four-petaled flowers bloom in May and June.

Fruit: The fruit is a four-celled capsule. The seeds are 1/3 to 1/4 inch (5 to 6 millimeters) long.

Range and Habitat: Found in New Mexico, central and western Texas, Colorado, Utah, Arizona, and Chihuahua, Mexico, from 3,000 to 7,000 feet (900 to 2,100 meters) on rocky slopes and cliffs in the mountains of the Southwest, including those in the Chihuahuan Desert region.

Hardiness: Zone 4

Planting and Care: Seeds and plants are available at nurseries in the Southwest and through mail-order sources. The seeds are easily germinated following cold stratification of two to three months. The seeds can also be planted in the ground in the fall for germination the following spring. Cliff fendlerbush can also be grown from softwood cuttings. In lower elevations it requires extra watering; however, it is relatively drought tolerant and should be planted in well-drained soils. Prune it occasionally to keep it from getting too scraggly.

Remarks: Cliff fendlerbush is a small shrub well suited to today's smaller yards. In spring its showy flowers make it useful as an accent plant. The species name *rupicola* means "lover of rocks." Because it's thornless, cliff fendlerbush is a good choice for planting near patios and other areas where people congregate. Its fragrance will perfume the air nearby.

Fendlera rupicola
Cliff Fendlerbush

Species Name: *Larrea tridentata*

Family: Zygophyllaceae (Caltrop)

Common Name(s): CREOSOTE BUSH, CHAPARRAL, GREASEWOOD, HEDIONDILLA, GOBERNADORA

Description: *Larrea tridentata* is an evergreen shrub that grows up to 12 feet (360 centimeters) high, although it is usually much shorter, averaging 3 to 5 feet (90 to 150 centimeters). It is the most common and widespread shrub of the southwestern deserts, being found in practically pure stands in some parts of the region. Clones of creosote bush are among the oldest living things on earth.

Leaves: The small, bright green leaves occur in pairs joined at the base. They are 1/5 to 2/5 inch (5 to 10 millimeters) long.

Flowers: The tiny yellow flowers, which are 1/2 inch (1 centimeter) wide, have five petals. Creosote bush flowers intermittently during the growing season, particularly after rains, although its blooming period is from April through June. The flowers are primarily pollinated by bees, several species of which are entirely dependent on the nectar and pollen of creosote bush.

Fruit: The fruit of creosote bush is a small, rounded capsule that is covered with fuzzy white hairs. The fruit is about 1/5 inch (5 millimeters) in diameter and is divided into five hard carpels that contain one seed within each chamber.

Range and Habitat: Found in central and southern New Mexico, Trans-Pecos Texas, southern, central, and western Arizona, southern California, southern Nevada, southwestern Utah, and Mexico south to Durango below 6,000 feet (1,800 meters) on a variety of soils on sandy or gravelly slopes and mesas in the Chihuahuan, Sonoran, and Mojave deserts and the surrounding desert grassland.

Hardiness: Zone 7

Planting and Care: Creosote bush is often available as plants and sometimes as seeds at nurseries in the desert Southwest. It is offered by a few mail-order sources specializing in native plants of the Southwest. Creosote bush is easy to grow once it has been established, existing on harsh, hot, and dry sites where care will be minimal. Creosote bush is very difficult to transplant from the wild, and unfortunately it is equally difficult to start from seeds. The hard seed coat needs to be scarified by one of the following means: pricked with a pin, or worn down with sandpaper or acid scarification. After scarification, soak the seeds overnight and sow them the next day in a flat containing well-drained soil. The seeds will germinate sporadically over the course of the growing season.

Remarks: Creosote bush's aromatic fragrance is particularly strong after it rains; in fact, it is one of those sensory characteristics that make our deserts unique in our remembrances of the arid Southwest. In the desert creosote bush is so evenly spaced that various theories have been proposed to explain this, such as a chemical inhibitor being produced by the plant to suppress other plants. However, it seems more likely that the roots of creosote bush are so efficient at extracting water from the soil that nothing else can grow near it. This is something to consider when planting it in the landscape. Used as an accent plant or in groups, creosote bush will bring the fragrance of the desert to your garden.

Species Name: *Psorothamnus scoparia* (*Dalea scoparia*)

Family: Fabaceae (Leguminosae) (Pea); Subfamily: Papilionoideae (Bean)

Common Name(s): BROOM DALEA, PURPLE SAGE

Description: *Psorothamnus scoparia* is a collection of blue-green stems with very tiny leaves. Following spring or summer rains, it turns into a spectacular desert display of bluish purple, flower-covered shrubs. It grows 2 to 4 feet (60 to 120 centimeters) tall and wide.

Leaves: The minute blue-green leaves are 1/4 to 3/4 inch (6 to 20 millimeters) long.

Flowers: Broom dalea has purple flowers that are 1/2 inch (1 centimeter) wide. They appear in clusters in June and again in August and September during the summer monsoon season.

Fruit: The fruit is a small capsule that grows 1/8 inch (3 millimeters) long.

Range and Habitat: Found in central New Mexico, Trans-Pecos Texas, southeastern Arizona, and Chihuahua and Coahuila, Mexico, from 2,000 to 6,000 feet (600 to 1,800 meters) on sandy soils and dunes in the Chihuahuan Desert and the desert grassland.

Hardiness: Zone 7

Planting and Care: Finding seeds and plants of broom dalea for sale is difficult. Plants are occasionally offered in nurseries specializing in southwestern native plants. You'll probably have to collect seeds in the fall and start your own plants. The seeds germinate rapidly. Broom dalea is very drought tolerant and requires sandy, well-drained soils to survive and grow well.

Remarks: Broom dalea is native to the Rio Grande Valley from El Paso, Texas, to just north of Albuquerque, New Mexico, where it is often found in association with Indian rice grass and bush penstemon. When it's at its fullest bloom after the summer rains, this shrub, which normally goes unnoticed, suddenly catches everyone's eye. Because of its purple flowers and blue-green foliage, broom dalea is often called purple sage, although it is neither a true sage (*Salvia*) nor a sagebrush (*Artemesia*). Regardless of what you call it, broom dalea is a great plant for sandy soils.

Species Name: *Rhus microphylla*

Family: Anacardiaceae (Cashew)

Common Name(s): LITTLE-LEAF SUMAC, DESERT SUMAC, AGRITOS

Description: *Rhus microphylla* is a large, deciduous shrub that can grow 8 to 15 feet (240 to 450 centimeters) tall, though 4 to 6 feet (120 to 180 centimeters) is common; and although it can be up to 40 feet (1,200 centimeters) wide, 8 feet (240 centimeters) is a more typical width.

Leaves: The leaves, which are 2 inches (5 centimeters) long, are composed of five to nine leaflets that are only 1/4 inch (6 millimeters) in length, hence the common name little-leaf sumac.

Flowers: The tiny, whitish flowers, which are 1/8 inch (3 millimeters) wide, appear in the spring before the foliage. They occur in clusters which measure 2 to 4 inches (5 to 10 centimeters) and cover the shrub.

Fruit: The fuzzy, orange to bright red fruits, which are 1/4 inch (6 millimeters) long, occur in clusters from late summer into fall.

Range and Habitat: Found in central New Mexico; southern, western, eastern, and central Texas; southeastern Arizona; and northern Mexico from 2,000 to 6,000 feet (600 to 1,800 meters) on sandy or gravelly hills and mesas of the Chihuahuan and upper Sonoran deserts, the desert grassland, and Great Plains grasslands.

Hardiness: Zone 7

Planting and Care: Little-leaf sumac is occasionally offered as plants by nurseries specializing in native plants of the Southwest. Seeds are rarely available for sale. You'll most likely need to collect them yourself. The sumacs require scarification or after-ripening (given one or more years of storage) of the seeds followed by three months of cold stratification. Once planted in pots, the seedlings are rapid growers. Because little-leaf sumac grows to a large size, be sure to give it ample space in the garden.

Remarks: Little-leaf sumac is also known as desert sumac because of its ability to grow under arid conditions. The flowers are pretty, but the bright red fruits are the real attraction. They can literally cover the bush in masses of berry clusters. They are eaten by many kinds of wildlife, including birds and rodents. Little-leaf sumac is a good shrub for a hedge. Requiring minimal amounts of water and care, little-leaf sumac is the perfect plant for the desert garden. This is especially true for those who want a low-maintenance landscape in the arid Southwest.

Related Species: The desert sumacs are a varied group of shrubs with many desirable qualities as garden ornamentals. Three-leaf sumac, agrillo (*Rhus trilobata*), is a fast-growing shrub with very attractive foliage, especially in the fall when the leaves turn

Rhus microphylla • *page 176* ▶

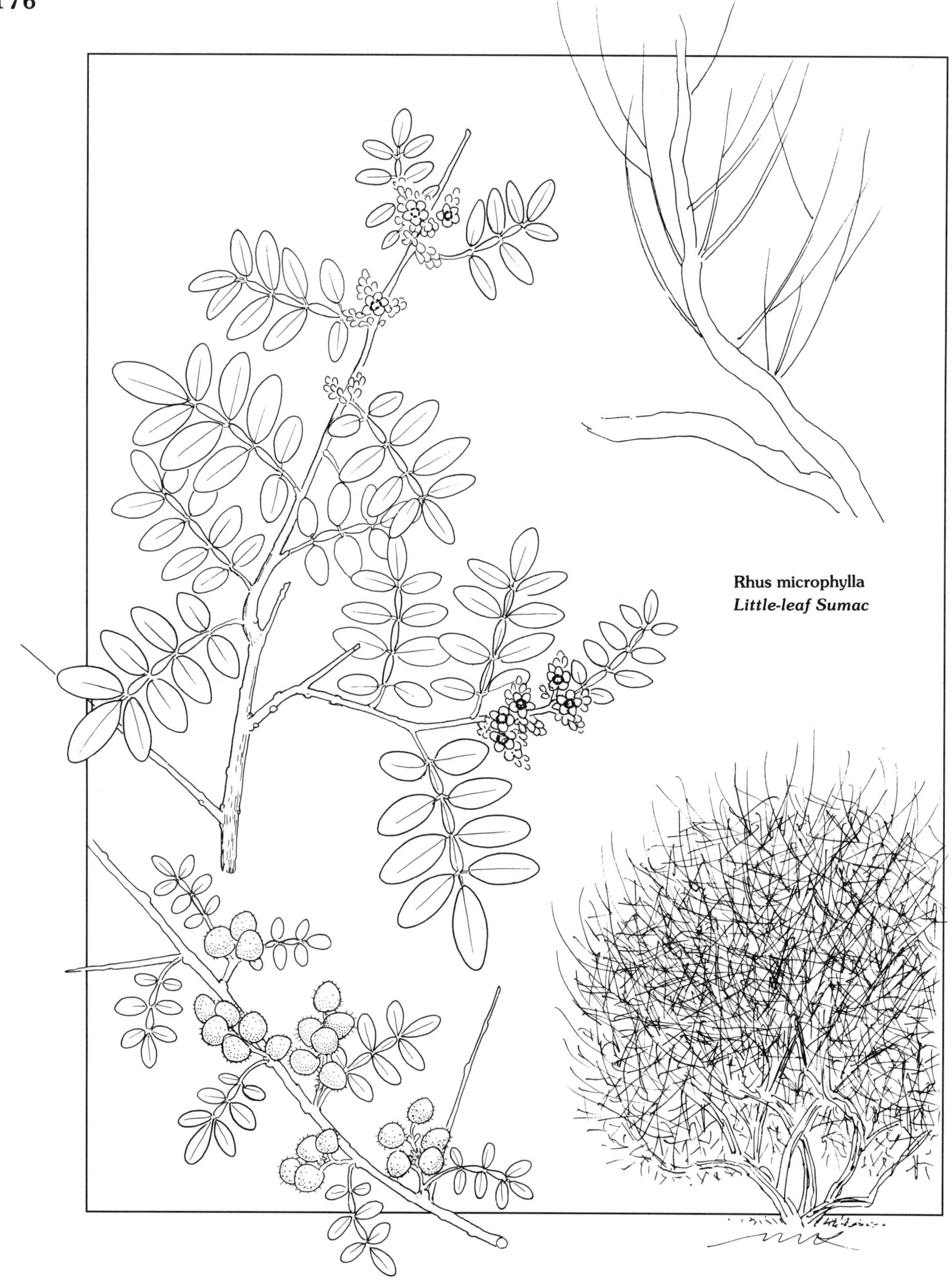
Rhus microphylla
Little-leaf Sumac

various shades of orange and red. The whitish flowers are 1/8 inch (2.5 millimeters) long and bloom from March into June. Hardiness: Zone 4.

Prairie flame-leaf sumac (*Rhus lanceolata*) grows into a medium-sized tree with beautiful fall color. The greenish white flowers are 1/8 inch (2.5 millimeters) long and bloom from June into August. It's an ideal tree for small areas and lots. Hardiness: Zone 7.

Evergreen sumac, zumaque (*Rhus virens*), is a very attractive shrub due to its evergreen nature. The white flowers are slightly larger than 1/8 inch (3 millimeters) long and bloom in July and August. It is less cold hardy than the previously mentioned, deciduous sumacs. Hardiness: Zone 8.

All the sumacs listed here have red fruits that are very attractive to wildlife.

Species Name: *Senna wislizenii* (*Cassia wislizenii*)

Family: Fabaceae (Leguminosae) (Pea); Subfamily: Caesalpinoideae (Bird-of- Paradise)

Common Name(s): SHRUBBY SENNA

Description: *Senna wislizenii* is a shrubby senna of the Chihuahuan Desert with bright yellow flowers 1½ inches (4 centimeters) wide. It grows from 4 to 9 feet (120 to 360 centimeters) tall.

Leaves: The dark green foliage consists of four to six tiny, oblong leaflets per leaf that grow from 1/5 to 1/3 inch (5 to 8 millimeters) long.

Flowers: The clusters of five-petaled yellow flowers are 1½ inches (4 centimeters)

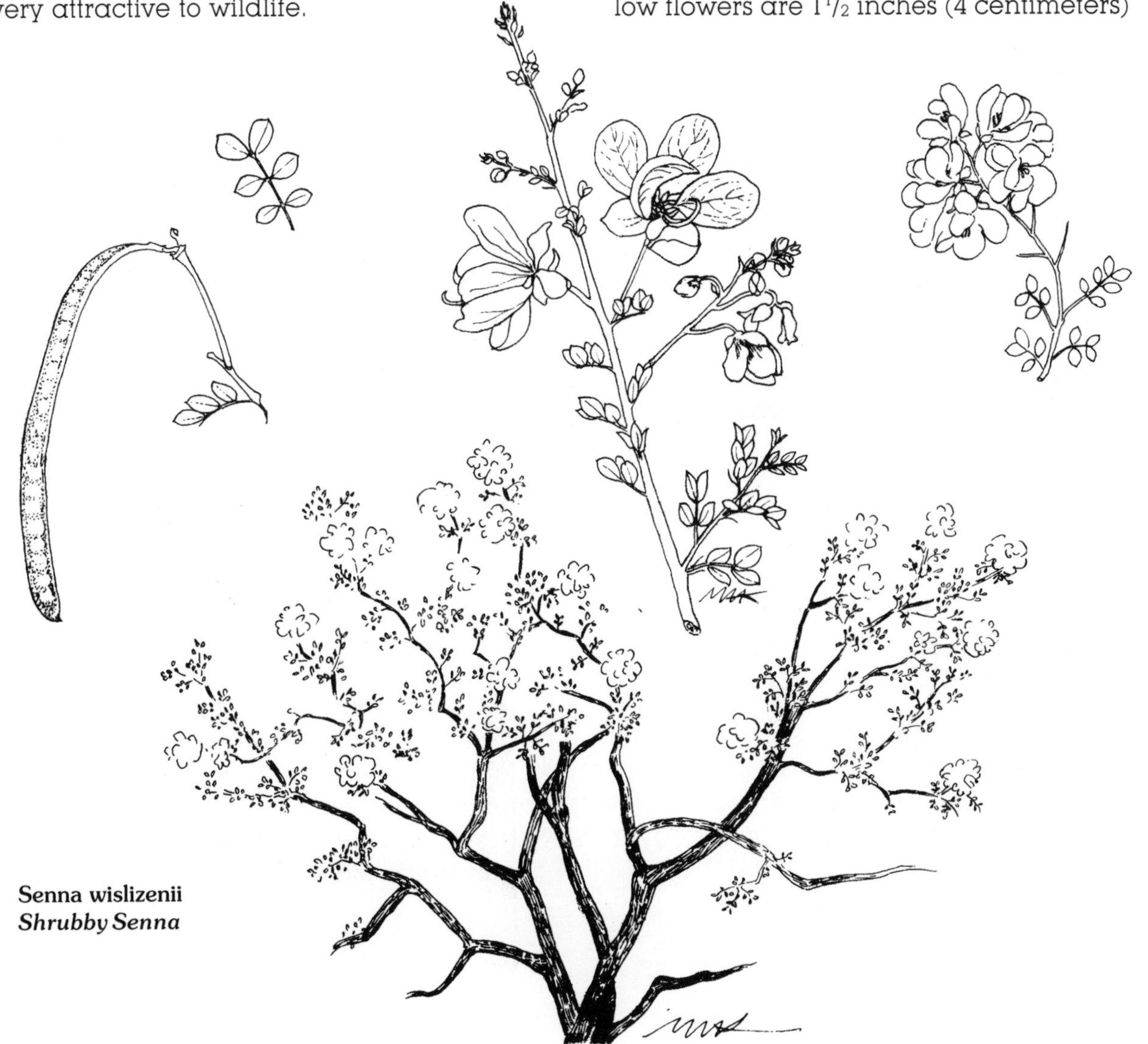

Senna wislizenii
Shrubby Senna

wide and bloom all summer from May to September.

Fruit: The shiny black fruit is a pod which is 2 3/4 to 4 inches (7 to 10 centimeters) long.

Range and Habitat: Found in southwestern New Mexico, southeastern Arizona, Trans-Pecos Texas, and northern Mexico up to 6,000 feet (1,800 meters) on dry, rocky slopes and mesas in the Chihuahuan Desert and desert grassland.

Hardiness: Zone 8

Planting and Care: Plants are often available at nurseries throughout the desert Southwest. Although seeds are sometimes listed by mail-order seed companies in the area, it is more likely that you will need to collect your own seeds if you want to start your own plants. The seeds don't require any special treatment; however, like most legumes, they should be planted in deep containers, as shrubby senna has a fast-growing taproot. It requires full sun in the garden.

Remarks: Shrubby senna is a bright, cheery bush that is drought tolerant. In nature it blooms after periods of rainfall. When covered with yellow blossoms, shrubby senna is an outstanding attraction in the landscape.

Species Name: *Sophora secundiflora*

Family: Fabaceae (Leguminosae) (Pea); Subfamily: Papilionoideae (Bean)

Common Name(s): TEXAS MOUNTAIN LAUREL, FRIJOLILLO, MESCAL BEAN

Description: *Sophora secundiflora* is a beautiful evergreen shrub or small tree that grows up to 15 feet (450 centimeters) tall. The fragrant, purple flowers cover the shrub in early spring.

Leaves: The dark green leaves are 4 to 6 inches (10 to 15 centimeters) long. There are five to thirteen leaflets 1 to 2 1/2 inches (2.5 to 6 centimeters) long and 1/2 to 1 1/2 inches (1 to 3.5 centimeters) wide.

Flowers: The flowers hang in clusters 3 to 7 inches (8 to 18 centimeters) long. Texas mountain laurel blooms in March and April.

Fruit: The fruit is a large bean 1 to 5 inches (2.5 to 13 centimeters) long. The bright red seeds are 1/2 inch (1 centimeter) long and poisonous.

Range and Habitat: Found in southeastern New Mexico, Texas, and northern Mexico from sea level to 5,000 feet (1,500 meters) on limestone hills and soils in the Chihuahuan Desert and other habitats.

Hardiness: Zone 8, warmer parts of zone 7

Planting and Care: Seeds are available by mail order and at nurseries in the Southwest. Plants are also available at regional nurseries where Texas mountain laurel is hardy. The hard seed coat must be penetrated in order to allow water to reach the seed's embryo. Mechanical scarification of the seeds by nicking them, a hot water bath, or a combination of the two is required for germination. Sow in large containers such as 1 gallon (3.8 liters) or bigger to accommodate the large root system.

Texas mountain laurel's major drawback is that this otherwise gorgeous landscape specimen is only hardy down to 15°F (9°C). It is relatively slow growing, and extra watering will help promote faster growth and better health in the desert garden. It can be selectively pruned into a small tree.

Remarks: Texas mountain laurel has drooping, wisterialike clusters of flowers that are fragrant with the scent of grapes. This is an excellent accent shrub or tree for use around patios, foundations, or as a hedge. The glossy, dark green leaves make Texas mountain laurel a handsome plant year-round.

DESERT TREES

Primarily found along washes, arroyos, and other waterways, desert trees tend to be small in stature, sometimes nothing more than large shrubs. This tendency makes them a good choice for the small lots common today.

The majority of these trees have showy flowers. Not only does this make them attractive garden choices, but it usually means less pollen and, therefore, less likelihood of creating problems for allergy suffers. Trees with conspicuous flowers are usually insect- or hummingbird-pollinated and, therefore, have no need to produce and release large amounts of pollen into the air. Trees with inconspicuous flowers usually produce large amounts of pollen, which is carried from plant to plant on the wind. The pollen is also carried to the noses and eyes of those susceptible to hay fever.

Two desert trees, netleaf hackberry and western soapberry, get quite large and are, therefore, good for shade. Some of the smaller trees, such as desert willow, can also be used for light shade once they have attained some age and height. Other uses for desert trees include windbreaks, revegetation, screening out unsightly views, and as accent plants.

Trees are the largest plants in the desert garden. It is important to remember this when planting them, especially when they are small seedlings. It is always a pleasure to see mature trees that were correctly placed when planted.

Desert trees can provide shade for other desert plants. In nature they often shelter seedlings of young cacti. Such a tree is called a nurse plant. In the garden they can shelter small cacti such as mammillarias or young seedling barrel cacti. Desert trees not only provide shelter for plants but also for people. Now they can inspire us with their beauty and endurance.

Species Name: *Acacia greggii*

Family: Fabaceae (Leguminosae) (Pea); Subfamily: Mimosoideae (Mimosa)

Common Name(s): CATCLAW ACACIA, UNA DE GATO

Description: *Acacia greggii* usually grows as a shrub; however, it can grow into a tree up to 30 feet (900 centimeters) tall. Its common name, catclaw acacia, is derived from its curved, catclawlike prickles.

Leaves: The leaves are 1 to 3 inches (2.5 to 8 centimeters) long. There are usually two to six primary leaflets and six to fourteen secondary leaflets up to $^{1}/_{4}$ inch (6 millimeters) long.

Flowers: The fragrant, pale yellow flowers are about $^{1}/_{2}$ inch (1 centimeter) wide and up to $2^{1}/_{2}$ inches (6 centimeters) long. Catclaw acacia blooms between April and October, depending upon the temperature and rainfall.

Fruit: The fruit consists of large beans, which are 2 to 5 inches (5 to 13 centimeters) long and $^{3}/_{4}$ inch (2 centimeters) wide. The dark brown seeds are flat and circular shaped.

Range and Habitat: Found in central and southern New Mexico, Trans-Pecos Texas to the Gulf Coast, southern and western Arizona, southern Nevada, southwestern Utah, southern California, Baja California, Sonora, Chihuahua, and Coahuila, Mexico, from sea level to 5,000 feet (1,500 meters) on gravelly slopes and along washes in the Chihuahuan Desert, desert grassland, Sonoran Desert, Mojave Desert, and other habitats.

Hardiness: Zone 7

Acacia greggii • *page 180* ▶

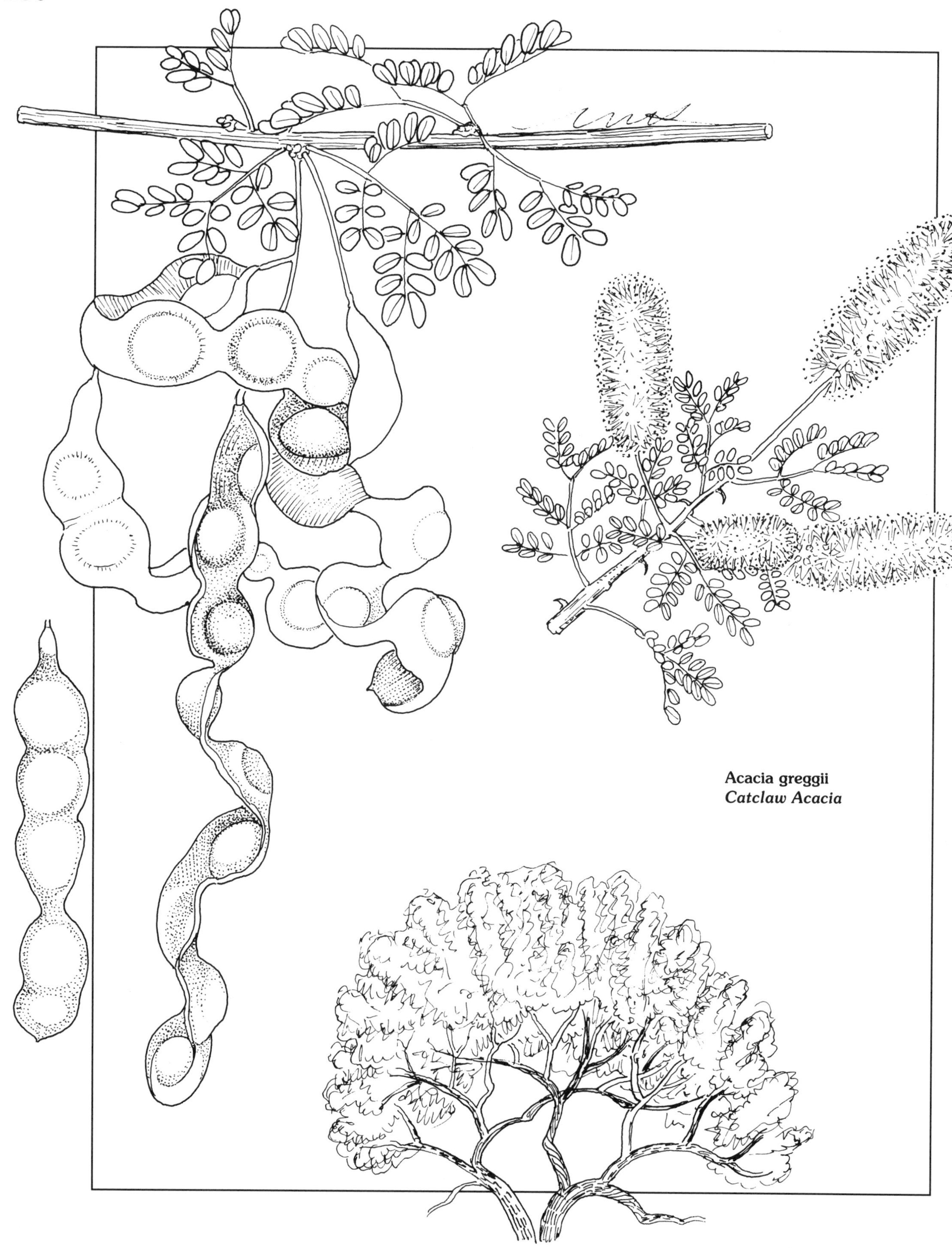
Acacia greggii
Catclaw Acacia

Planting and Care: Catclaw acacia is often found as plants in nurseries in the desert Southwest. Seeds are available from southwestern mail-order sources. As with other legumes, a hot water bath is the easiest treatment for getting the seeds to germinate. Growth is rapid. Catclaw acacia is one of the most cold hardy of the acacias. It is a good idea to grow plants started from seeds in containers for planting the following season. Protect young plants over the winter in a greenhouse or other warm location. Larger plants planted in late spring or early summer are more likely to survive in colder areas.

Be sure to plant catclaw acacia in an area where people aren't likely to brush up against the prickles. Given full sun and an occasional watering, catclaw acacia will quickly become a handsome specimen addition to your desert garden.

Remarks: Catclaw acacia is a plant of many uses. From time to time it has been used for fuel wood, as a bee plant for honey, and its seeds as food. Native Americans of the Southwest ground the seed into a meal to which they added water. The resulting mush was known as *pinole*.

Species Name: *Arbutus texana*

Family: Ericaceae (Heath)

Common Name(s): TEXAS MADRONE, MADRONO

Description: *Arbutus texana* is a small tree, usually multitrunked, which grows 20 to 30 feet (600 to 900 centimeters) tall. In the woodlands where it grows, Texas madrone is easily spotted by its smooth bark, which changes from a cream color to a dark red with age.

Leaves: The evergreen leaves are 1 to 3 inches (2.5 to 8 centimeters) long and up to an inch (2.5 centimeters) wide. They are dark green, thick, and leathery.

Flowers: The tiny, white to pale pink flowers, which are 1/2 inch (1 centimeter) long, are borne on clusters about 2 1/2 inches (6 centimeters) long. Texas madrone blooms in February and March.

Fruit: The red fruit, which is 1/4 to 1/3 inch (6 to 8 millimeters) wide, is borne in clusters on the tree. Inside there are many small, white seeds.

Range and Habitat: Found in southeastern New Mexico, central and Trans-Pecos Texas south through Mexico to Guatemala from 4,500 to 6,500 feet (1,350 to 1,950 meters) on limestone or volcanic soils in wooded, rocky canyons from the Chihuahuan Desert into the mountain woodlands.

Hardiness: Zone 7

Planting and Care: As plants, Texas madrone is becoming more available at nurseries in the Southwest, especially in Texas and New Mexico. Seeds are hard to find, and it's best to collect your own. Texas madrone is difficult to get started from seeds. The seeds should be sown in containers shortly after ripening or they will need cold stratifying for spring sowing. The seedlings are subject to damping off. Try using a biodegradable fungicide or garlic powder as a preventive. When transplanting Texas madrone into the garden, be sure to give it plenty of water until it is well established. This can take up to five years.

Remarks: Texas madrone is an outstanding ornamental. It has very attractive bark. The outer, papery skin peels away each year. The new bark is cream colored but changes through various shades to a beautiful, dark reddish brown. Hardy, broad-leaved evergreens such as Texas madrone are valued for their foliage during the winter season. While the flowers are attractive, it is the bright red clusters of fruit that steal the show.

Texas madrone is a woodland plant that barely enters the edges of the Chihuahuan Desert where the mountain canyons and washes empty into the lowland desert. As such,

Arbutus texana • *page 182* ▶

Arbutus texana
Texas Madrone

it needs extra watering in the desert garden. Texas madrone is one of the most beautiful trees in the world. Use it as a focal point to add a unique touch to your garden.

Species Name: *Celtis reticulata* (*Celtis laevigata* var. *reticulata*)

Family: Ulmaceae (Elm)

Common Name(s): NETLEAF HACKBERRY, PALO BLANCO

Description: *Celtis reticulata* is a large, deciduous shrub or medium-sized tree of riparian areas and desert washes. It can grow up to 30 to 50 feet (900 to 1,500 centimeters) tall.

> ***Leaves:*** The yellowish green saw-toothed leaves are $1^1/_8$ to $2^1/_4$ inches (3 to 6 centimeters) long and $^1/_2$ to $1^1/_2$ inches (1 to 4 centimeters) wide.
>
> ***Flowers:*** The small greenish yellow flowers are inconspicuous when they bloom in the spring. They are $^1/_{25}$ to $^3/_{25}$ inch (1 to 3 millimeters) in diameter.
>
> ***Fruit:*** The fruit, known as a hackberry, is actually a drupe (a fleshy fruit surrounding a seed). It is about $^1/_4$ inch (6 millimeters) in diameter.

Range and Habitat: Found in New Mexico, Oklahoma, Colorado, Texas, Arizona, California, and south into Mexico from 2,500 to 6,000 feet (750 to 1,800 meters) along streams and in canyons of the Chihuahuan, Sonoran, and Mojave deserts, the desert grassland, and other habitats.

Hardiness: Zone 6

Planting and Care: Netleaf hackberry is rarely offered by nurseries as either seeds or plants. Collect the berries in late summer and fall, and cold stratify the seeds over the winter outdoors or in the refrigerator. Netleaf hackberry is a fast-growing tree when given the extra water it needs.

Remarks: The berries were eaten by Native Americans of the area. They are also a favorite food for songbirds, especially if fermenting occurs during the fall.

Netleaf hackberry is one of the few trees we have in the Chihuahuan Desert region that reaches a fairly large size. As such, its cooling shade is a valued addition to our desert landscapes.

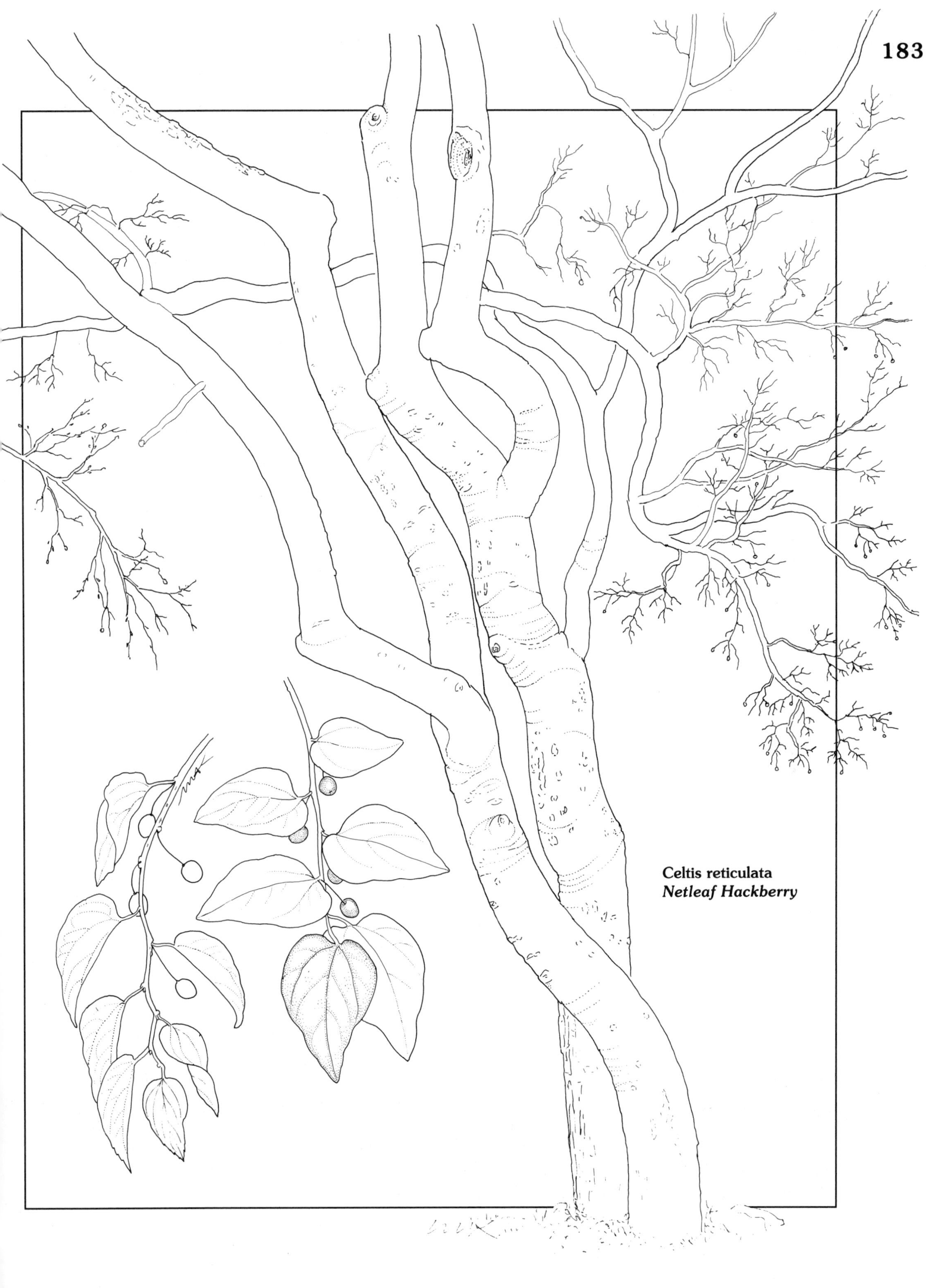

Celtis reticulata
Netleaf Hackberry

Chilopsis linearis
Desert Willow

Species Name: *Chilopsis linearis*

Family: Bignoniaceae (Trumpet-creeper)

Common Name(s): DESERT WILLOW, MIMBRE, FLOR DE MIMBRE, DESERT CATALPA

Description: *Chilopsis linearis* is a large shrub or small tree that can grow up to 25 feet (750 centimeters) or more tall. It is usually multitrunked, although it can be pruned to a single trunk.

Leaves: The bright green, linear leaves grow up to 3 to 6 inches (8 to 15 centimeters) long and 3/8 inch (1 centimeter) wide. The leaves resemble those of a willow; however, desert willow is not a willow at all. It is a member of the same family as the familiar catalpa tree.

Flowers: The flowers are one of the reasons desert willow has become a very popular ornamental in the Southwest. The purple to pink to pure white flowers resemble orchids. They are sweet-scented, 1 to 1 1/4 inches (2.5 to 3 centimeters) long, and tubular; they bloom in May and June and periodically after summer rains.

Fruit: The seed capsules are very long, 4 to 8 inches (10 to 20 centimeters), and 1/4 inch (6 millimeters) wide. The slender pods split along the sides when the seeds are ripe.

Range and Habitat: Found in central and southern New Mexico, central and Trans-Pecos Texas, southern Arizona, southern California, and northern Mexico from 1,500 to 5,000 feet (450 to 1,500 meters) along arid desert washes and dry arroyos in the Chihuahuan and Sonoran deserts, desert grassland, and other habitats.

Hardiness: Zone 7

Planting and Care: Since it has become such a standard in the nursery trade here, desert willow is sold at nurseries throughout the Southwest. Seeds are easy to purchase, or they can be collected when the pods dry in the fall. It is easily propagated from seeds, which need no special pretreatment and can be sown as any other seeds. With extra watering, the seedlings grow rapidly, and if started early, desert willow will bloom the first year from seed. Once they are established, the trees can withstand considerable drought.

Remarks: Desert willow is one of the best native plants in many ways. Its lovely flowers are attractive to both humans and wildlife, particularly hummingbirds. The flowers also attract bees and make good honey. Desert willow is useful for windbreaks, erosion control, and blocking out unwanted views. Its light shade makes this small tree a wonderful plant for sitting under on a hot summer's day.

Related Species: Yellow bells, tornadora (*Tecoma stans* var. *angustata*), is a shrubby relative of desert willow. As its name implies, it has bright yellow, trumpet-shaped flowers which bloom from April through November when given extra waterings. This drought-tolerant native of southern New Mexico, Trans-Pecos Texas, Arizona, and Mexico is more tender than desert willow. It will freeze to the ground in cold winters but grows back quickly in the spring and flowers the same season. Yellow bells is a striking addition to any desert garden. Hardiness: Zone 8.

Species Name: *Forestiera neomexicana*

Family: Oleaceae (Ash)

Common Name(s): DESERT OLIVE, NEW MEXICO OLIVE, NEW MEXICO PRIVET, PALO BLANCO

Description: *Forestiera neomexicana* is an attractive, bright green deciduous shrub or small tree that grows up to 15 feet (450 centimeters) tall and 10 feet (300 centimeters) wide. It has pretty gray to whitish bark.

Leaves: The leaves are 1/2 to 1 1/2 inches (1 to 3.5 centimeters) long and 1/4 to 3/4 inch (6 to 20 millimeters) wide. They turn a pretty yellow in the fall.

Flowers: The inconspicuous yellow to cream-colored flowers have no petals. Male and female flowers are borne on separate plants. Desert olive blooms from March into May.

Fruit: The blue-black berry grows 1/5 to 1/3 inch (5 to 8 millimeters) long. It matures on female plants from June into September.

Range and Habitat: Found in New Mexico, central and Trans-Pecos Texas, Arizona, southwestern Colorado, southeastern Utah, southern California, and Chihuahua, central and northern Coahuila, and Baja California, Mexico, from 3,000 to 7,000 feet (900 to 2,100 meters) along streams and on mesas and hillsides in the Chihuahuan and Mojave deserts, the desert grassland, and various woodlands.

Hardiness: Zone 4

Planting and Care: Seeds and plants are widely available at nurseries and by mail order. The seeds will germinate easily following one month of cold stratification. They can also be planted in the fall to achieve the same results. If seeds are old, a hot water bath before stratifying may increase germination. The plants grow rapidly when young. They will require supplemental irrigation during their lifetimes in areas with less than 10 to 20 inches (25 to 50 centimeters) of yearly precipitation. Occasional fertilizing with nitrogen will stimulate the growth of young plants.

Desert olive is also known as New Mexico privet since it can be sheared into a mounded form or hedge. To maintain it as a tree, desert olive can be trained by pruning young trees into multitrunked specimens.

Remarks: Desert olive is a versatile landscape plant. Its bright green foliage is unusual for normally olive or gray-green desert plants. Use it as a background plant or as a specimen plant or focal point in its own right. Desert olive is a good choice for erosion control along arroyos and other riparian areas. With irrigation it is useful for windbreaks and for screening out unwanted views.

As wildlife habitat it provides cover and blue-black fruit that is relished by birds. In

Forestiera neomexicana • *page 186* ▶

Forestiera neomexicana
Desert Olive

cold winter areas of the Southwest and elsewhere, it is a good substitute for creosote bush; however, desert olive is deciduous.

For all of these reasons it has become a popular ornamental in the Albuquerque and Santa Fe areas. Desert olive is well on its way to becoming a standard in the nursery industry in the Southwest.

Species Name: *Fraxinus cuspidata*

Family: Oleaceae (Ash)

Common Name(s): FRAGRANT ASH, FRESNO

Description: *Fraxinus cuspidata* is a small deciduous tree growing 10 to 20 feet (300 to 600 centimeters) tall and 8 feet (240 centimeters) wide. It is unusual for an ash in that it has fragrant flowers and petals.

> ***Leaves:*** The dark green leaves, which are 3 to 5½ inches (8 to 14 centimeters) long, are divided into five to seven leaflets.
>
> ***Flowers:*** The fragrant, four-petaled flowers are ½ inch (1 centimeter) wide. The white blossoms occur in clusters 2 to 4 inches (5 to 10 centimeters) long in April and May.
>
> ***Fruit:*** The fruit is a typical ash samara, a wing and seed together, ¾ to 1¼ inches (2 to 3 centimeters) long.

Range and Habitat: Found in New Mexico, Arizona, Trans-Pecos Texas, and Chihuahua, Coahuila, and Nuevo León, Mexico, from 2,400 to 7,000 feet (1,050 to 1,650 meters) on dry, well-drained soils of mountains and canyons in the Chihuahuan Desert region and other habitats.

Hardiness: Zone 5

Planting and Care: Seeds and sometimes plants are becoming available in nurseries specializing in southwestern native plants. The seeds should be warm, moist stratified for one month, followed by three months of cold stratification before planting. Seeds can take several months to germinate. Although fragrant ash tolerates drier conditions than other ashes, it grows better and faster with extra watering.

Remarks: Fragrant ash's small size makes it a good choice for yards, near patios, and other sites where a larger tree would be unsuitable. The leaves turn yellow in the fall. Fragrant ash is a beautiful accent shrub or tree. Mass fragrant ash with trees of similar size, such as golden ball leadtree and New Mexico buckeye, for a colorful spring blooming display.

Species Name: *Leucanea retusa*

Family: Fabaceae (Leguminosae) (Pea); Subfamily: Mimosoideae (Mimosa)

Common Name(s): GOLDENBALL LEADTREE

Description: *Leucanea retusa* is a large shrub or small tree valued in the landscape for its large, round flower heads. It can grow up to 15 feet (450 centimeters) tall and 15 feet (450 centimeters) wide.

> ***Leaves:*** The leaves are 3 to 8 inches (8 to 20 centimeters) long and 4 to 5 inches (10 to 13 centimeters) wide. There are usually four to ten primary leaflets and six to sixteen secondary leaflets.
>
> ***Flowers:*** The sweet-scented, yellow flowers are globe shaped and are 1 inch (2.5 centimeters) wide. They bloom anytime between April and October as long as there is ample warmth and moisture.
>
> ***Fruit:*** The large seeds, which are ⅓ inch (8 millimeters) long by ¼ inch (6 millimeters) wide, are borne in pods up to 10 inches (25 centimeters) long.

Range and Habitat: Found in southeastern New Mexico, central and Trans-Pecos Texas, and northern Mexico from 3,000 to 6,500 feet (900 to 1,950 centimeters) on well-drained soils of canyons and hillsides in the Chihuahuan Desert.

Fraxinus cuspidata • *page 188* ▶
Leucanea retusa • *page 189* ▶

Fraxinus cuspidata
Fragrant Ash

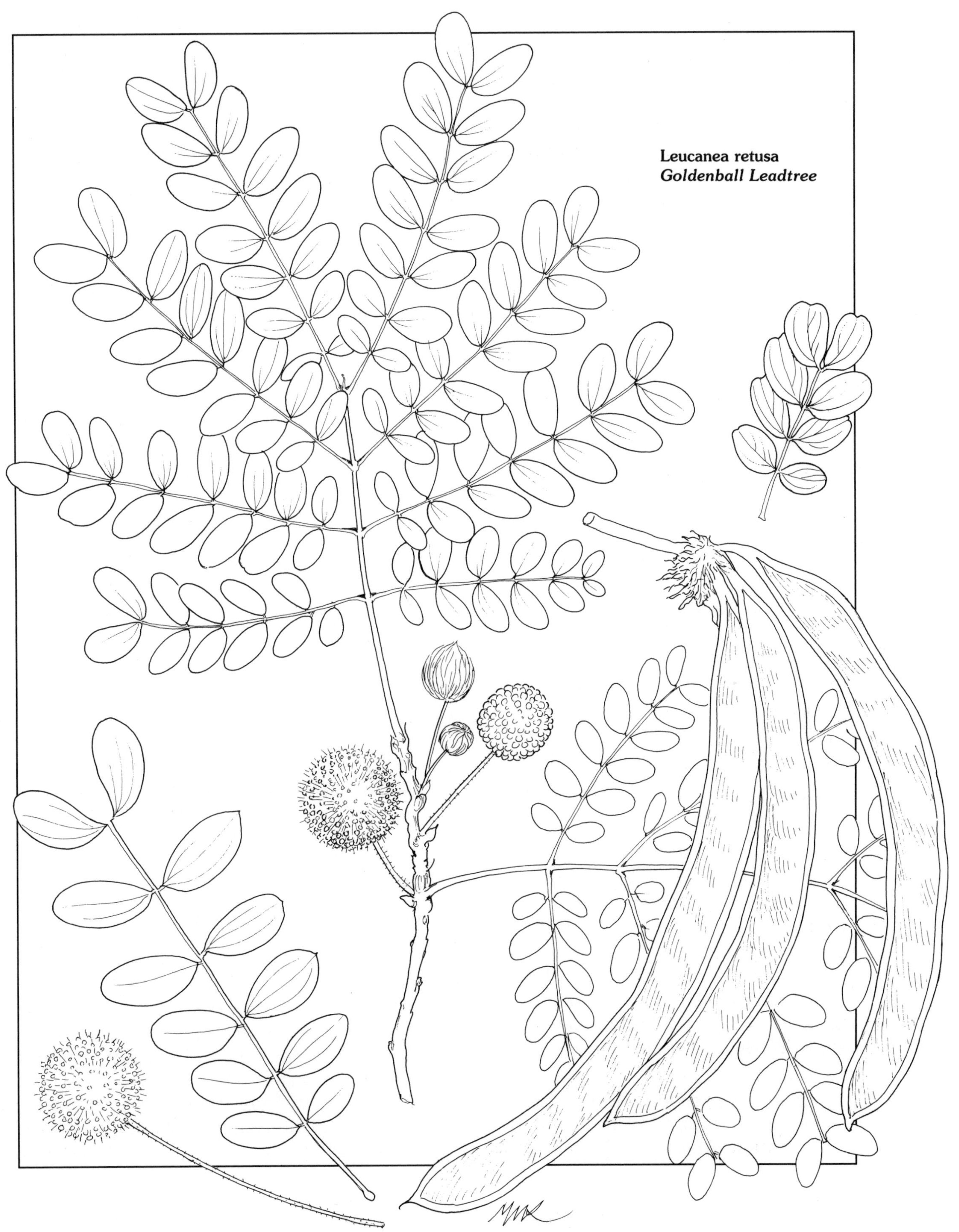
Leucanea retusa
Goldenball Leadtree

Hardiness: Zone 7

Planting and Care: Goldenball leadtree is rarely available as plants, and the seeds are even more difficult to find for sale. You'll most likely need to collect your own seeds. Goldenball leadtree is propagated by using a hot water bath to get the seeds to germinate. The small tree grows relatively fast if given extra water. For that dry, rocky place where you're trying to get something to grow, goldenball leadtree is a good choice.

Remarks: Goldenball leadtree has several attributes that make it a wonderful plant for landscaping. Unlike its cousins, the acacias and mimosas, goldenball leadtree doesn't have thorns. This is a plus for plantings near patios and walkways. The addition of fragrant, showy, yellow pompon flowers and large, decorative seedpods make this an ideal tree for the desert garden. Usually multitrunked, its small size lends itself well to today's smaller yards. With so many things going for it, goldenball leadtree deserves to be more widely used.

Species Name: *Prosopis glandulosa* (*Prosopis juliflora*)

Family: Fabaceae (Leguminosae) (Pea); Subfamily: Mimosoideae (Mimosa)

Common Name(s): MESQUITE, HONEY MESQUITE, MEZQUITE

Description: *Prosopis glandulosa* is a large shrub or small tree that grows up to 20 feet (600 centimeters) wide and 32 feet (960 centimeters) tall. It has straight, sharp thorns on gnarled, drooping branches that give a rounded appearance. Mesquite is known for its drought resistance, which is the result of its radially spreading root system with deep taproots.

Leaves: The light to dark green, bipinnate leaves emerge late in the season, usually after the last frost. Mesquite is deciduous. There are two varieties of *Prosopis glandulosa*, var. *glandulosa* (honey mesquite) and var. *torreyana* (western honey mesquite), the main difference being smaller leaflet size in var. *torreyana*, 3/5 to 1 inch (1.5 to 2.5 centimeters), as compared to 1 1/5 to 2 inches (3 to 5 centimeters) long in var. *glandulosa*.

Flowers: The creamy white to yellowish flowers are borne on fuzzy-looking spikes. The fragrant blossoms are very attractive to bees, and mesquite honey is a valuable product of this plant. Mesquite blooms intermittently from May to September, depending upon rainfall.

Fruit: The flat seedpods, which are 4 to 9 inches (10 to 23 centimeters) long, occur in loose clusters of straw- or rose-speckled beans. The shiny, brown seeds are encased in a fibrous, spongy tissue.

Range and Habitat: Var. *glandulosa*: Found in eastern and southern New Mexico, southwestern Kansas, Texas, southeastern Colorado, southwestern Oklahoma, parts of Louisiana, to Arizona, and northern Mexico from 2,000 to 5,000 feet (600 to 1,500 meters) on plains, prairies, washes, and river valleys in the Chihuahuan Desert, the desert grassland, and the Great Plains grassland.

Var. *torreyana*: Found in central to south-central and southwestern New Mexico, Trans-Pecos Texas, Arizona, and southeastern California and adjacent Mexico from 3,500 to 6,000 feet (1,050 to 1,800 meters) on plains, bottomlands, and mesas in the Chihuahuan and Sonoran deserts, the desert grassland, other grasslands, and other habitats.

Hardiness: Zone 6

Planting and Care: Mesquite is fairly easy to find as plants at nurseries in the desert Southwest. Seeds are not often available for sale; however, in most years they are abundant enough that you can gather your own. Mesquite is easily started from fresh seeds without treatment. Stored, dry seeds should be scarified by a hot water treatment. The seeds should be planted in deep containers with a well-draining soil mix as the seedlings have a long initial root. In warm soil the seeds will germi-

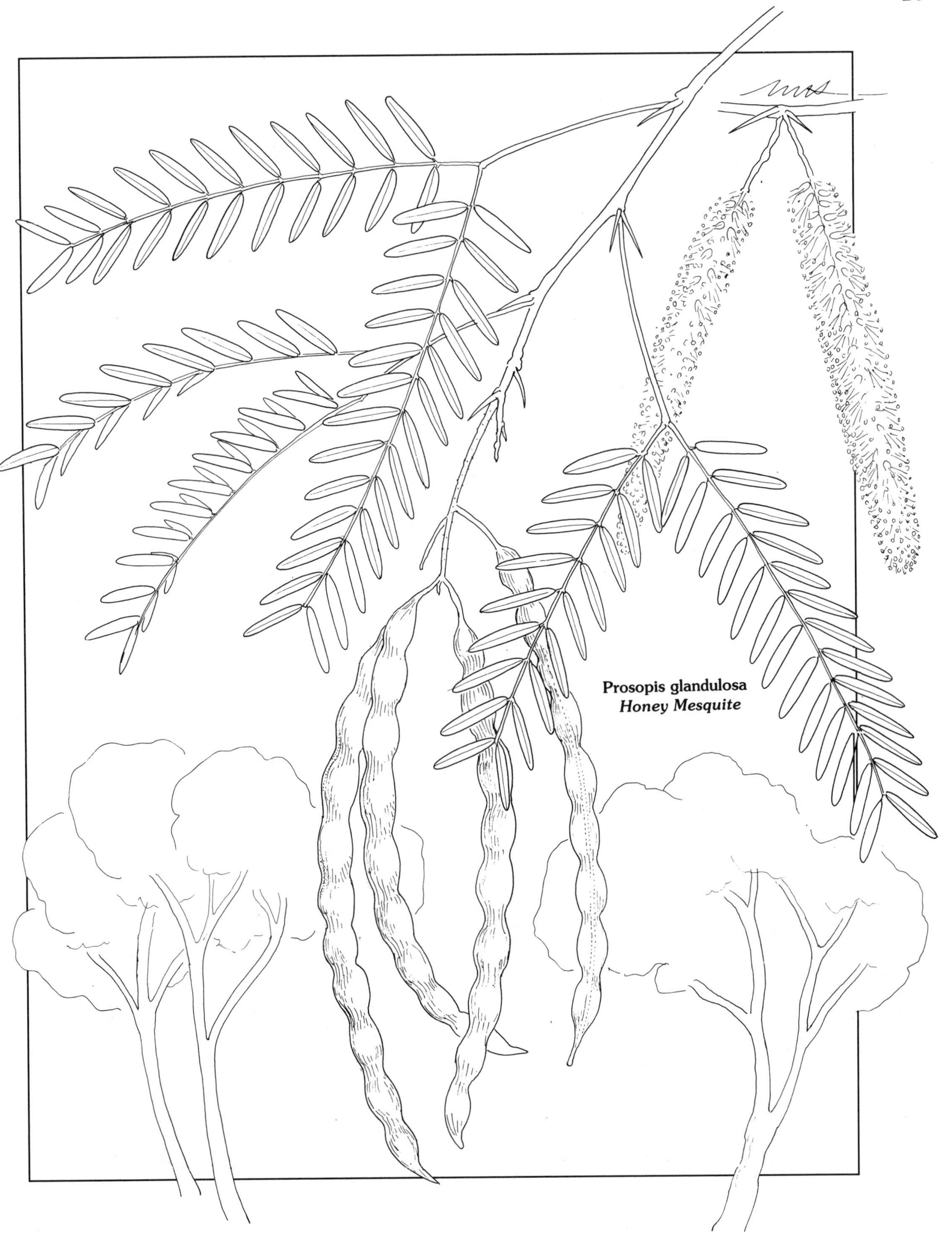
Prosopis glandulosa
Honey Mesquite

nate in ten days or so. Mesquite has nitrogen-fixing roots and requires little or no fertilizer in the garden. Keep it well watered and pruned until your tree has reached its desired size. After that, it can exist on its own and will require watering only during extreme drought. Mesquite is subject to attack by a stem-girdling insect that causes die-back of the tips. Clip off the affected tips when damage is noticed. The stems will releaf at this point. Properly pruned and watered, mesquite can grow into a nice shade tree. If kept shrubby, it should be placed where the thorns can be avoided.

Remarks: Mesquite beans were an important staple in the diet of early Native Americans of the Southwest. In the desert garden mesquite will attract a wide variety of wildlife such as quail, other small birds, and small mammals that feed on the seeds. The wood has been used for a variety of things, including fence posts, fuel, furniture, and charcoal.

In the Southwest mesquite is used as a guideline as to when to plant warm season vegetable crops. Once it has leafed out it is generally assumed that there will be no more frosts. With its airy foliage it is an attractive addition to the desert landscape. Mesquite is considered a pest on the rangelands, but in the desert garden it can provide a refreshing touch of leafy green.

Species Name: *Prosopis pubescens*

Family: Fabaceae (Leguminosae) (Legume); Subfamily: Mimosoideae (Mimosa)

Common Name(s): SCREWBEAN, TORNILLO, SCREW-POD MESQUITE, TWISTED BEAN

Description: *Prosopis pubescens* is a large shrub or small tree that grows up to 32 feet (960 centimeters) tall with more delicate leaves than honey mesquite.

Leaves: The bipinnate leaves are 1 1/2 to 3 inches (4 to 8 centimeters) long. The leaflets are 1/4 to 2/3 inch (6 millimeters to 2 centimeters) long and occur in pairs of five to eight.

Flowers: The greenish white or yellowish white flower spikes are 1 1/2 to 3 inches (4 to 8 centimeters) long. The flowers are among the showiest of the genus and make screwbean a useful plant in areas too cold for acacias. It blooms in spring and summer.

Fruit: The common name screwbean comes from the tightly coiled bean pods. The yellow to brown screwbeans grow up to 2 inches (5 centimeters) long and to 1/4 inch (6 millimeters) wide. The tan seeds are 1/16 to 1/12 inch (2 millimeters) long.

Range and Habitat: Found in central and southern New Mexico, Trans-Pecos Texas, Arizona, southern Nevada, southwestern Utah, southern California, and adjacent Mexico from 3,500 to 4,500 feet (1,050 to 1,350 meters) along streams, washes, and arroyos in the Chihuahuan, Sonoran, and Mojave deserts.

Hardiness: Zone 6

Planting and Care: Screwbean is sometimes available as plants at nurseries in the Southwest. Seeds are also available from a few mail-order sources. The seeds require a hot water treatment in order to germinate. As with other legumes, the seeds should be planted in large containers to allow for root development. Screwbean requires more watering than honey mesquite; however, it is probably more cold hardy.

Remarks: Screwbean wood has been used, as have other mesquites, for fuel, tool handles, fence posts, and so forth. Quail feed on the beans, and a ground meal from the beans was made into bread by Native Americans.

Screwbean tends to be a multitrunked, vase-shaped tree. It lends itself well to planting in smaller gardens as well as larger landscapes. In the garden screwbean and other mesquites make good plants for those cacti that like semishade or need support for their stems.

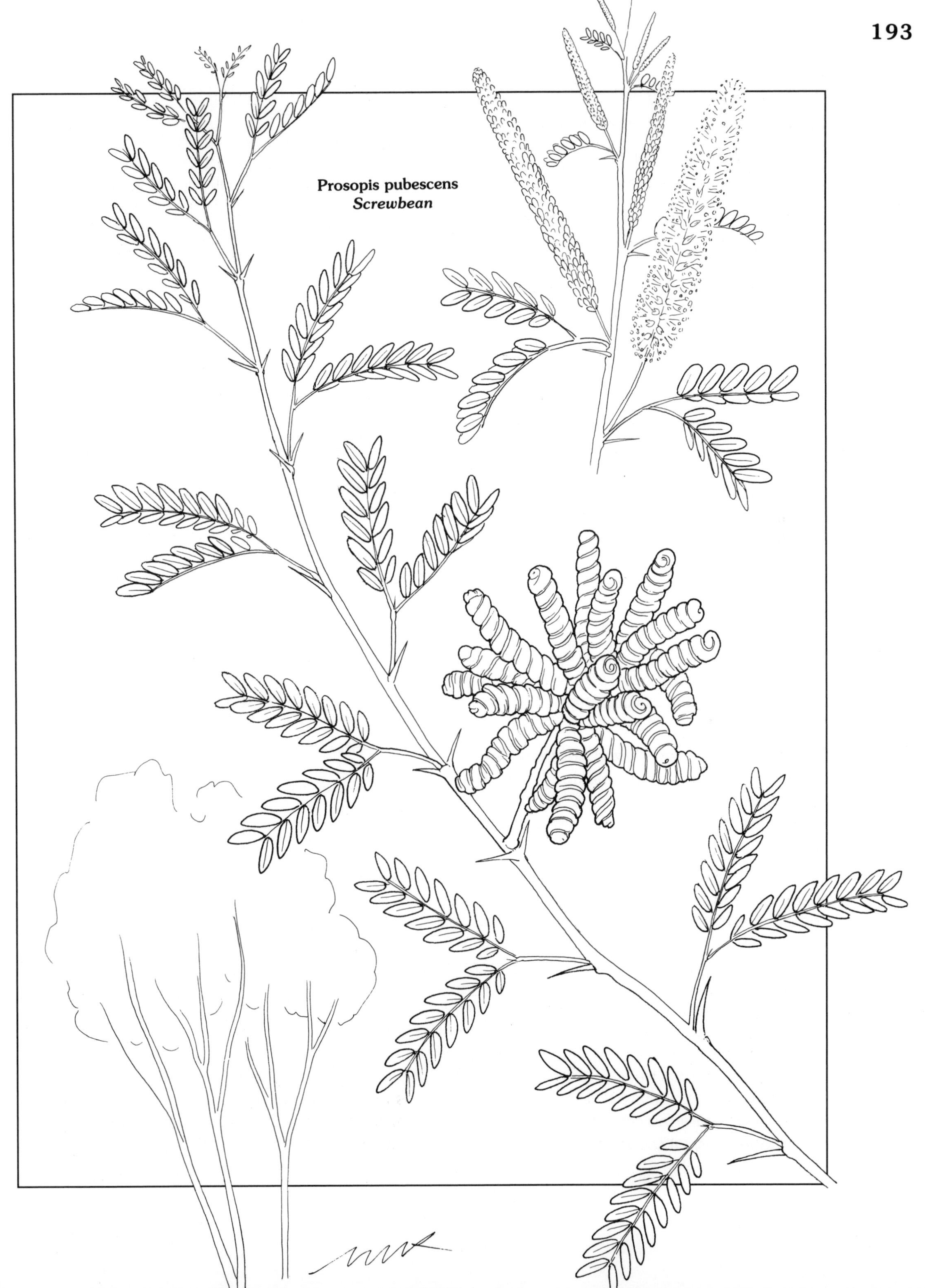
Prosopis pubescens
Screwbean

Species Name: *Sambucus mexicana*

Family: Caprifoliaceae (Honeysuckle)

Common Name(s): MEXICAN ELDER, DESERT ELDERBERRY, FLOR SAUCO

Description: *Sambucus mexicana* is a small to medium-sized tree that grows up to 35 feet (1,050 centimeters) tall with a canopy spread of 15 to 25 feet (450 to 750 centimeters). It is semievergreen, being partially deciduous in late summer and fall. In late winter or early spring it releafs.

Leaves: The opposite, odd-pinnately compound leaves are divided into three to five pale green, thick, leathery leaves. The leaves grow up to 3 inches (8 centimeters) long.

Flowers: The tiny flowers, which are 1/4 inch (6 millimeters) wide, occur in flat, creamy white clusters, 2 to 6 inches (5 to 15 centimeters) wide. Mexican elder blooms mainly from April to June; however, it can bloom at other times of the year after rains.

Fruit: The dark blue, edible fruit is 1/4 inch (6 millimeters) in diameter.

Range and Habitat: Found in southern New Mexico, southwestern Texas, southern Arizona, southern California, and Mexico from 1,200 to 5,000 feet (360 to 1,500 meters) along streams and other riparian areas in the Chihuahuan and Sonoran deserts and the desert grassland.

Hardiness: Zone 7

Planting and Care: Plants of Mexican elder are regularly available at nurseries throughout the Southwest. Seeds are practically impossible to find for sale, so you'll need to collect your own. Mexican elder is easily grown from seeds and can be propagated from cuttings also. Cuttings of the softwood taken in late summer root readily in a moist medium, such as sand or vermiculite. Young trees require lots of water until they are established. Mexican elder requires deep watering on a regular basis; however its shade-giving canopy will provide welcome relief from the hot desert sun and is worth the extra water.

Remarks: Mexican elder's fruits can be used in jellies, pies, and so forth. They are an excellent wildlife food, particularly for birds. Mexican elder has been used in New Mexico from Albuquerque south as an ornamental.

Species Name: *Sapindus saponaria* var. *drummondii*

Family: Sapindaceae (Soapberry)

Common Name(s): WESTERN SOAPBERRY, JABONCILLO, PALO BLANCO

Description: *Sapindus saponaria* var. *drummondii* is usually a small tree 6 to 15 feet (180 to 450 centimeters) high, but in favorable situations it can grow up to 50 feet (1,500 centimeters) tall. The berries were once used for soap in Mexico and the early American West.

Leaves: The leaves, which are 5 to 18 inches (13 to 46 centimeters) long, are composed of thirteen to nineteen leaflets, which are 1 1/2 to 4 inches (4 to 10 centimeters) long and 1/4 to 3/4 inch (6 millimeters to 2 centimeters) wide. They are yellowish green, turning bright yellow to gold in the fall.

Flowers: The tiny white flowers are borne on dense panicles, which are 5 to 10 inches (13 to 25 centimeters) long. Western soapberry blooms from May to June.

Fruit: The large, translucent amber, fleshy fruit surrounds a large, dark brown seed 2/5 to 1/2 inch (10 to 12 millimeters) in diameter, which ripens from September into October. The fruit contains saponin, a substance that makes a good lather in water.

Range and Habitat: Found in central, southern, and eastern New Mexico, central and southeastern Arizona, throughout Texas, eastward to Kansas and Louisiana, and northern Mexico from 2,500 to 6,000 feet (750 to 1,800 meters) on a variety of soils found along various riparian areas and canyonsides of the Chihuahuan and Sonoran deserts, the desert grassland, and Southwest woodlands.

Hardiness: Zone 6

Planting and Care: Western soapberry can be found on occasion at nurseries specializing in native southwestern plants. Seeds are hard to find for sale, and you will probably need to collect your own. The seeds need scarification and stratification for three months in order to germinate. With extra water western soapberry will grow into a beautiful tree.

Remarks: Western soapberry is one of our best desert trees for providing shade in the garden. With its attractive foliage, rough, gray bark, and pretty amber fruit, this tree should be used more extensively in the Southwest. It is a perfect example of an underutilized native plant that could be planted instead of a non-native exotic.

Sambucus mexicana
Mexican Elder

Sapindus saponaria • *page 196* ▶

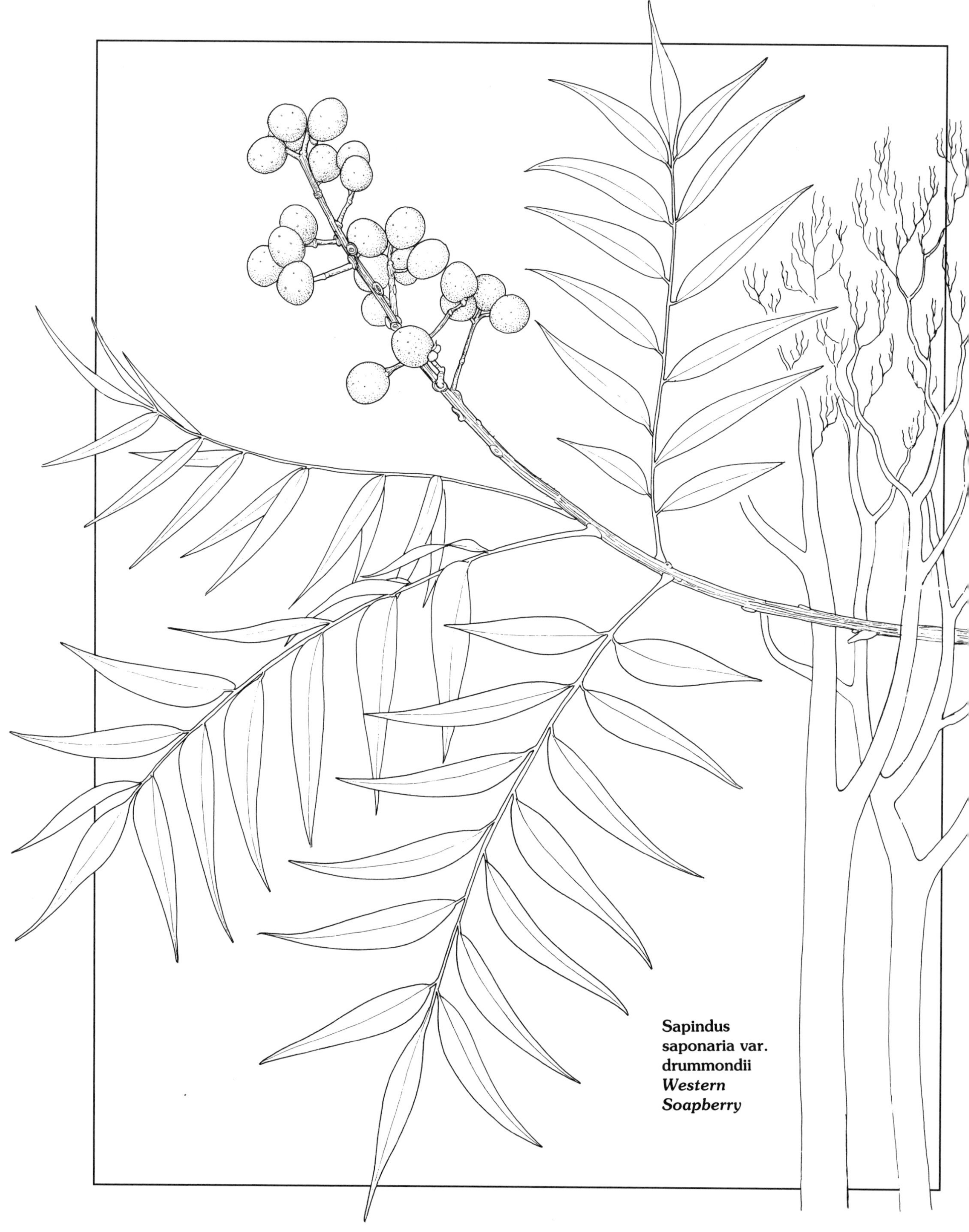

Sapindus saponaria var. drummondii
Western Soapberry

Species Name: *Ungnadia speciosa*

Family: Sapindaceae (Soapberry)

Common Name(s): NEW MEXICO BUCKEYE, MEXICAN BUCKEYE, TEXAS BUCKEYE, MONILLO

Description: *Ungnadia speciosa* is a shrub or small tree with clusters of bright pink flowers that bloom before the leaves appear in the spring. It can grow up to 30 feet (900 centimeters) tall, but it is usually a much smaller, multitrunked tree.

Leaves: The deciduous, serrated, light green leaves are compound with five to seven leaflets which are up to 5 inches (13 centimeters) long.

Flowers: The small flowers, approximately 1 inch (2.5 centimeters) wide, bloom in the spring from March to June. These fragrant, rose-colored flowers are often described as being similar to a redbud's.

Fruit: The three-celled woody pods contain two to three round, shiny, black seeds which are poisonous to humans. The seeds are about 2/5 inch (10 millimeters) in diameter.

Range and Habitat: Found in southern New Mexico, central and West Texas, and Mexico from 4,500 to 6,000 feet (1,350 to 1,800 meters) on limestone soils on rocky hills in the Chihuahuan Desert.

Hardiness: Zone 8, warmer parts of zone 7

Planting and Care: New Mexico buckeye is becoming more widely available at nurseries in the Southwest, particularly those that specialize in native plants. The seeds are sometimes offered for sale; however, you may need to collect your own in the fall. New Mexico buckeye is easily propagated from seeds, which should be sown in deep containers, 1 gallon (3.8 liters) or larger. This drought-tolerant tree is very adaptable and will grow in dry or moist, clay or sandy soils.

Remarks: Highly ornamental, New Mexico buckeye should be used more in our desert landscapes. Use it as an accent plant, especially to show off its beautiful spring flowers. Its small size makes it suitable for small gardens and spaces such as patios and courtyards. New Mexico buckeye is one of our best native plants.

Ungnadia speciosa • *page 198* ▶

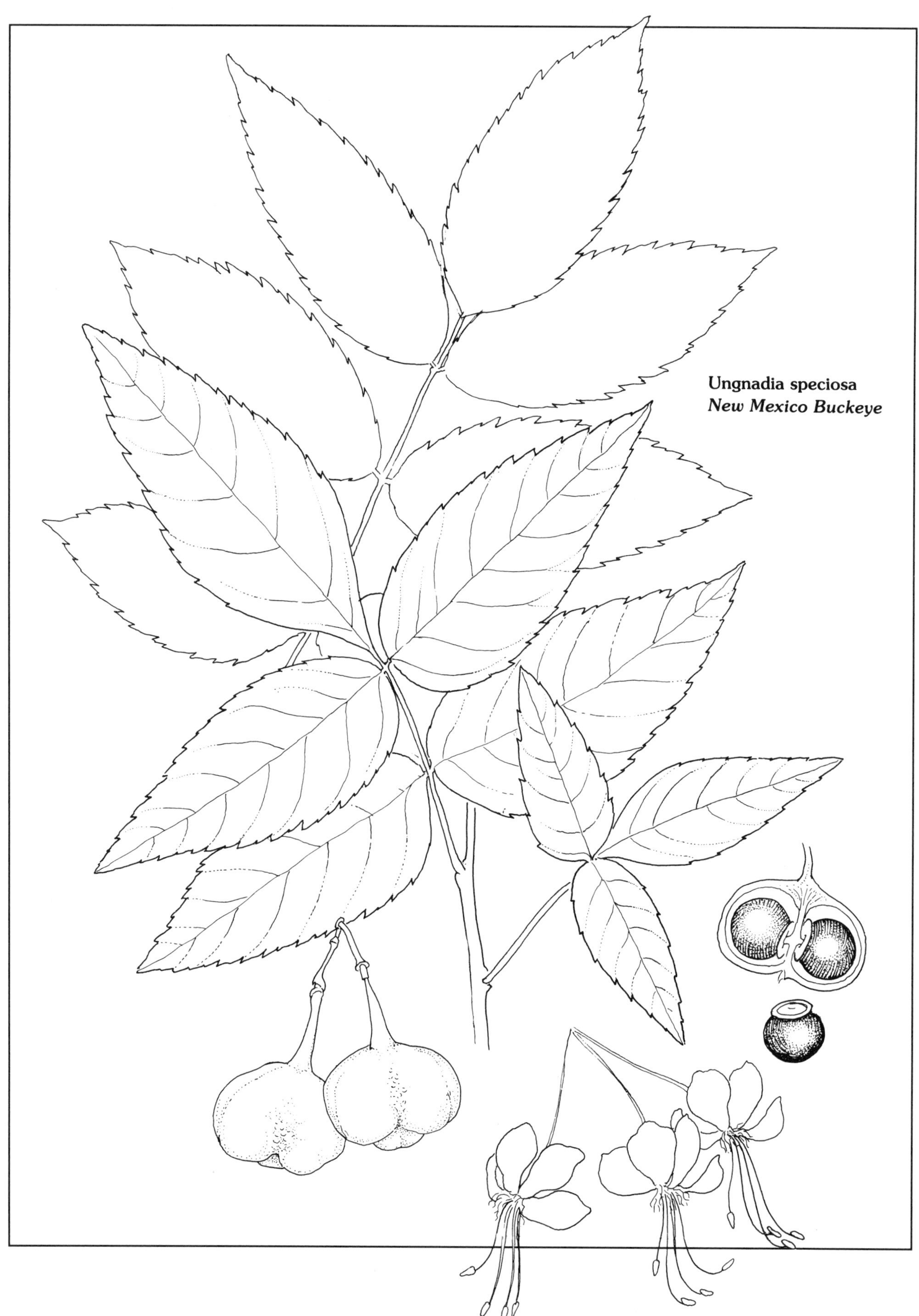
Ungnadia speciosa
New Mexico Buckeye

APPENDIX I:

Locations for Viewing Native Plants

The following is a list of places, such as parks, wildlife refuges, and botanical gardens, where plants of the Chihuahuan Desert can be seen growing, either in the wild or in cultivation.

Arizona

Arizona Cactus and Succulent Research Botanical Garden, Bisbee

On the western edge of the Chihuahuan Desert region, this garden features a wide variety of native species of cacti and succulents.

Boyce Thompson Southwestern Arboretum, Superior

The arboretum has a loop trail through a planting of Chihuahuan Desert plants. It is a good place to see both the differences and similarities between the Chihuahuan and Sonoran deserts.

Desert Botanical Garden, Phoenix

As part of its displays of different deserts around the world, the Desert Botanical Garden has a section of Chihuahuan Desert plants. In addition to displays of desert plants in natural settings, there are ethnobotanical and home landscape exhibits using native plants.

Tohono Chul Park, Tucson

This gem of a botanical garden has a display of Chihuahuan Desert plants, along with an exhibit gallery, bookstore, gift shop, and, of course, an outstanding collection of Sonoran Desert plants.

New Mexico

Aguirre Springs National Recreation Area, eastern slope of the Organ Mountains near Las Cruces

With the jagged spires of the Organ Mountains creating a dramatic backdrop, this area of hiking trails in the lower Tularosa Basin is an excellent area to see many of the plants mentioned in this book.

Albuquerque Police Department Memorial Xeriscape Garden, Albuquerque

Located at the corner of Osuna N.E. and Wyoming N.E., this garden features many of the plants listed in the "Desert Plant Encyclopedia."

Bosque del Apache National Wildlife Refuge, south of Socorro

There is a section of Chihuahuan Desert plants within a larger planting of native plants at the visitor center and parking area. Here the visitor experiences the added bonus of viewing plenty of wildlife, especially birds.

Carlsbad Caverns National Park, Carlsbad

Famous for its caves and bats, Carlsbad Caverns National Park has turnouts for cars along the drive in Walnut Canyon and trails through an excellent example of Chihuahuan Desert, which occupies the surface of the land above the caves.

City of Rocks State Park, north of Deming

Known for its unusual rock formations that rise from the desert floor, the park also has a small cactus garden.

Dripping Springs Natural Area, Las Cruces

Dripping Springs Natural Area is managed by the Bureau of Land Management in cooperation with the Nature Conservancy. In addition to nature trails throughout the refuge, the visitor center is landscaped with native plants.

Living Desert Zoological and Botanical State Park, Carlsbad

This park is a good introduction to the plants and animals of the Chihuahuan Desert, which it showcases. It sits atop a desert hill with beautiful views of the Pecos Valley below.

Oliver Lee State Park, Alamogordo

The visitor center and Dog Canyon trail are located on the spectacular Sacramento Escarpment; there is a wealth of Chihuahuan Desert species in the park.

Pancho Villa State Park, Columbus

Commemorating Pancho Villa's raid on the town of Columbus, the park has an extensive cactus and succulent garden.

Quebrados Road Backcountry Byway, Escondida, north of Socorro

This drive passes through rugged, rocky Chihuahuan Desert country with the stark Sierra de las Canas looming above. Be sure to check on road conditions, especially during the late summer monsoon season.

Rio Grande Botanical Gardens, Albuquerque

Opening in the summer of 1996, these gardens will feature a unique conservatory with Sonoran Desert plants on the inside, blending into a Chihuahuan Desert exhibit on the outside.

Rock Hound State Park, Deming

While viewing the desert plants here, including large barrel cacti, you can also look for rocks, which you're allowed to take home.

Valley of Fires Recreation area, Carrizozo

Located at the northern end of the Tularosa Basin, this recreation area features black basalt that is among the most recent lava flows in the continental United States. It is a natural rock garden full of Chihuahuan Desert cacti and other plants.

White Sands National Monument, Alamogordo

The shining white gypsum sand dunes fit the image most people have of deserts. Few plants can grow in the heart of the dunes. Those that do must continually push upwards as they get buried with new waves of sand. A good place to look at desert plants in the monument is around the edges of the dunes.

Texas

Barton Warnock Environmental Education Center, Lajitas

There is an extensive collection of Chihuahuan Desert cacti and other plants here, as well as exhibits on the geology, archaeology, and history of the Big Bend area.

Big Bend National Park, south of Alpine

This is the largest preserve of Chihuahuan Desert in the United States. It is an incredibly scenic place to view a wide variety of desert plants, some unique to the park.

Chihuahuan Desert Arboretum and Visitor Center of the Chihuahuan Desert Research Institute, Fort Davis

The 507–acre center has a 40–acre arboretum representing fifty–seven plant families with over four hundred species. It is one of the best places for information on the Chihuahuan Desert and its flora.

Guadalupe Mountains National Park, south of Carlsbad, New Mexico

This is an amazing place where maples and agaves grow side by side. McKittrick Canyon is one of the region's best hikes, especially in the fall when the canyon is full of color.

Hueco Tanks State Park, east of El Paso

This 860–acre desert park has unique rock formations and is known for its use in the past by the Native Americans of the area. While viewing plants, you can also look at over two thousand pictographs made by these ancient people.

APPENDIX II:

Mail–order Sources for Seeds and Plants

The following list consists of nurseries, seed companies, and other sources of seeds and plants of species listed in the "Desert Plant Encyclopedia." There are also other nurseries as well as botanical gardens and native plant societies in the Southwest that sell native plants. Some suppliers charge for their catalog.

Agua Fria Nursery
1409 Agua Fria Street
Santa Fe, New Mexico 87501
Native and other plants; wide selection of penstemons.

Aztekakti
11306 Gateway East
P.O. Box 26126
El Paso, Texas 79927
Seed list of cacti and succulents, including Chihuahuan Desert species.

Desert Moon Nursery
P.O. Box 600
Veguita, New Mexico 87062
Specializing in cacti, succulents, and other native plants of the Chihuahuan Desert and the Southwest.

Desert Nursery
1301 South Copper
Deming, New Mexico 88030
Cacti and succulents of the Southwest and elsewhere.

Diamond JK Nursery
HCR 389
Elgin, Arizona 85611
Source of hard to find trees, shrubs, and succulents. Many are salvaged plants.

Forestfarm
990 Tetherow Road
Williams, Oregon 97544–9599
Trees, shrubs, and wildflowers from around the world, including a good selection from the Southwest.

Gunsight Mountain Ranch & Nursery
P.O. Box 86
Tarpley, Texas 78883
Container–grown native plants of Texas, including Plants of the Chihuahuan Desert.

Mesa Gardens
P.O. Box 72
Belen, New Mexico 87002
Extensive catalog of cacti and succulents from around the world.

New Mexico Cactus Research
P.O. Box 787
Belen, New Mexico 87002
Cacti and succulents, including a large selection of prickly pears.

Plant Delights Nursery at Juniper Level Botanic Gardens
9241 Sauls Road
Raleigh, North Carolina 27603
Trees, shrubs, and flowers from areas around the world, including the Southwest and Mexico.

Plants of the Southwest
Agua Fria, Rt. 6 Box 11A
Santa Fe, New Mexico 87505
Plants and seeds of many native trees, shrubs, and wildflowers.

Rocky Mountain Rare Plants
P.O. Box 200483
Denver, Colorado 80220
Seeds of alpine, cushion, and xeric plants.

Schulz Cactus Growers
1095 Easy Street
Morgan Hill, California 95037
Cacti and succulents from around the world.

Semillas Solanas
Sunny Land Seeds
P.O. Box 385
Paradox, Colorado 81429
Seeds of many Chihuahuan Desert species, and species from other areas of the Southwest and from Ecuador.

Southwestern Native Seeds
Box 50503
Tucson, Arizona 85703
Extensive list of seeds from plants of the Southwest and Mexico.

Wild Seed, Inc.
P.O. Box 27751
Tempe, Arizona 85285
Large selection of seeds of Chihuahuan and Sonoran Desert species.

Yucca Do Nursery at Peckerwood Gardens
P.O. Box 655
Waller, Texas 77484
Wildflowers, cacti, succulents, shrubs, and trees (many rare) of the Southwest, Mexico, and elsewhere.

GLOSSARY OF TERMS

Achene. A dry, one-seeded fruit with the wall free from the seed. The fruit does not split open when ripe.

After-ripening. A process in which seeds are aged, usually for one or more years, in order to break down inhibitors to germination.

Anthers. The parts of the stamen containing the pollen.

Areole. The area on a cactus stem from which the spines arise.

Biennial. A plant whose life span is two years.

Bipinnate. Twice pinnate.

Bract. A modified leaf, usually found under a flower or cluster of flowers.

Caliche. A hard, calcareous soil that often forms an impermeable layer underlying other soil above.

Calyx. The outer whorl of a flower consisting of the sepals.

Carpel. A simple pistil.

Corolla. The inner whorl of a flower consisting of the petals.

Crusher fines. The fine, almost powderlike siftings left after crushing gravel.

Cultural requirements. The needs of a plant for optimum growth in cultivation.

Damping off. A fungus that girdles and kills young seedlings.

Deciduous. Plants which lose their leaves in response to climatic factors.

Dish garden. A collection of plants arranged in a container.

Disk flowers. The central flowers of a composite flower.

Drought deciduous. Plants which drop their leaves in order to conserve moisture in times of drought.

Drupe. A fleshy fruit surrounding a seed.

Endemic. Native to a specific area. Often an indication of rarity.

Garden rooms. Spaces created by dividing the garden into separate areas, or "rooms."

Germinate. To begin to grow or sprout.

Glochid. A minute, barbed prickle or spine found on prickly pear cacti and chollas.

Inflorescence. A flower cluster.

Iron chlorosis. A harmful condition, caused by a lack of available iron, in which leaves turn yellow while veins remain green.

Island bed. A planting bed that is isolated by lawn, gravel, or other materials.

Lanceolate. A lance-shaped leaf.

Leggy. Excessive, rank growth of a plant, usually caused by overwatering and/or too much fertilizer.

Moon garden. A garden planted entirely with white flowers intended to be viewed in the moonlight.

Nitrogen-fixing. A plant, often a legume, which has the ability to extract nitrogen from the air via a symbiotic relationship with bacteria.

Nurse plant. A plant, usually a shrub, that provides shelter to developing seedlings of other plants.

Odd-pinnate. A compound, pinnate leaf with a terminal leaflet.

Offsets. Small plants produced around the base of a larger, mature plant.

Ovate-lanceolate. A lance-shaped leaf that is broad to oval at the wide end.

Panicle. Several clusters of flowers.

Perennial. A plant whose life is longer than two years.

Perianth. The calyx and corolla together.

Pinnate. Compound leaves with the leaflets arranged in two rows along a common axis.

Pistil. The female reproductive part of the flower, consisting of the ovary and the stigma.

Propagation. The act of producing plants from seeds or cuttings.

Radicle. The first, or embryonic, root that emerges from a seed.

Ray flowers. The individual flowers that grow around the perimeter of the disc of a composite flower; the "petals" of a daisy or sunflower.

Rhizome. An underground stem.

Rib. The stems which are divided into linear ridges on some cacti.

Riparian. A term for plant life that grows along the side of a stream, river bottom, or other aquatic area.

Samara. A dry, winged fruit that does not split open when ripe.

Scarification. A seed treatment which seeks to break down a hard seed coat by mechanical means.

Scoria. Crushed volcanic rock.

Sepals. Units of the calyx, usually green, which protect the emerging flower bud. Sometimes colored like, and supplementing or replacing, the petals.

Softwood cutting. A cutting off the season's newly formed growth taken for propagation.

Spine. A structure developed from a leaf or a part of one.

Stamen. The male, pollen-producing part of a flower.

Staminode. A sterile stamen.

Stomata. Minute openings on the epidermis of a leaf.

Stratification. A seed treatment to break down chemical inhibitors that prevent germination.

Succulent. Any plant that has modified, thick, fleshy stems or leaves which can store moisture.

Taproot. The main or primary root.

Trans-Pecos Texas. Texas west of the Pecos River.

Tubercle. A projection on the stem of some cacti which bears an areole.

Xeriscape. A gardening philosophy that seeks to conserve water in the landscape.

BIBLIOGRAPHY

Atkinson, Richard. *White Sands, Wind, Sand and Time.* Globe, Ariz.: Southwest Parks and Monuments Association, 1977.

Barr, Claude A. *Jewels of the Plains.* Minneapolis: University of Minnesota Press, 1983.

Benson, Lyman. *The Cacti of the United States and Canada.* Palo Alto, Calif.: Stanford University Press, 1982.

Benson, Lyman, and Robert A. Darrow. *Trees and Shrubs of the Southwestern Deserts.* Tucson, Ariz.: University of Arizona Press, 1981.

Bowers, Janice Emily. *100 Desert Wildflowers of the Southwest.* Tucson, Ariz.: Southwest Parks and Monuments Association, 1989.

———. *100 Roadside Wildflowers of the Southwest Woodlands.* Tucson, Ariz.: Southwest Parks and Monuments Association, 1987.

Brown, David E. *Biotic Communities of the American Southwest—United States and Mexico.* "Desert Plants," vol. 4, nos. 1–4. Superior, Ariz.: University of Arizona, Boyce Thompson Arboretum, 1982.

Brown, Lauren. *The Audubon Society Nature Guides: Grasslands.* New York: Alfred A. Knopf, 1985.

Castetter, Edward F., Prince Pierce, and Karl H. Schwerin. "A Reassessment of the Genus Escobaria." *Cactus and Succulent Journal* 47(1975): 60–70.

Champie, Clark. *Cacti and Succulents of El Paso.* Santa Barbara, Calif.: Abbey Garden Press, 1974.

———. *Strangers in the Franklins.* El Paso, Tex.: Guynes Printing Company, 1973.

Crockett, James Underwood. *Wildflower Gardening.* New York: Time–Life Books, Inc., 1977.

Desert Botanic Garden Staff. *Arizona Highways Presents Desert Wildflowers.* Phoenix, Ariz.: Arizona Highways, 1988.

Dodge, Natt N. *100 Roadside Wildflowers of Southwest Uplands in Natural Color.* Globe, Ariz.: Southwest Parks and Monuments Associations, 1967.

———. *100 Desert Wildflowers in Natural Color.* Globe, Ariz.: Southwest Parks and Monuments Association, 1963.

———. *Flowers of the Southwest Deserts.* Tucson, Ariz.: Southwest Parks and Monuments Association, 1985.

Fisher, Pierre. "Varieties of *Coryphantha vivipara.*" *Cactus and Succulent Journal* 52 (1980): 86–91.

Garden Design. New York: Simon and Schuster, 1984.

Gentry, Howard Scott. *Agaves of Continental North America.* Tucson, Ariz.: University of Arizona Press, 1982.

Hobhouse, Penelope. *Garden Style.* Boston: Little, Brown and Company, 1988.

Hodoba, Theodore, and Candace Hodoba. *Desert Moon Nursery 1989 Plant List.* Veguita, N.M.: Desert Moon Nursery, 1989.

Hortus Third. New York: Macmillan Publishing Co., 1976.

Kearney, Thomas H., and Robert H. Peebles. *Arizona Flora.* Berkeley: University of California Press, 1969.

Knox, Kimberley M., ed. *Landscaping for Water Conservation: Xeriscape.* Aurora, Colo.: City of Aurora and Denver Water Department, 1989.

Lamb, Edgar, and Brian Lamb. *Colorful Cacti of the American Deserts.* New York: Macmillan Publishing Co., 1974.

Lamb, Samuel H. *Woody Plants of the Southwest.* Santa Fe, N.M.: Sunstone Press, 1975.

Leighton, Phebe, and Calvin Simonds. *The New American Landscape Gardener.* Emmaus, Pa.: Rodale Press, 1987.

Little, Elbert L. *Southwestern Trees.* Washington, D.C.: U.S. Department of Agriculture, 1950.

MacMahon, James. *The Audubon Society Nature Guides: Deserts.* New York: Alfred A. Knopf, 1985.

Martin, Laura C. *The Wildflower Meadow Book.* Charlotte, N.C.: East Woods Press Book, 1986.

Martin, William C., and Charles R. Hutchins. *Fall Wildflowers of New Mexico.* Albuquerque: University of New Mexico Press, 1988.

———. *Summer Wildflowers of New Mexico.* Albuquerque: University of New Mexico Press, 1986.

———. *Spring Wildflowers of New Mexico.* Albuquerque: University of New Mexico Press, 1984.

———. *A Flora of New Mexico.* Vaduz, Germany: J. Cramer, 1981.

Mielke, Judy. *Native Plants for Southwestern Landscapes.* Austin: University of Texas Press, 1993.

The Native Plant Society of New Mexico. *Native Plants for Landscaping in Southern New Mexico.* Santa Fe, N.M.: The Native Plant Society of New Mexico, 1978.

New Mexico Native Plant Protection Advisory Committee. *A Handbook of Rare and Endemic Plants of New Mexico.* Albuquerque: University of New Mexico Press, 1984.

Nokes, Jill. *How to Grow Native Plants of Texas and the Southwest.* Austin, Tex.: Texas Monthly Press, 1986.

Phillips, Judith. *Southwestern Landscaping with Native Plants.* Santa Fe, N.M.: Museum of New Mexico Press, 1987.

Plants of the Southwest. *Plants of the Southwest 1989 Catalog.* Santa Fe, N.M.: Plants of the Southwest, 1989.

Quiros, Alice, and Barbara L. Young. *The World of Cactus and Succulents and Other Water-thrifty Plants.* San Francisco, Calif.: Ortho Books, 1977.

Sacamano, Charles M., and Warren D. Jones. *Native Trees and Shrubs for Landscape Use in the Desert Southwest.* College of Agriculture, Cooperative Extension Service. Tucson, Ariz.: University of Arizona, 1975.

Smith, Ken. *Western Home Landscaping.* Tucson, Ariz.: H. P. Books, 1978.

Smyser, Carol A. *Nature's Design.* Emmaus, Pa.: Rodale Press, 1982.

Spellenberg, Richard. *The Audubon Society Field Guide to North American Wildflowers, Western Region.* New York: Alfred A. Knopf, 1979.

Sunset Western Garden Book. Menlo Park, Calif.: Lane Publishing Co., 1988.

Symposium on the Biological Resources of the Chihuahuan Desert Region, United States and Mexico, Sul Ross State University, 1974. *Transactions of the Symposium on the Biological Resources of the Chihuahuan Desert Region, United States and Mexico, Sul Ross State University, Alpine, Texas, 17–18 October, 1974.* Washington, D.C.: U.S. Department of the Interior, 1974.

Taylor, Nigel P. *The Genus Echinocereus.* Portland, Oreg.: Timber Press, 1985.

Vines, Robert A. *Trees, Shrubs, and Woody Vines of the Southwest.* Austin: University of Texas Press, 1960.

Warnock, Barton H. *Wildflowers of the Big Bend Country, Texas.* Alpine, Tex.: Sul Ross State University, 1970.

Wasowski, Sally, and Julie Ryan. *Landscaping with Native Texas Plants.* Austin, Tex.: Texas Monthly Press, 1985.

Wauer, Roland H. *Naturalist's Big Bend.* College Station: Texas A & M University Press, 1980.

Weniger, Del. *Cacti of Texas and Neighboring States.* Austin: University of Texas Press, 1984.

Wirth, Thomas. *The Victory Garden Landscape Guide.* Boston: Little, Brown and Company,

INDEX

Numerals in **bold** indicate an illustration or photograph of the subject.

A

B

C